PERSONAL DEVELOPMENT *MADE EASY*

A STEP-BY-STEP GUIDE TO SELF IMPROVEMENT

Grandmaster
AVADHUT DAS

PRABHAT PRAKASHAN

Published by
PRABHAT PRAKASHAN PVT. LTD.
4/19 Asaf Ali Road,
New Delhi-110002 (INDIA)
e-mail: prabhatbooks@gmail.com

ISBN 978-93-5562-062-0
PERSONAL DEVELOPMENT MADE EASY
by *Grandmaster Avadhut das*

Edition
First, 2023

Price
₹ 600 (Rupees Six Hundred Only)

Printed at
Japan Art, Delhi

Author's Note

I have longed to write this book for some time. As a subconscious mind trainer and personal development coach, I have encountered numerous individuals who struggle to live their best lives. I strongly believe that personal development is the key to realizing one's potential and leading a fulfilling life.

This book is for anyone who is interested in self-improvement, whether you are starting your journey or have been on it for a while. I will guide you through a step-by-step process of personal development, starting with understanding what it is and why it is crucial, and then moving on to specific topics such as goal-setting, time management, building positive habits, and overcoming fear.

The purpose of this book is to equip you with practical tools and exercises that you can apply to enhance your personal development journey. Each chapter is designed to build upon the previous one, enabling you to make steady progress towards your goals. The book covers a broad range of topics, from understanding yourself to developing positive habits, effective communication, emotional intelligence, and much more.

This book is divided into twelve chapters, each focusing on a particular aspect of personal development. Each chapter includes exercises, case studies, and personal stories that will help you relate to the concepts and apply them to your life. These case studies and personal stories are from real people who have attained success through personal development, including my personal experiences.

To use this book effectively, I recommend that you read it from cover to cover first to gain a comprehensive understanding of the concepts. Then, you can revisit each chapter, concentrating on the exercises and case studies that are relevant to your personal development journey. You can also use the book as a reference guide to revisit specific topics as required.

It is essential to note that personal development is an ongoing journey that requires effort and commitment. This book is not a quick fix, and it will take time and effort to see tangible results. Additionally, while the techniques and strategies presented in the book have proven successful for many, they may not work for everyone. It is important to approach personal development with an open mind and be willing to adapt and adjust the strategies to suit your unique circumstances.

It is also important to acknowledge that personal development is not a substitute for professional help. If you are struggling with mental health issues or any other serious problems, seeking the assistance of a professional is essential. Personal development can be a helpful tool for managing your mental health, but it is not a replacement for therapy or medication.

I hope that this book will inspire and motivate you to take control of your personal development journey and achieve your goals. Remember, personal development is a lifelong journey, and the first step is the most critical.

Best wishes on your journey to self-improvement.

Sincerely,

Grandmaster Avadhut das
Kolkata

Acknowledgments

My gratitude to Srila Prabhupada, my mentor. He has helped shape my thoughts and actions, and for that, I am deeply grateful. I also offer my loving gratitude to Vamsidhari Gopal, the guiding light of my journey. His loving handholding has been instrumental in bringing this book to fruition. Without His presence, this book would not have been possible.

I am especially grateful to my daughter Puja, who has been a constant source of love, encouragement, and inspiration. Her unwavering support and belief in me has been invaluable, and her enthusiasm for this project has helped to keep me motivated during the most challenging times. She has provided valuable feedback, offered helpful insights, and her love and encouragement has been a source of strength and comfort.

I am immensely proud of her and grateful for her presence in my life. She is a shining light, and I am blessed to have her as my daughter.

I humbly express my gratitude to the many researchers and authors whose work has informed and influenced my own understanding of personal development.

I would like to express my gratitude to my students, and those who have shared their stories and experiences with me, and to the many researchers, authors, and thought leaders whose work has informed and influenced my own understanding of personal development.

Most importantly, thank you dear reader for joining me on this journey of personal development. Remember that you have the power to achieve your goals and live a fulfilling life. Keep exploring, and keep growing. May you find strength, wisdom, and success on every step of your journey!

❑

Introduction

Growing up, I struggled with low self-esteem and a lack of direction in life. I constantly found myself comparing myself to others and feeling like I didn't measure up. It wasn't until I discovered the power of personal development that I was able to break free from these limiting beliefs and create a life that I truly love.

Personal development involves more than just improving your skills and achieving your goals. It's about tapping into your true potential and becoming the best version of yourself. It involves developing the mindset, habits, and relationships that will support you in creating a purposeful and fulfilling life.

In this book, I'll share with you the insights, tools, and strategies that have helped both myself and my clients transform our lives. Each chapter will guide you through a different aspect of personal development, from discovering your true self to cultivating meaningful relationships. I've included personal stories and case studies to help you relate to the concepts and see how they can be applied in real-life situations. You'll also find practical exercises and reflection questions to help you apply the ideas to your own life.

Personal development is a lifelong journey of self-discovery and growth. It involves exploring your inner world, discovering your unique talents and strengths, and cultivating the habits and relationships that will support you in creating a purposeful and fulfilling life. While the path of personal development may not always be smooth, it's important to remember that every challenge and obstacle is an opportunity for learning and growth. By embracing challenges, you can develop resilience, learn new skills, and deepen your understanding of yourself and your potential.

To succeed in personal development, it's crucial to have a growth mindset. This means seeing failures as opportunities to learn and viewing setbacks as temporary obstacles that can be overcome with effort and persistence. In this book, I'll guide you through a step-by-step process of personal development, covering topics such as goal-setting, time management, positive habits, effective communication, emotional intelligence, and meaningful relationships. Along the way, you'll gain insights from personal stories and case studies, and you'll have the opportunity to reflect on your own experiences and goals.

However, personal development is not just about acquiring knowledge and skills. It is also about taking action and making positive changes in your life. This requires commitment, dedication, and a willingness to step outside your comfort zone.

My hope is that this book will inspire and empower you to take control of this journey and create the life that you truly desire. Remember, personal development is not a one-time event but a lifelong journey of growth and discovery, so let's embark on this journey together!

Remember to stay focused on your goals and believe in your ability to achieve them. It's important to be patient with yourself, as personal growth takes time and effort. With the right mindset, tools, and strategies, you can overcome any obstacle and become the best version of yourself. So, let's commit to this journey and create a life that exceeds our wildest dreams. The power is in your hands, so let's make it happen!

❑

Contents

Exercises in this Book

❑

CHAPTER 1

Personal Development Unveiled

"If you want to change the world, change yourself."
– Mahatma Gandhi

Introduction

Are you looking to make positive changes in your personal and professional life? If so, investing in yourself is the key to success.

In this chapter, we will explore what it means to invest in yourself and why it is essential for your growth. We will discuss the concept of personal development, and the many benefits that come with it, such as gaining self-awareness, confidence, and resilience.

We will also explore the factors that shape our personalities and perspectives, including upbringing and experience. Through this, we will help you understand why self-improvement is critical in shaping your life in a positive direction.

This book covers various aspects of personal development, including career, relationships, health, and spiritual growth. In this chapter, we will introduce you to different methods of self-improvement, such as stepping out of your comfort zone and trying new things.

Our goal is to provide you with practical ideas for creating a personal development plan, which can help you kick-start your journey towards growth. Throughout this chapter, we will share examples and insights from successful individuals who have achieved their goals through self-improvement.

By the end of this chapter, you will have a solid understanding of personal development, its importance, and how you can begin your journey. Remember, the power of self-improvement lies within you, and it's time to start using it to realize your full potential.

What is personal development?

Personal development refers to the process of improving oneself through various means. It involves setting goals, identifying areas for improvement, and taking steps to enhance personal skills and abilities. It is a lifelong journey that can bring about positive changes in every aspect of one's life, including personal relationships, career, health, and overall well-being.

The importance of personal development lies in the fact that it enables individuals to reach their full potential. When we invest in our personal growth and development, we become more self-aware, confident, and resilient. We are better equipped to handle life's challenges and can make informed decisions that lead to success and fulfillment.

However, personal development can mean different things to different people. For some, it may involve improving their professional skills or achieving a specific career goal. For others, it may be about developing their spiritual or emotional well-being. Some may see personal development as a means to improve their physical health, while others may focus on developing their social skills.

Regardless of how we define personal development, the journey towards achieving it is unique to each individual. It is essential to identify our goals and values and create a roadmap that aligns with them. We need to be mindful of our strengths and weaknesses, and focus on improving areas that need attention.

Understanding Your Potential

Every individual has unique skills, talents, and abilities that they can develop further to reach their full potential. However, many people may not realize their full potential due to limiting beliefs or lack of self-confidence. Personal development can help individuals overcome these barriers and unleash their hidden potential.

Self-Awareness: Self-awareness is the first step towards personal development. It involves understanding oneself, including one's strengths, weaknesses, values, and beliefs. When individuals become more self-aware, they can identify areas for improvement and take steps to enhance their skills and abilities. Self-awareness can be developed through practices such as meditation, journaling, and seeking feedback from others.

Goal-Setting: Setting goals is a powerful tool for personal development. It provides direction and motivation, and helps individuals focus their efforts towards achieving specific outcomes. When setting goals, it is essential to ensure that they are specific, measurable, achievable, relevant, and time-bound (SMART). By setting and achieving goals, individuals can boost their self-confidence and build a sense of accomplishment.

Continuous Learning: Personal development is an ongoing process that requires individuals to be open to learning and growth. Continuous learning can take various forms, such as reading books, attending seminars, or taking courses. By acquiring new knowledge and skills, individuals can expand their horizons, increase their value in the job market, and improve their overall quality of life.

Taking Action: Personal development is not just about acquiring knowledge and skills; it also involves taking action towards achieving one's goals. Individuals must take consistent and deliberate action towards their goals to make progress. Taking action can be challenging, but it is essential to overcome the fear of failure and step out of one's comfort zone.

Achieving Your Goals Through Personal Development

Personal development, at its core, serves as a guiding compass that helps you navigate the path to your goals. This process is much like equipping yourself with a sharpened axe; it facilitates the journey by honing your skills, fostering a resilient mindset, and bolstering your capacity to deal with adversities. When you engage in personal development, you are essentially setting the stage to bring your dreams to fruition. It's about molding your potential into palpable success by actively seeking growth and improvement.

When you immerse yourself in personal development, you will uncover hidden strengths and learn to transform weaknesses into opportunities. The beauty of this process is that it's not just about skill acquisition; it's about cultivating a positive attitude, unwavering determination, and a profound belief in your capabilities. These traits become your guiding stars, transforming every challenge into a stepping stone and every setback into a lesson. Through personal development, the journey to your goals becomes less burdensome, more manageable, and profoundly enriching.

Personal Story

Sunita, who is from Goa, India, talks about how personal development helped her achieve her goals and achieve her full potential.

I have always been interested in running my own business, but I didn't have the skills and knowledge to do so. That's when I decided to put money into my growth. I took business management, marketing, and finance classes and went to networking events to meet other business owners.

Through personal development, I learned how to set clear goals and come up with plans to achieve those goals. I also learned how to stay focused on my goals and keep going even when things didn't go as planned.

Because of my journey to improve myself, I was able to start my own business and be successful. I owe my success to personal development, which gave me the tools, skills, and plans I needed to achieve my goals and live up to my full potential.

Personal development is a lifelong process that can help people achieve their goals and achieve their full potential. People can become the best versions of themselves and achieve their goals by getting to know themselves better, setting clear goals, learning new skills and competencies, building relationships with other people, and learning how to deal with challenges and setbacks.

Why Personal Development is Important

Personal development helps individuals enhance their skills, knowledge, and mindset. By investing in personal growth, individuals can improve their ability to succeed in every area of life, be it in their personal relationships, career, or other areas. Personal development can also help individuals identify and overcome limiting beliefs and negative self-talk that may be holding them back from achieving their goals.

Personal development also fosters self-awareness, which is essential for understanding oneself and one's purpose in life. By gaining a deeper understanding of oneself, individuals can align their goals and actions with their values and passions, leading to a sense of fulfillment and purpose in life. Personal development also promotes continuous learning, which is crucial for staying relevant in a rapidly changing world and remaining competitive in the job market.

Examples of Successful Individuals Who Prioritize Personal Development:

Many successful individuals prioritize personal development as a key component of their success. Here are some examples:

Oprah Winfrey

Oprah Winfrey is one of the most successful and influential people in the world. She credits her success to personal development, which has helped her overcome adversity, build resilience, and achieve her goals.

Elon Musk

Elon Musk is a visionary entrepreneur who has achieved incredible success with his companies, such as SpaceX and Tesla. He is known for his relentless pursuit of personal development and is constantly learning and growing.

Tony Hsieh

Tony Hsieh was the CEO of Zappos, an online retailer. He was known for his commitment to personal growth and development and encouraged his employees to invest in their personal growth. He believed that personal growth was essential to building a successful business.

Case study: A successful entrepreneur shares how personal development helped her build her business

Hello, I'm Khushi Mehta, and I run a garments exporting business that I started five years ago. When I first began, I faced many challenges, but I was determined to succeed. I realized that to be successful, I needed to invest in personal development and continuously improve myself.

To begin with, I attended various workshops and seminars related to business and entrepreneurship. I learned new skills, gained knowledge, and developed a growth mindset. I also worked on building my communication and networking skills, which helped me establish strong relationships with clients and suppliers.

In addition to attending workshops and seminars, I also spent a lot of time reading books and articles on personal development, business, and leadership. I learned from successful entrepreneurs and business leaders and applied their strategies to my own business.

My dedication to personal development paid off. I was able to overcome the challenges I faced and grow my business steadily. My strong leadership skills, growth mindset, and effective communication skills were critical factors in my success.

Today, I continue to invest in personal development and encourage my employees to do the same. I believe that continuous learning and growth are essential for personal and professional success. My story is a testament to the importance of personal development in achieving success as an entrepreneur.

The Benefits of Personal Development

Increased self-awareness: Personal development allows individuals to gain a deeper understanding of themselves, their values, and their beliefs. By exploring their inner selves, individuals can identify areas where they need to grow and work towards becoming their best selves. This increased self-awareness can lead to greater confidence, resilience, and a sense of purpose.

Improved relationships: Personal development can also improve the quality of relationships individuals have with others. By developing skills such as effective communication, empathy, and active listening, individuals can build stronger and more meaningful connections with the people in their lives. This can lead to better collaboration, increased trust, and more fulfilling relationships.

Enhanced well-being: Engaging in personal development activities can have a positive impact on an individual's physical, emotional, and mental well-being. For example, regular exercise and healthy eating habits can improve physical health, while practices such as meditation and journaling can promote emotional and mental wellness. Additionally, personal development activities can reduce stress and increase overall life satisfaction.

How personal growth can help you be successful:

In the professional realm, personal development can help individuals advance their careers and achieve success. By developing skills such as time management, effective communication, and leadership, individuals can become more valuable to their organizations and increase their chances of promotion. Additionally, personal development can help individuals identify their career goals and develop a plan to achieve them, whether it's starting their own business or pursuing a new career path.

Personal development can also lead to success in relationships. By developing skills such as empathy, active listening, and conflict resolution, individuals can build stronger and more fulfilling relationships with family, friends, and romantic partners. Personal development can also help individuals identify and overcome limiting beliefs or negative patterns that may be affecting their relationships, leading to greater happiness and connection with others.

Furthermore, personal development can lead to success in personal growth and overall well-being. By engaging in activities such as meditation, exercise, and self-reflection, individuals can improve their physical, emotional, and mental health. Personal development can also help individuals develop a growth mindset that enables them to approach challenges with resilience and perseverance.

Personal story: An individual shares how personal development helped him overcome personal challenges and achieve his goals

Meet Jayesh Modi, a 32-year-old software engineer from Mumbai. He was born and raised in a middle-class family and has always been passionate about technology. Jayesh always knew that he wanted to pursue a career in software engineering, so he worked hard and earned a degree in Computer Science. Here is his personal story:

A few years after graduating from college, I went through a difficult time in my personal life. I had just gone through a painful breakup, and I was struggling with depression and anxiety. I found it hard to focus on my work and felt constantly overwhelmed.

It was during this time that I started exploring the concept of personal development. I began reading self-help books, listening to podcasts, and attending workshops and seminars. I realized that I needed to make some changes in my life. I needed to develop a more positive mindset, improve my communication skills, and learn how to manage my emotions better.

Through personal development, I learned how to identify my strengths and weaknesses and work on improving them. I also gained more self-awareness and learned how to take responsibility for my own happiness and success. With a clearer understanding of who I was and what I wanted, I was able to set clearer goals for myself and work towards achieving them.

Personal development helped me overcome my personal challenges and achieve my goals. It allowed me to develop a stronger sense of self and become a better version of myself. I believe that personal development is essential for anyone who wants to lead a fulfilling and successful life.

Factors That Influence Personal Development

Personal development is a journey that can be influenced by various factors like, genetics, environment, and experiences as they shape who we are and the way we interact with the world around us.

Genetics play a significant role in shaping our personality traits, cognitive abilities, and emotional intelligence. For instance, some people may be naturally more optimistic, while others may have a predisposition to anxiety or depression. However, it is important to note that genetics do not determine our fate. We have the power to shape our thoughts and behaviors through personal development and self-improvement.

Environment also plays a crucial role in our personal development. Our upbringing, culture, and social surroundings shape our values, beliefs, and attitudes towards life. The people we interact with and the environments we inhabit can either support or hinder our personal growth. It is important to surround ourselves with positive influences that motivate and inspire us to be the best version of ourselves.

Experiences are another important factor that can influence our personal development. Our experiences shape our perspectives, beliefs, and behaviors. Positive experiences such as success, love, and happiness can boost our confidence and self-esteem, while negative experiences such as failure, rejection, and trauma can affect our mental health and well-being. However, it is important to acknowledge that even negative experiences can be transformative and lead to personal growth and resilience.

Taking Control of Personal Development

Taking control of personal development means taking an active role in shaping one's own growth and progress towards their goals. It involves making conscious and intentional choices that lead to personal growth and development. One of the first steps towards taking control of personal development is setting clear and specific goals. Goals give direction and purpose to one's efforts, and help to focus energy and attention on the things that truly matter.

Another important aspect of taking control of personal development is developing self-awareness. This means becoming more conscious of one's thoughts, feelings, strengths, weaknesses, and motivations. Self-awareness is essential for understanding one's own tendencies, habits, and behaviors, and for identifying areas where growth and improvement are needed. Developing self-awareness can be done through practices such as mindfulness, journaling, or working with a coach or mentor.

In addition to setting goals and developing self-awareness, taking control of personal development also involves making intentional choices about how to spend time and energy. This means being deliberate about the activities one engages in, the relationships one cultivates, and the habits one forms. It means being willing to step outside of one's comfort zone and take risks in pursuit of personal growth and development. It also means being open to feedback and willing to learn from mistakes and setbacks.

Self-Reflection Exercise

We suggest the following self-reflection exercise to help you figure out your goals and areas of focus for personal growth:

1. Think about what you believe and what you value. What's most important to you? How do you want your life to turn out?
2. Figure out what your good points and bad points are. What do you do well? Where do you need to get better?
3. Think about what you've done in the past. What are the most important things you've done in your life? What did they do to you?
4. Set personal development goals that are clear, measurable, doable, relevant, and have a deadline. What are your short-term and long-term goals?

Personal growth is a complicated and multifaceted process that is affected by many things, like genes, the environment, and life experiences. Even though these things can affect how a person grows, that person has the power to take charge of their growth. By setting goals, making habits, and asking for feedback, people can make choices that will help them achieve their personal development goals. The self-reflection exercise can help people figure out their goals and areas of focus for personal growth. By investing in themselves and committing to personal growth, people can achieve their full potential and live happier lives.

Different Areas of Personal Development

One of the most fundamental aspects of personal development is physical health. Taking care of one's body by eating a balanced diet, getting enough exercise, and getting adequate rest can greatly contribute to overall well-being. It can increase energy levels, improve mental health, and help individuals feel more confident in their abilities.

Emotional well-being is also a critical aspect of personal development. It involves developing emotional intelligence, self-awareness, and empathy towards others. By learning how to manage emotions effectively, individuals can better handle stress, communicate more effectively, and build more meaningful relationships.

Career development is another vital area of personal development, as individuals spend a significant amount of time at work. Developing skills, setting goals, and continuous learning can help individuals progress in their careers and achieve success. It is also essential to find a career that aligns with one's values and passions to achieve fulfillment and satisfaction in life.

Personal relationships are an integral part of life and require ongoing attention and effort. Developing healthy communication skills, empathy, and trust can help individuals build deeper connections and create meaningful relationships. It can also lead to greater personal growth and development as individuals learn from their interactions with others.

How to prioritize different areas of personal development

One way to prioritize areas of personal development is to consider one's long-term goals. For instance, if an individual wants to advance their career, they may need to focus on developing specific skills or acquiring certain knowledge. In this case, career development may be the top priority for personal development. On the other hand, if an individual is experiencing emotional distress, they may need to prioritize their emotional well-being by seeking therapy or practicing self-care.

Another way to prioritize areas of personal development is to consider one's current needs. For instance, if an individual is struggling with a physical health condition, they may need to prioritize their physical health by adopting healthy habits or seeking medical treatment. Similarly, if an individual is experiencing relationship issues, they may need to prioritize their personal relationships by seeking therapy or improving communication skills.

It is important to note that personal development is not a linear process, and priorities may shift over time. What is important today may not be as important tomorrow. Therefore, it is essential for individuals to regularly evaluate their priorities and make adjustments as needed.

Case study: Nitu shares how she prioritized personal development in her career and achieved success

Hi, my name is Nitu Shindhe, and I am the spa manager at a prestigious 5-star hotel. Throughout my career, personal development has been a top priority for me, and I have made intentional choices to pursue opportunities for growth and learning.

When I first started working in the hospitality industry, I knew that I wanted to excel in my role and progress in my career. However, I quickly realized that simply working hard was not enough. To truly stand out and make a difference, I needed to continuously develop my skills and knowledge.

One of the first areas I focused on was my communication skills. As a spa manager, I needed to be able to effectively communicate with my team, guests, and other departments in the hotel. I invested time and effort in learning how to listen actively, give and receive feedback, and communicate clearly and professionally.

Another area I prioritized was staying up-to-date with industry trends and best practices. I attended conferences, workshops, and training sessions to learn about the latest techniques, products, and technologies in the spa industry. This helped me not only improve the services we offered at the spa but also made me a more valuable employee to the hotel.

I am able to see that prioritizing personal development has helped me achieve success in my career. By continuously learning, growing, and improving, I have been able to take on new challenges and responsibilities, and contribute to the success of the hotel. I highly recommend that anyone looking to excel in their career make personal development a priority.

Approaches to Personal Development

There are various approaches that individuals can take to help them achieve their personal development goals. One of the most popular approaches is self-help books, which are widely available and cover a broad range of topics, from building self-confidence to improving relationships. Self-help books can be an affordable and accessible way to gain knowledge and insights into personal development.

Another approach to personal development is coaching. Coaching is a process where individuals work with a coach to identify their goals, strengths, and areas for improvement. The coach provides guidance and support to help individuals reach their goals and overcome any obstacles that may arise. Coaching can be particularly effective for individuals who want to achieve specific goals, such as career advancement or improved communication skills.

Therapy is another approach to personal development that focuses on mental and emotional well-being. Therapy can help individuals address any underlying issues that may be holding them back from achieving their personal development goals. A therapist can provide tools and strategies to help individuals manage stress, anxiety, and other mental health issues that may be impacting their personal development.

Mentorship is one other approach to personal development that involves seeking guidance and advice from someone with more experience and knowledge in a particular field or area of interest. A mentor can provide valuable insights and feedback to help individuals grow and develop in their chosen career or personal pursuits.

Choosing the Approach That Works Best for You

One of the first things to consider is your learning style. Some people prefer to read books and articles, while others may benefit more from one-on-one coaching or therapy. If you're a visual learner, you might find it helpful to watch videos or attend workshops. Similarly, if you prefer hands-on learning, you might benefit from mentorship or apprenticeship programs.

Another factor to consider is the type of development you're looking for. If you're interested in improving your emotional well-being, therapy or coaching might be a good choice. On the other hand, if you're looking to develop specific skills or knowledge, such as public speaking or financial management, you might benefit from workshops, classes, or mentorship.

It's also important to consider your budget and availability. Personal development can come with a wide range of costs, from free online resources to expensive coaching or therapy programs. Make sure to choose an approach that fits within your budget and schedule. Additionally, it's important to consider the time and effort required for the approach you choose. Some approaches, such as therapy or coaching, require regular appointments and a significant time commitment.

Implementing the Approach

Once you've decided how you want to improve yourself, it is important to do it well. Here are some tips for carrying out the plan:

- ❖ Make a plan of action and set clear goals.
- ❖ Figure out what tools and help you need to achieve your goals.
- ❖ Keep track of your progress and make changes as you need to.
- ❖ Stay motivated and on track by celebrating your successes and learning from your mistakes.
- ❖ Ask others for feedback and change your plan as needed.
- ❖ Don't give up on your journey to improve yourself, and be patient with yourself.

Exercise

Dear Reader, you are encouraged to look into different ways to improve yourself and choose one to try. Here are some steps you need to take:

- Make a list of the personal development goals you want to achieve. These could be goals for your career, relationships, health and wellness, spirituality, or any other area of your life where you want to grow and improve.
- Next, look into the different ways to improve yourself that were discussed in this chapter and any others that interest you. Use books, online resources, and experts in personal development to find out more about each method. Write down the pros, any possible cons, and any examples of how the idea has been used successfully.
- Think about your values and interests, and consider which methods fit with them. Ask yourself which approach makes you feel the most inspired, energized, or connected to your goals and dreams.
- Choose a personal development method that interests you and make a plan for putting it into practice in your life. Find specific steps you can take to use this method in your daily life or other situations.
- Put your plan into action and promise to use the chosen method for a certain amount of time, such as 30 or 60 days. Note any changes in your mood, behavior, or outlook, as well as any problems or successes you face along the way.
- At the end of the set time, evaluate how well the approach worked by thinking about how you changed and whether or not you met your personal development goals. If you think the approach worked, keep doing it or think about trying something else. If not, you should try a different approach.

Case Study: My Path to Personal Growth

I am Mira, and I have always been interested in improving myself. Over the years, I have read a lot of books, gone to a lot of seminars, and tried out a lot of different techniques and ways of doing things. But despite everything I did, I still felt stuck in some parts of my life and didn't know how to move on.

One day, I found an online seminar on self-reflection put on by Subconscious World and decided to give it a try. As the seminar suggested, I started keeping a regular journal and making time every day to think about my thoughts, feelings, and experiences. At first, it was hard to get into the habit of doing this new thing, but as I started to see the benefits, it got easier.

I learned more about myself and what drives me by taking time to think about myself. I was able to see patterns in my behavior and thoughts that were holding me back and keeping me from achieving my goals. By noticing these patterns and working to change them, I was able to move forward in areas of my life where I had previously felt stuck.

I also started to see the value in other ways to improve myself, like setting goals and learning new skills. By setting clear, measurable goals and working to learn new skills, I was able to make real progress and feel like I had done something good.

As I kept looking into different ways to improve myself, I realized that each one had its own set of pros and cons. But I was able to create a more well-rounded and effective plan for my personal development by using several different methods.

I still work on my personal growth and make it a top priority in my life. I can live a more fulfilling and successful life by regularly reflecting on myself, setting goals, learning new skills, and doing other things that help me grow as a person.

Building a Personal Development Plan

A personal development plan is a set of steps that a person can follow to achieve their goals and make their lives better. It involves making goals that are clear, measurable, and doable; finding the resources needed to achieve those goals; and coming up with a plan to achieve them. In this section, we will talk about how important it is to set goals that are clear, measurable, and attainable. We will also show you step-by-step how to make your own personal development plan.

Importance of Setting Specific, Measurable, and Achievable Goals

Without clear and measurable goals, it can be hard to stay motivated and on track, and it can be hard to see how far you've come. Here are some reasons why it is important to set goals that are clear, measurable, and doable:

First, having clear and focused goals brings clarity. When you have a clear goal in mind, you can put all of your time and energy towards achieving it. Having clear goals also helps you figure out what success means, which can give you motivation and a sense of purpose.

Second, goals that can be measured let you keep track of your progress and change your plan as needed. When you have a goal that can be measured, you can keep track of your progress and change your plan if you aren't making the progress you wanted. Measurable goals also give you a feeling of success when you achieve certain points along the way.

Third, it is important to have goals that are attainable because they make you feel like you can achieve them. When goals aren't realistic or are too hard to achieve, it can be discouraging and make you feel like you've failed. Setting goals that are hard but not impossible to achieve can make you feel good and give you more confidence in your ability to succeed.

How to set specific, measurable, and achievable goals

To set specific goals, you need to be clear about what you want to achieve. For example, if your goal is to improve your communication skills, you should be clear about which aspects of communication you want to work on. For instance, you might want to work on improving your public speaking, writing, or interpersonal communication skills. Once you know what you want to improve, you can make a plan to help you achieve that goal.

Measurable goals are those that can be measured or judged using objective criteria. Measurable goals give you a way to track your progress and see if you are getting closer to your goal. To make goals that can be measured, you need to decide on the specific criteria that will be used to measure your progress. For example, if your goal is to improve your public speaking skills, you could make it a measurable goal by setting a target for the number of speeches you will give in a certain amount of time or the number of people you will talk to.

Achievable goals are those that are realistic and can be achieved with the resources and time you have. When setting goals that can be achieved, it is important to think about your current skills, resources, and time constraints. If your goal is too big or requires resources that you don't have, you may get discouraged and lose motivation. On the other hand, if your goal is too easy, you may not feel challenged and may not make any progress toward your personal development.

Here are some examples of personal development goals that are specific, measurable, and attainable:

Example 1: Education Goal

- **Goal:** to finish a bachelor's degree in psychology in three years.
- **Specific:** The goal is specific because it clearly states what the person wants to do, which is getting a bachelor's degree in psychology.
- **Measurable:** The goal is measurable because it has a specific outcome, which is getting the degree in three years.
- **Achievable:** The goal is attainable because it is a common amount of time to earn a bachelor's degree and the person has researched the program and knows what they are capable of.

Example 2: Career Goals

- **Goal:** To get a promotion to a senior project manager position in the next two years.
- **Specific:** The goal is specific because it says exactly what the person wants to achieve, which is to get a promotion to a senior project manager position.
- **Measurable:** The goal is measurable because it has a clear deadline: within the next two years.
- **Achievable:** The person has looked over the requirements and responsibilities of the job and talked to their boss about their career goals, so the goal is doable.

Example 3: Relationship Goals

- **Goal:** To improve communication with my partner by going to couples therapy once a week for six months.
- **Specific:** The goal is specific because it clearly states what the person wants to achieve, which is to improve communication with their partner by going to couples therapy sessions.
- **Measurable:** The goal is measurable because it has a clear time frame, such as once a week for six months.
- **Achievable:** The goal is attainable because the person has talked to their partner about their concerns, and together they have agreed to go to therapy to work on their communication skills.

Creating a Personal Development Plan

The first step in creating a personal development plan is to identify specific goals that one wants to achieve. These goals should be challenging yet achievable, and align with one's values and interests. The next step is to break down the goals into smaller, manageable steps that can be achieved over time. It is important to set a timeline for achieving these steps to keep oneself accountable and motivated.

Another important aspect of creating a personal development plan is to identify the resources required to achieve the goals. This could include books, courses, workshops, or mentorship. One should also consider the potential obstacles that may arise and plan for how to overcome them.

Tracking progress is an important part of the personal development plan. Regularly monitoring one's progress towards achieving the goals helps to stay motivated and make necessary adjustments to the plan. Celebrating small wins along the way can also help to maintain momentum and positivity.

A step-by-step guide to creating a personal development plan:

Step 1: Reflect on Yourself

The first step in making a personal development plan is to think about your current situation and where you want to be. Ask yourself questions such as:

- ❖ What are my strengths and what are my weaknesses?
- ❖ What do I enjoy doing?
- ❖ What are my short and long-term goals?
- ❖ What are the obstacles that keep me from achieving my goals?
- ❖ What skills and knowledge do I need to learn or build to achieve my goals?

By thinking about these questions, you can get a better idea of what you want to achieve and what areas you need to focus on for personal development.

Step 2: Set Specific Goals

After you've thought about your current situation, the next step is to come up with specific goals you want to achieve. Make sure that these goals are specific, measurable, achievable, relevant, and time-bound (SMART). Write down your goals and be as specific as you can about what you want to achieve.

Step 3: Make an Action Plan

After you've decided on your goals, it is time to make a plan for how to achieve them. This should include specific steps you will take to achieve each goal, as well as a timeline and milestones for keeping track of your progress.

- ❖ Some things to think about when creating your action plan are:
- ❖ What resources or help will I need to achieve my goals?
- ❖ What obstacles or challenges might I face, and how can I get past them?
- ❖ What specific steps will I take to achieve each goal?

Step 4: Implement Your Plan

Once you have made your action plan, it is time to start carrying it out. Start taking the specific steps you've listed in your plan, and keep track of your progress toward each goal. Make changes as needed based on your progress and any problems you run into.

Step 5: Review and Change Your Plan

Review your progress often and adjust your plan as needed. As you achieve some of your goals, you may find that you need to change your plan to reflect new goals or priorities. Reviewing and changing your plan often will help you stay on track and keep making progress toward your personal development goals.

Exercise: Create Your Own Personal Development Plan

Follow the steps above to make your plan for personal development. Take some time to think about your goals and objectives, and use the SMART criteria to make them specific, measurable, achievable, relevant, and time-bound. Find the resources you will need and the problems you will have to solve to achieve your goals. Then, make an action plan with the steps you need to take to achieve each goal. Put your plan into action, keep track of your progress, and make changes as needed. Celebrate your progress along the way and use it to push you forward.

Author's Personal Story: "The Impact of Personal Development on My Life Journey"

As a child, I always felt like something was missing from my life, but I couldn't figure out what it was. Even though I had a good family and a good education, I didn't know what I wanted to do with my life. But when I found the world of personal development, everything changed.

I became obsessed with learning everything I could about growing and changing as a person. I read a lot of books and went to seminars because I was eager to achieve my full potential and find my calling. The plan worked! I was amazed by how my life changed when I started to see things differently.

I didn't just want to learn, though. If I wanted to change my life, I knew I had to use what I had learned. So, I made plans and worked hard to achieve my goals. And when I saw the results of my work, I felt like I had a purpose and was happy in a way I had never felt before.

I didn't take long to realize that I wanted to help other people go through the same kind of change. So I became a trainer of the subconscious mind and a motivational speaker. I share my knowledge and experience with anyone who wants to achieve their goals and achieve their full potential.

Personal development has helped a lot of people become successful and change their lives over the years. It has been an amazing journey, and I feel lucky to be able to do what I love every day.

Personal development has not only impacted my career, but it has also impacted every aspect of my life. It has taught me to live intentionally, to pay attention to my thoughts and actions, and to always try to grow and get better.

If you feel like your life is missing something, you should look into the world of personal development. It can change your life in ways that you never thought were possible. So start your journey today by taking the first step.

Exercises for you

- Think about why you want to improve yourself as a person.
- Make a list of the possible benefits you might get from achieving your full potential.
- Write down three specific goals for how you want to grow as a person.

Share your Thoughts

Congratulations, you've made it to the end of the chapter! I hope you found this chapter helpful in understanding what personal development is all about. If you are like me, you might be thinking, "Wait, why do I need personal development? I'm already perfect!" (cue eye roll). But in all seriousness, personal development is an essential aspect of living a fulfilling life.

If you enjoyed this chapter and found it helpful, I would love it if you could leave a review on Amazon. Not only does it help other readers decide if this book is right for them, but it also helps me as an author to know what I am doing right and what I can improve on. Share your own personal experiences with personal development in your review, and let us start a conversation about how we can all grow and improve.

Writing a review is easy - just head over to Amazon, find the book, and click on the 'Write a Customer Review' button. And don't worry if you are not a professional writer or if you are not sure what to say. Just be honest and share your thoughts. I promise it will mean the world to me.

As an incentive for leaving a review, I would like to offer you the 'Author's Draft' of this chapter. The Author's Draft contains extended details and research on the chapter that may not have made it into the final published version. All you have to do is write a review and inform our office at sworld.mind@gmail.com about the review. We will then send over the 'Author's Draft' to you. So, what are you waiting for? Leave a review and get the 'Author's Draft'!

Conclusion

In this chapter, we have discussed the importance of personal development and its numerous benefits. We have also explored the different factors that influence personal development and identified the various areas and approaches that can be taken to achieve personal growth.

Understanding your potential is crucial in personal development. It enables individuals to identify their strengths, weaknesses, values, and goals. Personal development helps individuals build their self-awareness, boost their confidence, and create a positive outlook towards life. Through personal development, individuals can achieve personal and professional growth, improve their relationships, and live a more fulfilling life.

Remember that personal development is a continuous journey that requires effort, dedication, and patience. There is no one-size-fits-all approach to personal development, and individuals should tailor their approach to their unique needs and goals. Creating a personal development plan and seeking support from mentors, coaches, or like-minded individuals can help individuals stay on track and achieve their goals.

Wrap Up

Congratulations again, on taking the first step towards personal development! It takes courage to acknowledge that you want to improve yourself and take control of your life. Now it is time to talk about the most important aspect of personal development - your commitment to it. Personal development is not a one-time event; it's a journey that requires constant attention and effort. You need to make a commitment to yourself to continue growing and improving every single day.

It is easy to get caught up in the busyness of everyday life and neglect our personal development. We may feel like we don't have the time, energy, or resources to invest in ourselves. But I am here to tell you that investing in yourself is the best investment you can ever make.

The benefits of personal development are limitless. It can help you become more confident, resilient, and productive. It can also lead to a more fulfilling and purposeful life. But it all starts with a commitment to yourself.

Make a pledge to commit yourself to personal development. Take small steps every day to improve yourself in some or the other area of your life, whether it is your physical health, emotional well-being, relationships, or career. Keep learning, growing, and challenging yourself. Remember, personal development is not a destination, but a journey that you must embrace wholeheartedly.

It won't always be easy, but it will always be worth it. Personal development is not just about achieving success; it is about becoming the best version of yourself. So, take a deep breath, make a plan, and commit yourself to personal development. The journey may be long, but the rewards are endless.

"Personal development is a major time-saver. The better you become, the less time it takes you to achieve your goals."

– Brian Tracy

❑

CHAPTER 2

Knowing Your True Self

"Knowing yourself is the beginning of all wisdom."

– **Aristotle**

Introduction

Have you ever found yourself in a situation where you were not sure how to react or respond? Perhaps you felt overwhelmed or unsure of yourself? Understanding yourself is an essential component of personal development. By developing a deep sense of self-awareness, you can gain a better understanding of who you are, what you stand for, and what you want in life.

In the previous chapter, we discussed the importance of personal development and how it can help you achieve your goals and live a fulfilling life. In this chapter, we will explore the concept of self-awareness and its importance in personal development. We will discuss the benefits of developing self-awareness and provide practical tips on how to cultivate it. You will learn how to identify your strengths and weaknesses, understand your values and beliefs, and overcome limiting beliefs that may be holding you back.

By the end of this chapter, you will have a better understanding of yourself, and you will be well on your way to unlocking your full potential. We will also share personal stories and case studies to help you gain a deeper understanding of the power of self-awareness in personal development. So, let's get started!

II. Defining Self-Awareness

Self-awareness is the ability to recognize and understand your own emotions, thoughts, and behaviors, and is the foundation of personal development because it enables individuals to identify their strengths, weaknesses, and values. By having a clear understanding of oneself, we can make conscious decisions that align with our personal goals and values, leading to a more fulfilling life. Being self-aware helps individuals gain a deeper understanding of their thoughts, feelings, and actions, and equips them to manage their emotions and handle challenging situations. It also allows individuals to take responsibility for their own behavior and make positive changes to improve themselves.

Understanding our strengths is essential to personal development because it helps us identify what we are good at and what we can leverage to achieve our goals. When we know our strengths, we can focus on developing them further, which can lead to increased confidence and success.

On the other hand, identifying our weaknesses can be difficult but is equally important. Acknowledging our weaknesses allows us to work on them, which can help us grow and improve. It also helps us understand our limitations and recognize when we need to seek help from others.

Values are the guiding principles that define who we are and what we stand for. They influence our decisions and actions, and having a clear understanding of our values can help us live a more purposeful life. When we align our actions with our values, we are more likely to feel fulfilled and satisfied with our choices.

The Benefits of Self-Awareness

Self-awareness leads to improved decision-making skills because it enables individuals to recognize their biases and consider multiple perspectives. By understanding our thoughts, feelings, and actions, we can make decisions that align with our values and goals. This helps us make better choices, resulting in more positive outcomes and less regret.

Being self-aware helps us understand our own emotions and behaviors, which in turn, helps us understand others. This allows us to build stronger and more meaningful relationships. Self-awareness also helps us communicate better, which reduces misunderstandings and conflicts. When we are able to communicate effectively and empathetically, we can build more trusting relationships.

Self-awareness helps individuals identify their strengths and weaknesses. By focusing on their strengths, individuals can increase their confidence and self-esteem. On the other hand, by acknowledging their weaknesses, individuals can work on improving themselves and building their self-confidence. Self-awareness also allows individuals to set realistic goals, which helps them feel a sense of accomplishment, leading to increased confidence.

Self-awareness helps individuals manage their emotions, leading to reduced stress and anxiety. By understanding our triggers and how we respond to them, we can develop coping mechanisms that help us manage stress and anxiety. This leads to a more peaceful and balanced life.

Personal story

Sara, a fashion designer, talks about how knowing herself helped her deal with problems and achieve her goals.

As a fashion designer, I have always loved being creative and letting my ideas come out through clothes. But as I started to work in the industry, I realized that not knowing myself was stopping me from achieving my goals.

I had always been a perfectionist who worried about every little detail of my designs and looked to others for approval. But this way of doing things left me feeling and thinking empty. If I wanted to do well in my career, I knew I had to make some changes.

One day, I decided to take a step back and think about how I designed clothes. I first asked myself why I was so focused on being perfect and looking for approval from other people. I realized that I had been trying to meet other people's expectations instead of embracing my own creativity and unique point of view.

Through this process of self-reflection, I began to develop a greater sense of self-awareness. I started to recognize my strengths as a designer, such as my eye for color and my ability to create bold, statement pieces. I also started to see my flaws, like how I tend to overthink and second-guess my ideas.

Now that I knew more about myself, I was able to start making changes to how I design. I started to trust my gut more, take more risks, and accept my unique point of view. I also started to ask for feedback from others more helpfully, focusing on how to use their ideas to make my designs better instead of trying to get their approval.

As I started to make these changes, my career started to move forward in a real way. My designs got bolder and more expressive, and people started to notice them more. I also started to feel more confident in my skills as a designer and didn't need outside approval to feel like I was doing well.

When I look back, I see that knowing myself was the key to my success. Without it, I would have kept trying to be perfect and looking for approval, and I would have never fully accepted my unique ideas and creativity. But it helped me get a better sense of who I was and make positive changes in my approach to design. Today, I continue to prioritize self-awareness in my work and personal life, knowing that it will always be an essential tool for achieving my goals and overcoming personal challenges.

Developing Self-Awareness

One way to develop self-awareness is through self-reflection. It is an effective way to develop self-awareness because it allows individuals to analyze their experiences and gain insight into their behavior. Journaling, meditating, or simply taking a few minutes to reflect on your day are all examples of self-reflection. By consistently engaging in self-reflection, individuals can gain a deeper understanding of themselves and their emotions.

Mindfulness too is an effective way to develop self-awareness because it helps individuals become more attuned to their thoughts and emotions. Mindfulness meditation, yoga, or simply focusing on your breath are all examples of mindfulness practices. By regularly practicing mindfulness, individuals can become more aware of their thought patterns and emotional responses, leading to increased self-awareness.

Another effective way to develop self-awareness is to seek feedback from others. This involves asking for honest and constructive feedback from trusted friends, family members, or colleagues. By receiving feedback, individuals can gain valuable insight into their behavior and identify blind spots that they may not have been aware of. It is important to be open-minded and non-defensive when receiving feedback, as this will help individuals learn and grow.

Journaling and Meditation

Journaling involves writing down your thoughts and feelings in a notebook or journal. It is a powerful tool for self-reflection and self-awareness because it allows individuals to track their emotions, identify patterns, and gain insights into their behavior. By consistently journaling, individuals can develop a deeper understanding of their thoughts and emotions, which can help them make more informed decisions.

Meditation involves training your mind to focus on the present moment and observe your thoughts and emotions without judgment. It is an effective way to develop self-awareness because it helps individuals become more attuned to their thoughts and emotions. By regularly practicing meditation, individuals can gain a deeper understanding of their thought patterns and emotional responses, which can help them make better decisions and manage their emotions more effectively.

Both journaling and meditation provide an opportunity to develop self-awareness by creating space for reflection and introspection. By taking time to reflect on our thoughts and emotions, we can identify areas where we need to grow and make positive changes in our lives. These practices can also help us develop greater self-acceptance and compassion as we learn to observe our world with greater clarity and understanding.

Exercise: A guided meditation for readers to increase their self-awareness

To start your journey towards more self-awareness, it is important to find a place where you can sit or lie down comfortably and where there aren't any distractions. It is important to create an environment that is peaceful and relaxing so that you can fully focus on your inner self. Once you've found a peaceful place, take a few deep breaths and let yourself fully relax, letting go of any tension or stress in your body.

After you've achieved a state of relaxation, turn your attention to your thoughts. Take note of any thoughts that come up, but don't actively follow them. Instead, picture your thoughts as clouds floating across the sky, and just watch them as they come and go.

Now is the time to focus on your feelings. Let yourself feel any emotions that come up without judging or criticizing yourself. It is important to accept and acknowledge all of your emotions, whether they are positive or negative, and to know that they are a natural part of being human.

Next, bring your attention to your body. Start at the top of your head and slowly move down to your toes, paying attention to any areas of tension or discomfort. With each exhale, let go of any tension you feel, allowing your body to fully relax.

As you continue to focus on your breath, imagine that you are stepping outside of your body and looking at yourself from a distance. Observe your thoughts, words, and actions without criticizing or judging them. This point of view will help you understand your behavior and how you interact with the world around you better.

In this time of reflection, ask yourself a few important questions that can help you learn more about yourself. What are your strong and weak points? What are your main values and beliefs? What are your hopes and goals? Let these questions lead you to deeper self-reflection and awareness. Take some time to think about these questions, and let the answers come to you naturally, without forcing them.

As you think about these questions, it is important to give yourself plenty of time to think and to let your answers come to you naturally, without any sense of pressure or expectation. You may find it helpful to keep focusing on your breath as you go through this process. The rhythm of your breathing can help you stay in the present moment.

When you are ready, you can slowly bring your focus back to your body and the world around you. Take a few deep breaths to bring yourself back to the present moment, and then slowly open your eyes. Take a moment to notice how you feel, both physically and emotionally, and be kind to yourself as you bring yourself back to the present.

Remember that developing self-awareness is a long-term process that requires constant work and attention. You can do this meditation exercise as often as you need to continue building your self-awareness and understanding of yourself. With each repetition, you may find that you can gain new insights and perspectives on your own life, which can help you live a more fulfilling and meaningful life.

Identifying Strengths and Weaknesses

Identifying your strengths is important because it allows you to focus on what you do well and build upon those skills. By identifying your strengths, you can capitalize on your natural talents and abilities, which can lead to increased confidence and success. Knowing your strengths can also help you make informed decisions about your career path or personal goals, as you can choose activities or opportunities that align with your strengths and interests.

Identifying your weaknesses is equally important because it allows you to address areas for improvement and develop new skills. By acknowledging your weaknesses, you can take steps to overcome them and become a more well-rounded individual. This can lead to increased self-awareness and personal growth. Additionally, identifying your weaknesses can help you avoid situations where you may struggle or feel overwhelmed, allowing you to focus on areas where you can thrive.

Identify Your Strengths and Weaknesses

Self-reflection is a powerful tool for identifying strengths and weaknesses because it allows individuals to gain a deeper understanding of themselves. To engage in self-reflection, individuals can set aside dedicated time to reflect on their experiences, ask themselves questions about their values and priorities, and evaluate their actions and decisions. This process can help individuals identify patterns in their behavior and pinpoint areas where they excel or struggle.

Another effective way to identify strengths and weaknesses is to seek feedback from others. Feedback can come from friends, family members, coworkers, or mentors. By asking for feedback, individuals can gain valuable insights into how others perceive them and their abilities. This can help individuals identify blind spots or areas where they may not be aware of their strengths or weaknesses. Additionally, receiving constructive feedback can provide individuals with new perspectives and ideas for personal growth.

Case study: How Self-Awareness Led Javed to a Fulfilling Career Path

Javed had just finished college and wasn't sure what he wanted to do with his life. He had a degree in business, but he didn't want to work in that field in a traditional way. Javed knew he had to figure out what he was good at and what he wasn't so he could figure out what career would be best for him.

Javed made a list of his strengths and weaknesses as a first step. He thought about his past and came up with a list of his strengths, such as being able to communicate well and having a strong work ethic. On the other hand, he also pointed out some of his weaknesses, such as not having enough technical skills in some areas and putting things off.

Javed also asked other people what they thought. He asked his friends and family to tell him what they thought were his best and worst traits. He was surprised to hear things he hadn't thought about before, like the fact that he was a natural leader and that he was too hard on himself.

Javed felt more confident in his ability to choose a career path that fit his strengths and interests after he thought about his strengths and weaknesses and asked for feedback from other people. He looked into different options until he found a career in marketing that let him use his communication skills and creativity while also giving him chances to improve in areas where he knew he was weak.

Javed's journey towards self-awareness and figuring out his strengths and weaknesses helped him find a fulfilling career path that fits with his values and allowed him to grow both personally and professionally.

Understanding Values and Beliefs

Values are principles or qualities that individuals hold dear and consider important. They guide an individual's behavior and decision-making, both personally and professionally. For example, some individuals may prioritize honesty, integrity, or loyalty. When an individual's actions align with their values, they experience a sense of fulfillment and purpose. On the other hand, when their actions conflict with their values, they may experience feelings of guilt or dissatisfaction. By understanding and aligning with their values, individuals can make choices that are in line with their priorities and lead to a more fulfilling life.

Beliefs are ideas or assumptions that individuals hold to be true, even in the absence of evidence or proof. They shape an individual's perspective and worldview, which in turn impacts their behavior and decision-making. For example, some individuals may believe that hard work always leads to success, while others may believe that luck plays a larger role. These beliefs can influence an individual's approach to work, relationships, and personal growth. By identifying and examining their beliefs, individuals can gain a deeper understanding of their thoughts and behaviors and make conscious decisions that align with their personal goals.

How to Identify Values and Beliefs

Self-reflection is a powerful tool for gaining insight into one's values and beliefs. By taking the time to reflect on their experiences and actions, individuals can gain a better understanding of what is truly important to them. This can involve asking oneself questions such as "What do I stand for?" and "What motivates me?". Through self-reflection, individuals can gain clarity on their values and beliefs and use this knowledge to guide their decisions and actions.

Another way to identify one's values and beliefs is by exploring one's life experiences. Our experiences shape our worldview and can offer clues as to what we find important. For example, if an individual consistently seeks out opportunities for personal growth, they may value learning and development. If an individual is always there to support their friends and family, they may value loyalty and relationships. By examining past experiences and identifying what was important in those moments, individuals can gain a deeper understanding of their values and beliefs.

Personal story: Lila, an architect, shares how understanding her values and beliefs helped her make a difficult career decision

When I woke up one morning, I felt very tired and unmotivated. As I dragged myself to work, I couldn't help but feel like something was missing. My job as an architect was safe, paid well, and well thought of by my friends, but it didn't make me happy like it used to. I felt like I was just going through the motions, and it was affecting my mental and emotional health.

I took a break from my work that day and went for a walk. As I walked through the park, I thought about my life and realized that I had been chasing success without thinking about what I believed in or what I valued. I was so busy trying to impress other people and meet their expectations that I forgot to check in with myself and see if what I was doing was in line with my values.

Then I decided to take a step back and look at what was most important to me. I started by writing down what really mattered to me: my family, my health, and my passion for making designs that are good for the environment and last a long time. I also thought about what made me want to become an architect in the first place: I wanted my work to make the world a better place.

As I thought more about what I value and what I believe, I realized that my current job didn't match them. I wasn't spending enough time with my family or taking care of my health because I was working long hours on projects that didn't satisfy my passion for sustainability. Even though it was hard to realize, I knew I had to make a change.

I started looking into different career paths that fit with what I cared about and what I was good at. After doing some research, I found a company that specializes in building and designing in a way that is good for the environment. I was interested in their goals and values, and I thought I could make a difference there. I also liked that they cared about balancing work and life, which was important to me.

Even though it meant leaving a safe and comfortable job, I decided to take a chance and apply for a job at the company. Even though the interview process was tough, I was sure I was making the right choice. In the end, I was offered a job as a senior architect where I could work on projects related to sustainable design, which I was very interested in.

I made the switch a year ago, and I couldn't be happier. I wake up every day eager to go to work and use my designs to make the world a better place. I have more time to spend with my family and take care of my health, and I feel like my life now has more meaning and purpose.

In retrospect, I realized that knowing what I valued and believed was the key to making that hard career choice. By putting what was most important to me first and finding a job that fits my interests, I am now able to live a more fulfilling and happier life.

Overcoming Limiting Beliefs

Limiting beliefs are beliefs that we hold about ourselves, others, or the world that constrain us in some way. They can hold individuals back from achieving their goals by creating self-doubt and fear. For example, an individual may believe that they are not capable of achieving a certain goal, leading to self-doubt and a lack of confidence. This can prevent them from taking the necessary steps to achieve their goal, as they may feel that they are not worthy or capable of success.

Limiting beliefs can also lead to a fear of failure. If an individual believes that they are not capable of achieving a certain goal, they may fear failure and avoid taking risks. This fear can prevent them from trying new things, taking on challenges, and pursuing their dreams.

If an individual holds negative beliefs about themselves or others, they may struggle to connect with others and build meaningful relationships. This can lead to a sense of isolation and loneliness, which can further reinforce their limiting beliefs.

How to Identify and Overcome Limiting Beliefs

One of the first steps in figuring out what limiting beliefs you have is to realize that you have them. To do this, one must be willing to look at their thoughts and beliefs and figure out which ones might be holding one back. Often, limiting beliefs are deeply rooted in a person's subconscious, and it can take some work to bring them to the surface.

One way to find limiting beliefs is to pay attention to the negative things you say to yourself. When we catch ourselves talking negatively to ourselves, it can help to question the truth of those thoughts and look at the evidence that backs them up. Most of the time, we will find that these beliefs are not backed up by much or any evidence.

Another helpful thing to do is to ask trusted friends or family members what they think. People who are close to us can often tell us things about how we think and act that we don't know ourselves. This feedback can help us find limiting beliefs that we might not have seen on our own.

Once we know what beliefs are holding us back, the next step is to work on getting rid of them. This could mean questioning the truth of our beliefs, looking for evidence that proves them wrong, and rethinking them in a more positive and empowering way. In some cases, it may also be helpful to work through these beliefs with the help of a therapist or coach, who can help us develop more positive and empowering ways of thinking.

Exercise: A self-reflection exercise to help you identify your limiting beliefs and develop strategies for overcoming them.

Step 1: Create a Safe and Quiet Space

For self-reflection to work, you need a safe, quiet space. Find a place where you feel safe and comfortable, where you can let go of any outside worries and just chill out. This could be a quiet room in your house, a park, or anywhere else where you can be alone and feel safe. Make sure the space is clean, comfortable, and free of anything that might get in the way. To create a calm atmosphere, you could light candles, play soft music, or use essential oils.

Step 2: Relax Your Body and Mind

For self-reflection to work, your body and mind need to be calm. Find a place to sit that's comfortable. Take some deep breaths and let your body calm down. Notice any tension in your body and do your best to let it go. You could also try some ways to calm down, like yoga, progressive muscle relaxation, or meditation.

Step 3: Identify Your Limiting Beliefs

The point of this exercise is to help you find your limiting beliefs. Limiting beliefs are the negative thoughts and ideas that keep you from achieving your goals and living a full life. They often come from past experiences, fears, or being taught by society. To figure out what your limiting beliefs are, ask yourself,

- What thoughts or beliefs have kept me from achieving my goals?
- What do I worry about or doubt about myself or my skills?
- What kind of negative self-talk do I do?

Write your answers down in a notebook or on a piece of paper. Be honest with yourself, and don't judge yourself for holding these beliefs. Give them your attention so you can move on to the next step.

Some examples of limiting beliefs:

- "I am not good enough"
- "I am not smart enough"
- "I don't deserve success."
- "I can't do it."
- "I am never going to be able to do it."
- "Nothing good ever happens to me."
- "I have had nothing but bad luck in my life."

Once you've found some beliefs that hold you back, try to figure out where they came from. Do you think about these things for a long time? Did someone else teach you those things? Do they come from a particular event? Knowing where your limiting beliefs come from can help you deal with and get rid of them.

Step 4: Challenge Your Limiting Beliefs

The key to getting rid of limiting beliefs is to question them. Once you know what beliefs are holding you back, ask yourself:

- Does this belief come from facts or personal opinions?
- Where did I get this idea from?
- What proof do I have that this belief is true?
- What proof do I have that this belief is wrong?
- What would I say to a friend who thought this way?

By asking yourself these questions, you can challenge your limiting beliefs and start to reframe them in a more positive and empowering way. For example, if you think you are not good enough to go after your dream job, challenge that belief by asking yourself if it is true or just a fear. Then, look for proof that this belief is wrong, like your past accomplishments and skills.

Step 5: Make Positive Affirmations

Once you've found and challenged your limiting beliefs, it is important to replace them with positive affirmations. Affirmations are positive statements that can help you stop talking negatively to yourself and help you believe good things about yourself. Here are some tips for making positive affirmations:

Make sure your affirmations are about you and your situation. For instance, instead of saying "I am successful," you could say "I am capable of achieving my goals."

Write in the present tense as if you've already achieved your goal. For example, instead of saying, "I will be confident and sure of myself," say, "I am confident and sure of myself."

Keep them brief and easy. It should be easy to remember and say your affirmations. Choose a few key phrases that you like and say them over and over.

Use positive language, rather than negative. For example, say "I am successful in everything I do" instead of "I am not a failure."

Here are some examples of positive affirmations:

- ❖ I know I can achieve my goals.
- ❖ I have faith in myself and my skills.
- ❖ I am deserving of love and respect;
- ❖ I am sure of my choices;
- ❖ I am strong and can handle hard things.

Step 6: Ask for Help from Other People

Getting rid of limiting beliefs can be hard, so it is important to get help from other people. This can be done with the help of friends, family, teachers, or a therapist. Here are a few ways to ask for help:

- ❖ Tell a friend or family member you can trust about your problems and ask for their help.
- ❖ Find a mentor who has experience in the area where you feel you need help and ask for advice.
- ❖ Think about going to therapy to work through deep-seated beliefs that hold you back.
- ❖ Ask a professional for help. A therapist or coach can help you work on getting rid of your limiting beliefs by giving you expert support and advice.
- ❖ Join a relevant support group to help you. Getting to know people who are going through similar problems can be a great way to feel better and get more done.

It is important to keep in mind that asking for help is not a sign of weakness but of strength. We all need help sometimes to get past our limiting beliefs and achieve our goals.

Step 7: Take Action

Taking action is the last step in getting rid of limiting beliefs. This means taking steps, no matter how small, toward your goals. Here are some ways to get things done:

- Break your goals into small steps that you can do. This will make them seem less hard and more doable.
- Give each step a realistic due date.
- Celebrate your wins, no matter how small they are. Recognize how far you've come and use that to push yourself to keep going.
- Keep track of how far you've come. Write down what you've done well and what's been hard, and think about what you've learned along the way.

Always keep in mind that taking action is what will help you get past your limiting beliefs and achieve your goals. Even if you run into problems, keep going and have faith in yourself. It may take time and work to get rid of limiting beliefs. But with the right mindset, support, and action, you can break free from the beliefs that have been holding you back and achieve your full potential.

Example: How to Recognize and Get Past a Limiting Belief

Let's say that one of your limiting beliefs is, "I am not good enough to go after my dream job." You realize that this belief comes from a fear of failure and a lack of confidence in your abilities. To test this idea, you can ask yourself the following:

- Is this thought real?

  No, I have skills and talents that are useful in my field of interest.

- Where is the evidence to support this belief?

  There is no hard evidence, only my doubts and fears.

- Is there any evidence to the contrary?

  Yes, I have gotten good feedback on my work and done well in other relevant experiences of my life.

- What would I tell a friend who thought this way?

  I would tell them to follow their dreams and remind them of all the good things they have done.

Based on this self-reflection, you realize that your limiting belief isn't based on reality but rather on fear and self-doubt. You start to replace negative self-talk with positive affirmations and look for supportive friends and mentors who believe in your abilities. With discipline, time, and practice, you will start to feel more confident about going after your dream job and go on to get the success you want.

Motivation

Here are some examples of people who have learned to understand themselves and have done well in their personal and professional lives as a result:

1. Nelson Mandela was a South African politician, an activist against apartheid, and a philanthropist. From 1994 to 1999, he was President of South Africa. People think of him as one of the best leaders in modern history because he fought against unfairness and racial inequality in his country. His willingness to forgive and make peace shows how self-aware and emotionally intelligent he was, and he continues to be an inspiration to many people all over the world.

   Self-awareness was a big part of Nelson Mandela's life. It helped him adapt to the culture of Johannesburg and survive 27 years in prison, among other things. He learned how to balance being from a tribe and living in the city, which was a big step in his personal growth. His inner strength and belief in what he believed helped him stay true to his beliefs while he was in prison. This made him a leader when he got out. As the first black president of South Africa, Mandela worked for peace and unity. He led his country through a peaceful change from apartheid to democracy by knowing his strengths and weaknesses.

2. Steve Jobs was an American businessman and inventor who helped start Apple Inc. and changed the way people use computers. He was known for being creative, coming up with new ideas, and inspiring and motivating his workers. People often say that he was successful because he knew himself well and worked on his growth and development.

   Self-awareness was a big part of Steve Jobs' success as an entrepreneur and innovator. It helped him see where he went wrong and change his strategy. Jobs was very focused on his vision for Apple and never wavered from it. He was also able to create a culture of innovation and collaboration by getting people with different skills and points of view to work together to make ground-breaking products. When the iPhone 4 had problems with reception, Jobs fixed the problem right away. This showed how self-aware he was and how committed he was to find a solution.

3. Richard Branson is a British business mogul, investor, and philanthropist who is best known for starting the Virgin Group, a group of more than 400 companies.

He is known for his unique way of doing business and his willingness to take risks. People often say that he was successful because he knew himself well and was able to stick to his values and beliefs.

Self-awareness played a big role in Richard Branson's success as an entrepreneur and leader. Even though he had trouble in traditional school settings because he had dyslexia, Branson knew his strengths and built on them. Being aware of himself also helped him stay focused on his goals and get past problems, like the tough competition he faced when he first started Virgin Atlantic. Self-awareness helped Branson be successful by keeping him true to his vision and helping him find ways to make his brand stand out.

Author's Personal Story: "Transformation Through Self-Awareness"

Sometimes it takes hitting rock bottom to realize that we need to start living with intention and self-awareness. I found this out the hard way - I was trapped in a job that left me feeling unfulfilled and disconnected from my true purpose. Day after day, I mechanically performed my job duties without any real passion or enthusiasm, feeling disconnected from my true self and lacking the energy, motivation, and purpose that I once felt. It wasn't until I hit this lowest point that I realized I needed to make a change. I knew deep down that I was destined for something greater, but I didn't know how to get there.

That's when I started to learn more about the idea of being self-aware. I started to look at myself and my actions more closely. I asked myself things like, "What am I good at?" and "What do I really like doing?" I took a personality test and found out what my values and beliefs are. This helped me figure out who I am and what motivates me.

As I learned more about myself, I began to change things in my life. I quit my job and tried to improve myself, especially, internally. Even though it was scary, I knew it was the right thing to do. I also started to put my personal relationships first, surrounding myself with people who helped me be my best self and pushed me to do better. My hard work was beginning to pay off. In a few years, my work as a subconscious mind trainer started to catch momentum.

Through my work, I have seen how being self-aware can affect other people. It is not always easy to be honest with ourselves and see our flaws, but it is a necessary step for growth and success. I want you to take the time to learn more about yourself, figure out your strengths and weaknesses, and make changes that fit with what you believe and value. Self-awareness is a journey you can start at any time, and the rewards are truly endless.

Exercises for you

- Complete a personality assessment, like the Myers-Briggs Type Indicator or the Big Five Personality Traits assessment.
- Make a list of the things you value and believe in.
- Ask people you can trust to tell you what your strengths and weaknesses are.

Share your Thoughts

As we come to the end of this chapter, I want to ask you: did you learn something new about yourself? Personal development is all about self-discovery, and I hope this chapter helped you on that journey. Whether you uncovered a new talent, discovered a hidden passion, or simply gained a better understanding of who you are, I would love to hear about it.

They say that knowing yourself is the first step to personal development, and I couldn't agree more. I remember the first time I discovered something new about myself - I was trying to learn how to play the guitar, and I realized that I had a terrible sense of rhythm. It was frustrating at first, but then I decided to embrace it and start exploring other creative outlets that didn't require a sense of rhythm. Now, I am proud to say that I am a pretty good writer - who knew?

If you found this chapter helpful in getting to know yourself better, please consider leaving a review on Amazon. Sharing your own personal discoveries not only helps other readers decide if this book is right for them, but it also helps me as an author to know what's working and what's not. Plus, I would love to hear about your own personal growth journey.

Writing a review is easy - just head over to Amazon, find the book, and click on the "Write a Customer Review" button. Don't be afraid to share your own story and how this chapter helped you get to know yourself better. Your review could inspire someone else to take that first step towards personal development.

And now for the incentive - if you write a review and then send an email to sworld.mind@gmail.com letting us know, we will send you the 'Author's Draft' of this chapter. This draft contains all the extended details and research that didn't make it into this final published version, so you'll get an even deeper understanding of this topic. It is a great way to continue your personal growth journey and learn even more about yourself. So go ahead and leave that review - I can't wait to read it!

Conclusion

In this chapter, we have explored the importance of self-awareness in personal development. We defined self-awareness as the ability to recognize and understand our own emotions, thoughts, and behaviors. We discussed the benefits of self-awareness, including improved decision-making, better relationships, and increased self-confidence. We also explored various methods for developing self-awareness, such as self-reflection, mindfulness, and seeking feedback from others. Additionally, we looked at how individuals can identify their strengths, weaknesses, values, beliefs, and limiting beliefs, and overcome the latter to achieve their personal and professional goals.

Through personal stories and case studies, we saw how self-awareness has helped individuals overcome challenges and achieve success in their lives. From identifying their passion and pursuing their dreams to becoming more effective leaders and communicators, these individuals have shown us the power of self-awareness in transforming our lives.

As you continue on your personal development journey, remember that self-awareness is the foundation upon which everything else is built. Therefore, it is essential that you take the time to reflect deeply on your thoughts, emotions, and actions, and remain truthful to yourself about your strengths, weaknesses, values, beliefs, as well as any limiting convictions that may hinder your growth. By doing so, you will be better equipped to recognize and leverage your strengths, overcome your limitations, and make informed choices that align with your personal aspirations and values.

Wrap up

Congratulations for finish this chapter! As you continue on this journey, remember that self-awareness is a continuous process, and it requires effort and commitment. But the rewards are worth it.

By developing self-awareness, you can identify your strengths and weaknesses, understand your values and beliefs, and overcome limiting beliefs that hold you back from achieving your goals. This, in turn, can lead to improved decision making, better relationships, and increased self-confidence.

I encourage you to take time for self-reflection, practice mindfulness, and seek feedback from others. Use journaling and meditation as tools to help you develop self-awareness, and don't be afraid to seek support from others when needed.

Remember, self-awareness is a journey, and it's okay to make mistakes and learn from them. Keep an open mind, stay curious, and embrace the process. You have the power to create the life you want, and developing self-awareness is a key step towards achieving your dreams.

Believe in yourself, and keep striving towards a better version of yourself every day. The journey of personal development may be challenging at times, but the rewards are worth it. You got this!

"The more you know yourself, the more clarity there is.
Self-knowledge has no end."

- Jiddu Krishnamurti

❑

CHAPTER 3

The Art of Goal-Setting and Planning

"Setting goals is the first step in turning the invisible into the visible."
– Tony Robbins

Introduction

What do you want to achieve in life? Do you have a dream that you want to turn into reality? Goal-setting is the key to turning your aspirations into achievable targets. In the previous chapter, we explored the importance of self-awareness and how it helps you understand yourself better. In this chapter, we will be discussing goal-setting and planning.

Goals are what give direction to our lives. They help us focus our time, energy, and resources towards achieving what we truly desire. In this chapter, we will be discussing how to define your goals, the benefits of goal-setting, setting SMART goals (Specific, Measurable, Achievable, Relevant, and Time-bound), developing a plan of action, overcoming obstacles, and staying on track.

We will also discuss the importance of celebrating your successes and reflecting on your progress. Celebrating your successes helps you stay motivated and feel a sense of accomplishment, while reflecting on your progress allows you to learn from your mistakes and make adjustments to your plan of action.

As always, we will be using personal stories and case studies to illustrate the concepts and make them relatable to your own life. Are you ready to turn your dreams into achievable targets? So, let's dive into this chapter and learn how to set and achieve goals that will help us live a fulfilling life!

Importance of Setting Goals

When we set goals, we define what we want to achieve and create a plan for how we will get there. This plan includes the steps we need to take, the resources we need to gather, and the timeline we will follow. By breaking down our goals into smaller, manageable tasks, we can make progress towards our objectives and build momentum.

Goals help us to prioritize our time and resources. When we have a clear idea of what we want to achieve, we can focus our efforts on the activities that will bring us closer to our goals. This means we can avoid distractions and activities that don't serve our purpose, and we can make the most of our limited time and energy.

By setting specific, measurable goals, we can track our progress towards our objectives and see how far we have come. This can be incredibly motivating, and it can help us to stay focused and committed to our goals, even when the going gets tough.

Setting goals can also help us to develop important personal qualities, such as discipline, resilience, and perseverance. When we set goals and work towards them, we learn to overcome obstacles and setbacks, and we develop the skills and mindset we need to succeed in life.

How Effective Goal-Setting Can Help Individuals Achieve Success

In the personal realm, effective goal-setting can help individuals to achieve their dreams and aspirations. Whether it's running a marathon, learning a new language, or starting a business, setting a goal can provide the motivation and direction needed to take action and make progress towards the desired outcome. By breaking down these larger goals into smaller, manageable tasks, individuals can make steady progress towards their objectives and build momentum.

By setting career goals and creating a plan to achieve them, individuals can focus their efforts on the skills and experiences needed to advance their careers. This can include setting goals related to job performance, acquiring new skills and knowledge, networking and building relationships within their industry.

By focusing on the activities and tasks that are most important to achieving their goals, individuals can avoid distractions and make the most of their limited time and energy.

Effective goal-setting also helps individuals to develop important personal qualities, such as discipline, resilience, and perseverance. By setting challenging goals and working towards them, individuals learn to overcome obstacles and setbacks, and they develop the skills and mindset needed to succeed in all areas of their lives.

Defining Goals

Goals are the desired outcomes or achievements that an individual sets for themselves in order to improve their personal and professional lives. They provide a clear direction and purpose to one's actions and help to ensure that they are working towards something that is meaningful and important to them. Setting goals is an important part of personal development, as it provides individuals with a roadmap for growth and improvement.

Goals can be short-term or long-term, depending on the timeline for achieving them. Short-term goals are those that can be accomplished in a relatively short amount of time, such as within a few days, weeks, or months. Long-term goals, on the other hand, may take several months or even years to achieve. Setting both short-term and long-term goals is important, as it allows individuals to make progress towards their objectives in a timely manner while also keeping their larger aspirations in mind.

Goals can be used to improve different areas of life, such as health, relationships, career, finances, education, and spirituality. Goals can also be used to improve relationships by setting a goal to spend more quality time with loved ones or to communicate more effectively.

Setting goals in these different areas of life can help individuals to create a sense of direction and purpose in their lives. By setting goals that are aligned with their values and priorities, individuals can ensure that they are working towards something that is meaningful and important to them. They can also use their goals as a framework for personal growth and development, by identifying the areas in which they want to improve and setting specific targets for achieving their objectives.

The Benefits of Goal-Setting

One of the most significant benefits of setting goals is increased motivation. When individuals have clear and specific goals, they are more likely to be motivated to take action and to make the necessary changes to achieve their objectives. Goals provide individuals with a sense of direction and purpose, and they can serve as a powerful motivator to keep individuals focused on their desired outcomes.

By setting specific goals, individuals can gain clarity on what they want to achieve and how they will get there. This can help to eliminate confusion and uncertainty, and can provide individuals with a clear path forward towards their objectives. Clarity can also help individuals to make better decisions and to stay focused on their priorities, which can be beneficial in both personal and professional settings.

Setting goals can also help individuals to stay focused and avoid distractions. When individuals have clear goals, they are less likely to be sidetracked by other activities or priorities that are not aligned with their objectives. This can help to ensure that individuals are making progress towards their desired outcomes and can lead to increased productivity and efficiency.

Personal story

Anika's story of how she overcame personal problems and achieved her dreams by setting goals is a great example of how to do this.

Hello, my name is Anika, and I would like to tell you a personal story about how setting goals helped me get through hard times and achieve my dreams.

I have always been interested in business, even when I was young. I loved coming up with new ideas and then making them happen. But as I got older and started to seriously think about starting my own business, I realized it wouldn't be easy.

Along the way, I had to deal with a lot of problems, both inside and outside of myself. Self-doubt and insecurity were some of the hardest things for me to deal with. I wasn't always sure I had what it took to be a successful business owner. I also had trouble with money because I didn't have a lot to put into my business. I didn't give up on my dreams, though, no matter how hard things got. I knew that if I wanted to make a difference in the world, I had to give myself goals that were clear and doable.

So, I started by learning more about setting goals and how they could help me achieve my dreams. I learned how important it is to have both short-term and long-term goals, and I started to think about what I wanted to do in the next few months and years.

I gave myself some specific, measurable goals, like meeting with possible investors, starting a marketing campaign for my business, and expanding my operations. I also made an action plan that would help me achieve these goals. I broke each goal down into smaller, easier-to-handle tasks and gave myself deadlines for each one.

I looked for tools and help to help me stay on track. I went to workshops and seminars on starting my own business, read books on business strategy and leadership, and met other people who were also working towards their dreams. The journey wasn't always easy, and I ran into many problems and setbacks along the way. At times, I wanted to just give up and go back to my old job. But I kept reminding myself of my goals and why they were important to me, and I worked through the problems.

I started to see progress over time. I was able to get a small investment for my business thanks to the people I knew. My marketing plan worked, and my sales and income went up as a result. As I achieved each goal, my confidence grew, and I became more and more sure that I could be a successful businesswoman.

When I look back on my journey, I can see how important it was for me to set goals. I was able to stay focused and motivated even when things were hard because I had specific, achievable goals. I was able to make steady progress toward my dreams because I broke each goal into smaller, more manageable tasks and looked for resources and help.

Today, I am proud to say that my business is doing well and that I am making a real difference in the world. And I know I wouldn't have made it this far without the power of setting goals.

Setting SMART Goals

The SMART framework is a popular and effective method for setting goals that are specific, measurable, achievable, relevant, and time-bound. This framework provides a structured approach to goal-setting, which can help individuals to create goals that are more likely to be achieved.

The first element of the SMART framework is **specificity**. This means that goals should be clear and specific, with a well-defined outcome. For example, instead of setting a goal to 'get in better shape,' a specific goal might be to 'lose 10 pounds by the end of the year.'

The second element is **measurability**. This means that goals should be measurable, so that individuals can track their progress and determine whether they have achieved their objectives. For example, a measurable goal might be to 'exercise for 30 minutes a day, five days a week.'

The third element is **achievability**. This means that goals should be realistic and achievable, taking into account an individual's skills, resources, and other factors. It's important to set goals that are challenging but also attainable. For example, setting a goal to 'run a marathon in one month' might not be achievable for someone who has never run before.

The fourth element is **relevance**. This means that goals should be relevant to an individual's values, priorities, and overall objectives. It's important to set goals that are aligned with one's long-term vision and that are meaningful and important to them.

The fifth and final element of the SMART framework is **time-bound**. This means that goals should have a clear deadline or timeframe for completion. This helps to provide individuals with a sense of urgency and can help to keep them on track and motivated. For example, a time-bound goal might be to 'save $5,000 for a down payment on a house in the next six months.'

By using the SMART framework, individuals can set goals that are clear, measurable, achievable, relevant, and time-bound. This can help to increase their chances of success and can provide them with a structured approach to goal-setting that can be used in all areas of life.

A worksheet to help you set your own SMART goals

IMPORTANT: As you fill out this worksheet, keep in mind that your goals should be challenging but also realistic and in line with your values and priorities.

Don't be afraid to ask for help from friends, family, or a coach to help you stay accountable and motivated as you work towards your goals. Remember that getting closer to your dreams starts with a single step and that setting SMART goals is a great way to take that first step. So, take a deep breath, grab a pen and paper, and let's start setting your SMART goals!

Specific

- ❖ What is your goal? Be as specific as possible.
- ❖ What exactly do you want to accomplish?
- ❖ Who is involved in your goal?
- ❖ What resources or limits do you need to consider?
- ❖ Why is this goal important to you?

Example:

- ❖ Goal: I want to improve my physical fitness.
- ❖ Specific: I want to be able to run a 5k without stopping within the next 3 months.
- ❖ Who: I will do this on my own, but my spouse will support me by joining me on runs occasionally.
- ❖ Resources: I will need to purchase new running shoes and set aside time for training.
- ❖ Why: I want to improve my overall health and feel more confident in myself.

Measurable

- ❖ How will you track your progress toward achieving your goal?
- ❖ How will you know when you have achieved your goal?
- ❖ What milestones can you set along the way to help you track your progress?

Example

- ❖ Track progress: I will use a running app to track my runs and monitor my progress.
- ❖ Know when achieved: I will know I have achieved my goal when I am able to run a 5k without stopping.
- ❖ Milestones: I will set weekly goals for distance and time, and aim to improve each week.

Achievable

- ❖ Is this goal realistic and possible for you to achieve?
- ❖ Do you have the resources, skills, and necessary support to achieve this goal?
- ❖ What potential obstacles might you face and how can you overcome them?

Example:

- ❖ Realistic: Running a 5k within 3 months is realistic for me based on my current fitness level.
- ❖ Resources: I have the necessary resources, including running shoes and access to a nearby park with a running path.

- Skills: I will need to improve my endurance and pacing, but I have the basic skills needed to start training.
- Obstacles: My schedule can be unpredictable due to work and family obligations, so I will need to plan my training around these events.

Relevant

- How does this goal align with your values and other priorities in your life?
- Why is achieving this goal important to you personally?
- How will achieving this goal benefit you in the short term and long term?

Example:

- **Values:** Physical fitness is important to me because it aligns with my values of health and self-care.
- **Personal:** Achieving this goal will make me feel more confident and improve my overall well-being.
- **Short-term benefits:** I will feel more energized and motivated as I begin to improve my fitness level.
- **Long-term benefits:** Improving my physical fitness will reduce my risk of health problems and allow me to continue enjoying physical activities as I age.

Time-bound

- When do you want to achieve this goal?
- What is the deadline for achieving each of the milestones you have set?
- Are your goals realistically achievable within the timeframe you have set?

Example

- Timeframe: I want to achieve this goal within 3 months.
- **Milestones:** I will aim to run 1 mile without stopping in the first week, 2 miles in the second week, and gradually increase my distance each week.
- **Realistically achievable:** This goal is realistically achievable within the timeframe I have set, as long as I stay committed to my training schedule and make adjustments as needed.

Remember to check in on your goals and your progress towards achieving them on a regular basis, and make changes as needed to make sure they are still relevant and attainable. Celebrate the things you did well along the way and think about the problems you faced and how you solved them.

Developing a Plan of Action

The first step in developing a plan of action is to break down the goal into smaller, more manageable tasks. This helps to make the goal less overwhelming and easier to tackle. For example, if the goal is to start a new business, the first step might be to research the market, followed by creating a business plan, securing funding, and so on.

Once we have identified the smaller tasks, we need to prioritize them in order of importance. This helps us to focus on the tasks that will have the greatest impact and ensures that we are using our time and resources efficiently.

The next step is to create a timeline or schedule for completing each task. This helps to ensure that we are making progress towards our goal and that we are staying on track. It's important to be realistic when setting deadlines, taking into account our other commitments and any potential obstacles that may arise.

Another important aspect of developing a plan of action is to identify any potential obstacles or challenges that we may encounter along the way. By anticipating these obstacles and developing strategies to overcome them, we can be better prepared and more resilient in the face of adversity.

Finally, it's important to regularly review and evaluate our progress towards our goals. This helps us to stay motivated and to make any necessary adjustments to our plan of action. We can ask ourselves questions like: "Am I making progress towards my goal?" and "What changes can I make to my plan to ensure that I am achieving my objectives?"

How to break down larger goals into smaller, manageable tasks

Breaking down larger goals into smaller, manageable tasks is an important step in achieving our objectives. When we face a big goal, it can be overwhelming and difficult to know where to start. By breaking it down into smaller tasks, we can make progress towards our goal and feel a sense of accomplishment along the way.

One way to break down a larger goal is to start by brainstorming all of the steps that need to be taken to achieve it. For example, if the goal is to run a marathon, we might list tasks such as building up endurance, finding a training plan, purchasing running gear, and registering for the race.

Once we have a list of tasks, we can then prioritize them in order of importance. This helps us to focus on the tasks that will have the greatest impact and ensures that we are using our time and resources efficiently. It's also important to consider any dependencies between tasks. For example, we might need to build up endurance before we can start following a training plan.

Next, we can break down each task into smaller, more manageable steps. For example, if the task is to build up endurance, we might break it down into steps such as running for 10 minutes each day for the first week, increasing to 15 minutes the second week, and so on.

When breaking down tasks into smaller steps, it's important to be realistic and consider our abilities and resources. It's also important to set achievable deadlines for each task to help us stay on track.

Case Study: How Developing a Plan of Action Helped Nisha Achieve Her Career Goal

I am a graphic designer, and my name is Nisha. I have always wanted to work for one of the best design agencies in my city. But it always seemed like a goal that couldn't be achieved. I didn't think I had what it took to join the agency because they were known for their creative designs and talented team.

But one day I decided I was sick of feeling stuck at my job and wanted to find something new. I wanted to give myself a challenge and try to achieve my goal of working at that agency. I knew I had to make a plan to make it happen.

Step 1: Setting a Clear Goal

The first step in making a plan of action was to be clear about what I wanted to do. I wanted to work at the best design agency in my city, but I had to be more specific. After doing some research, I learned that the agency was looking to hire a senior graphic designer. That became my goal: to work at the best design agency in my city as a senior graphic designer.

Step 2: Breaking Down My Goal

Once I knew what my goal was, I had to break it down into smaller tasks that I could do. I knew that becoming a senior graphic designer would take a lot of hard work and planning, so I broke my goal into several smaller goals:

1. Improve my design skills.
2. Work on high-profile projects to gain experience.

3. Make connections with people in the design industry.
4. Create a portfolio that showcases my work.

Step 3: Make a Plan of What to Do

Keeping my sub-goals in mind, I made a detailed plan for how to achieve my main goal. I broke each sub-goal down into smaller tasks and gave each task a due date. Here's an example of what my plan to improve my design skills looked like:

Sub-goal: Improve My Designing Skills

1. Research design trends and techniques (1 week)
2. Attend an online course about fonts (2 weeks).
3. Go to a conference and workshop on designing for one month.
4. Get used to designing for different types of media (ongoing)

Step 4: Taking Action

Making a plan of action was the easy part. The hard part was sticking to it. I promised myself that I would work on my smaller goals every day, even if it was only for a few minutes. I enrolled in the online course, went to the design conference, and designed every day. It wasn't always easy, but I kept going because I kept thinking about my end goal: to become a senior graphic designer at the best design agency.

Step 5: Celebrating Successes and Reflecting on Progress

I celebrated each important step along the way as I worked on my plan. I gave myself a day off to relax and recharge after I finished the online course. When I went to the design conference and workshop, I met other professionals in the field and made connections with them. As I did more design work, my skills got better and my portfolio grew.

During the process, I also took time to think about how far I had come. I looked over my plan often, changed my deadlines as needed, and made sure I was still on track to achieve my ultimate goal of becoming a senior graphic designer at the best design agency.

Step 6: Achieving My Goal

I finally achieved my goal after months of hard work and dedication. I applied to be a senior graphic designer at the best design firm and got the job. I was so happy;

it was like a dream come true. But when I looked back, I could see that it was all because of the plan I had made.

Creating a plan of action helped me divide my big goal into smaller, more manageable steps.

Obstacles and Staying on Track

One common obstacle that many individuals face is the lack of motivation or discipline needed to consistently work towards their goals. It's easy to lose sight of our goals or become distracted by other things going on in our lives. To overcome this, we need to develop a strong sense of motivation and discipline by breaking our goals down into smaller, achievable tasks, setting deadlines, and finding ways to hold ourselves accountable.

Another obstacle that we may encounter is a lack of resources, such as time or money, needed to achieve our goals. In such situations, it's important to find creative solutions and work with what we have. We can also try to develop new skills or seek out additional resources to help us achieve our goals.

Fear and self-doubt can also be significant obstacles to achieving our goals. We may be afraid of failure or uncertain about our ability to succeed. These feelings can hold us back and prevent us from taking action towards our goals. It's important to recognize and acknowledge these feelings, but also to challenge them and push ourselves to move forward.

External factors, such as negative feedback or criticism from others, can also pose challenges to achieving our goals. It's important to learn how to filter out unhelpful criticism and focus on constructive feedback that can help us improve and grow. Additionally, surrounding ourselves with a supportive network of family, friends, or mentors can provide the encouragement and motivation we need to persevere.

Unexpected circumstances such as illness, job loss, or family emergencies can also disrupt our progress towards our goals. In these situations, it's important to remain flexible and adaptable, adjusting our plans as needed while keeping our ultimate goal in mind.

Overcoming obstacles and staying on track with goal attainment

In order to overcome obstacles and stay on track with goal attainment, it's important to develop a mindset of resilience and determination. This means learning to overcome self-doubt, filtering out negative feedback, and surrounding ourselves with a supportive network. By building a strong sense of self-confidence and staying focused on our goals, we can overcome any challenges that come our way.

Another important aspect of staying on track with goal attainment is developing a plan of action. This means breaking down larger goals into smaller, manageable tasks, and setting specific deadlines for each task. By doing so, we can create a clear roadmap towards achieving our goals, and avoid feeling overwhelmed or discouraged by the enormity of the task.

Life is unpredictable, and it's likely that we'll encounter unforeseen obstacles or setbacks along the way. By remaining open to change and willing to adjust our plans as necessary, we can continue moving forward towards our goals even when things don't go as planned.

Maintaining Enthusiasm for Long-Term Goals

Maintaining enthusiasm and motivation over a prolonged period of time can be a challenge. One way to address this is to break down your goal into smaller, manageable tasks and to vary your approach as you work towards it. This can help to keep things interesting and prevent boredom from setting in. For example, if your goal is to run a marathon, you could vary your training routine by incorporating different types of workouts or running routes.

Stay connected to your 'why.' Remind yourself of why you set the goal in the first place. This can help to reignite your passion. Visualize how achieving the goal will positively impact your life, and keep this vision in mind as you work towards it.

Another helpful strategy is to track your progress towards the goal. Seeing the progress you've made can be a great motivator to keep going. Celebrate small wins along the way, and use them as a reminder of the progress you're making towards the larger goal.

In addition to tracking progress, it can also be helpful to find a support system. Surround yourself with people who believe in you and your goal, and who can offer encouragement and accountability. This can include friends, family members, or even a coach or mentor. Having someone to share your successes and struggles with can help to keep you motivated and on track.

Last but not the least, it is very important to take care of yourself physically and mentally. Eating a healthy diet, getting enough sleep, and engaging in regular exercise can all help to improve your overall well-being and keep your energy levels high. Additionally, taking time to relax and practice self-care activities such as meditation or yoga can help to reduce stress and maintain a positive mindset.

Personal story: Ravi Nayak, an awesome football player, shares how he overcame obstacles

I lived for football. I loved everything about it, from getting to know the other players to the thrill of scoring a goal. Since I was a little boy, I wanted to play professionally, and I worked very hard to make that happen. But when I was 18, I almost had to give up on my dreams.

During a game, I hurt my knee badly, which kept me from playing for months. I was very sad. Football was everything to me, and I didn't know if I'd ever be able to play again. I was angry and upset that something I couldn't change could ruin my plans.

I didn't want to give up, though. I knew I had to find a way to get around this problem so I could play football again. So, I started working with a physiotherapist to strengthen my knee and get it back to normal. Even though the process was slow and painful, I was still determined to get better.

I worked on other parts of my game while I was getting better. I watched game videos and focused on getting a better understanding of how the sport is played. I knew that even if I couldn't play, I could still train my mind and learn more about the game.

As I was getting better, I had to deal with another setback. I was having a hard time getting back to the level of fitness I needed to compete, so my team decided to let go of me. It was a crushing blow, but I wouldn't give up. I turned the setback into a reason to work even harder.

I kept training on my own and did everything I could to get stronger and better at my skills. I also tried to play with other teams and players to show that I still had something to offer on the field. I never lost sight of my goal, no matter how hard things got. I wanted to play football professionally, and I was willing to do whatever it took to get there. I spent a lot of time on the ground improving my skills and getting better at the game.

My hard work paid off in the end. When a local semi-professional team asked me to join, I jumped at the chance. From there, I kept getting better and got the attention of professional teams' scouts. I was finally signed by a professional team, and I got to play football at the highest level, which was my dream.

I am pleased with my accomplishments when I consider how far I have come. Injury and setbacks taught me how important it is to be strong and keep going. I learned that mistakes are just chances to learn and get better and that if you work hard and try your best, you can do anything. And most importantly, I learned that I have the strength and determination to get through any problem that comes my way.

Celebrating Successes and Reflecting on Progress

Achieving a goal can be a long and challenging journey. It can be easy to get caught up in the daily grind of working towards a goal and forget to celebrate our successes and reflect on our progress. Celebrating our successes can help us to stay motivated and energized, while reflecting on our progress can help us to make adjustments and continue moving forward.

Celebrating successes is a crucial part of goal-setting and planning. When we achieve a goal, no matter how small or big, it is important to take a moment to celebrate our accomplishment. Celebrating successes not only provides us with a sense of accomplishment and satisfaction but also helps us to stay motivated and enthusiastic about continuing our journey towards achieving our larger goals.

Reflecting on our progress is equally important. Taking a step back and objectively analyzing our progress towards our goals can help us to identify areas where we may be falling short and make the necessary adjustments to get back on track. It also helps us to recognize our strengths and weaknesses, which can help us to set more realistic and achievable goals in the future.

Exercise

An exercise to help you think about your progress and celebrate your successes:

1. Take some time to think about how far you've come towards your goals. Find a place that is quiet and comfortable where you can work.
2. Write down everything you've done well, big or small, in the last week, month, or year. This could be anything from finishing a project at work to just taking some time for yourself.
3. Take a moment to be proud of each of these accomplishments, no matter how small they seem. Let yourself be proud of what you've done, and don't forget how hard you worked to get there.
4. Think about how far you've come towards your bigger goals. Think about the steps you've taken and the problems you've solved along the way.
5. Write down any changes you've made to your plans and goals. Think about how these changes have helped you get closer to your goals or maybe even helped you find new ones.
6. Identify any areas where you feel stuck or where you still need to make progress. Think about what you can do to get past these problems and keep moving forward.

Personal and professional success

When individuals set clear and specific goals, they are more likely to achieve what they want, as they have a roadmap to follow. Planning is the process of identifying the steps necessary to achieve a specific goal. Effective planning helps individuals to anticipate and overcome obstacles, and to stay motivated and focused on their objectives.

One of the key benefits of goal-setting and planning is that it helps individuals to prioritize their time and resources. By identifying what is most important, individuals can make better decisions about how to allocate their time and effort. This leads to greater efficiency and productivity, and ultimately, to greater success in achieving their goals.

Effective goal-setting and planning also helps individuals to develop their skills and knowledge. When individuals set challenging goals and create a plan to achieve them, they are forced to step out of their comfort zone and try new things. This can lead to personal and professional growth, as individuals develop new skills and knowledge that can be applied in various aspects of their lives.

Case study: The story of a successful athlete who used goal-setting and planning to achieve his dreams

Michael Phelps is considered one of the greatest Olympic athletes of all time. He is a retired American swimmer who competed in five Olympic Games and won 23 gold medals, 3 silver medals, and 2 bronze medals.

Phelps' journey to success was not easy. He faced many obstacles and setbacks, including attention deficit hyperactivity disorder (ADHD) and tumultuous home life. However, he learned to set goals and make plans to achieve his dreams.

At the age of 11, Phelps set his sights on breaking the world record for the 200-meter butterfly. He wrote the record on a piece of paper and hung it on his bedroom wall as a constant reminder of his goal.

Phelps worked tirelessly to achieve his goal. He trained for six hours a day, six days a week. He also developed a routine to help him stay focused and organized. He broke his goals down into smaller, manageable tasks and tracked his progress regularly.

Phelps also visualized his success. He would close his eyes and imagine himself swimming in the perfect race. He would visualize the water, the stroke, and the finish line. This mental rehearsal helped him prepare for competitions and overcomes his nerves.

Phelps achieved his goal of breaking the world record for the 200-meter butterfly when he was just 15 years old. He went on to win his first Olympic gold medal at the 2004 Summer Olympics in Athens, Greece. Phelps continued to set goals and make plans for each competition, which helped him win a total of 28 Olympic medals throughout his career.

In addition to his success in the pool, Phelps has also been open about his struggles with mental health. He has used his platform to advocate for mental health awareness and to encourage others to seek help.

Phelps' story is a testament to the power of goal-setting and planning. By breaking down his goals into manageable tasks, visualizing his success, and staying focused and organized, he was able to achieve his dreams and become one of the greatest athletes of all time.

Author's Personal Story: "My Journey with Effective Goal-Setting and Planning"

Early on in my career, I had a vague idea of what I wanted to accomplish, but I didn't have a clear plan. I worked hard and put in long hours, but I never felt like I was getting closer to the life I wanted. I didn't start having real success until I started setting specific, measurable goals and making a detailed plan for how to achieve them.

One of my earliest goals was to become a certified mind trainer. I knew it would take a lot of time and work, but I was determined to make it happen. Under the guidance of my mentor, Dr. B. Rakshit, I set a specific date for finishing my training and made a plan that included daily study sessions and practice sessions with clients. By breaking up my big goal into smaller, more manageable tasks, I was able to stay focused and make steady progress. In the end, I passed my certification with flying colors.

Setting and achieving this goal was a big turning point for me. It made me feel more confident and motivated to set even bigger goals and create more specific plans on how to achieve them. I still use this method of setting goals and planning to be successful in both my personal and work life. Whether I want to learn a new skill or start a new task, I know that with the right goals and plan, I can do anything I set my mind to. Trust me, you too can.

Exercises for you

1. Write down three clear goals for the next month, the next year, and the next five years.

2. Break each goal down into smaller steps that you can take.
3. Figure out what could get in the way of you achieving your goals and think of ways to get around them.

Share your Thoughts

Congratulations on making it through the chapter on goal-setting and planning! Now, take a deep breath and ask yourself: Do you feel more confident about achieving your goals? If the answer is yes, then great job! If the answer is no, then maybe you need to set a new goal: read this chapter again. (I hope that brought a smile to your face!)

"A goal without a plan is just a wish." - Antoine de Saint-Exupéry. This quote reminds us that goal-setting is not just about dreaming big, but also about putting in the work to make those dreams a reality.

I would love to hear from you about your own personal goals and plans for development. Please leave a review and share your thoughts with me and others who may benefit from your experience.

Writing a review is easy! Simply go to the book's page on Amazon, click on 'write a review,' and let your thoughts flow. If you're not sure how to write a review, don't worry! Here are some questions to help guide you: What did you like about this chapter? What did you learn? How did it make you feel? Would you recommend this book to a friend? Remember, your review doesn't have to be long or formal -- just honest and helpful.

As a token of my appreciation for your review, I would like to offer you the 'Author's Draft' of this chapter. This draft contains additional details and research that may not have made it into this final published version. To claim your reward, simply send an email to sworld.mind@gmail.com after posting your review. Thank you for your support and dedication to your personal growth!

Conclusion

In this chapter, we explored the art of goal-setting and planning. We discussed the importance of defining goals, setting SMART goals, developing a plan of action, and overcoming obstacles. We also talked about the benefits of goal-setting and how reflecting on progress and celebrating successes can help us stay on track.

Effective goal-setting and planning are crucial to personal and professional success. By defining our goals, we can give ourselves direction and focus. By setting SMART goals, we can ensure that our goals are specific, measurable, achievable, relevant, and time-bound. By developing a plan of action, we can break down our goals into smaller, more manageable tasks, and by overcoming obstacles, we can stay on track even when things get tough. Finally, by reflecting on progress and celebrating successes, we can keep ourselves motivated and moving forward.

We hope that the insights shared in this chapter have given you a deeper understanding of the art of goal-setting and planning, and that you are now equipped with the tools you need to set and achieve your own goals.

Wrap up

Congratulations once again, on completing this chapter on the art of goal-setting and planning! By reading this chapter, you have already demonstrated your commitment to achieving your goals. Remember, goal-setting and planning are crucial tools for success, and it is essential to keep practicing and refining these skills.

As you continue on your journey of personal development, I encourage you to set high standards for yourself and strive towards achieving your goals. Remember, success is a journey, not a destination. It is essential to celebrate your successes along the way and reflect on your progress to ensure that you are on track towards achieving your goals.

I encourage you to continue developing your art of goal-setting and planning. The road ahead may be challenging, but I have no doubt that with your determination and commitment, you will achieve your goals and find success in all aspects of your life.

Always remember that you are the only one who can take the required steps towards creating a better version of yourself. Keep pushing forward and always strive for growth and improvement. The world needs your unique talents and contributions, so go out there and make a difference!

"If you want to live a happy life, tie it to a goal, not to people or things."

- Albert Einstein

❑

CHAPTER 4

The Growth Mindset Blueprint

"Believe you can and you are halfway there."

– Theodore Roosevelt

Introduction

Have you ever felt stuck in your personal or professional life, unable to make progress despite your efforts? Do you often find yourself giving up when faced with challenges or setbacks? Developing a growth mindset can help you overcome these obstacles and unlock your potential for success.

In the previous chapter, we discussed the importance of goal-setting and planning to achieve success in life. In this chapter, we will be exploring the concept of developing a growth mindset.

The way we think about ourselves and our abilities can either limit us or empower us to achieve our goals. This is where the concept of fixed mindset and growth mindset comes into play. A fixed mindset is when we believe that our abilities and traits are fixed and cannot be changed, while a growth mindset is when we believe that we can develop and improve our abilities through effort and dedication.

In this chapter, we will be discussing the benefits of having a growth mindset, identifying and overcoming limiting beliefs that hold us back, embracing challenges and failure as opportunities to learn and grow, and cultivating a growth mindset in our daily lives.

Remember, your mindset is a powerful tool that can either help or hinder your personal development journey. So, let's dive into this chapter and learn how to develop a growth mindset that will help us reach our full potential!

The Growth Mindset

A growth mindset is a set of beliefs that helps people see their skills and abilities as things that can be developed and improved over time with hard work, persistence, and dedication. People with a growth mindset see failure and setbacks as chances to learn and grow, not as proof that they are limited or have fixed skills. This way of thinking lets people face problems with excitement and a sense of possibility instead of fear or avoidance.

Carol Dweck, a psychologist, came up with the idea of a growth mindset. She found that people's beliefs about their intelligence and talent had a big effect on their academic and personal success. Dweck's research found that people who thought their intelligence and skills were fixed were more likely to give up when they ran into problems, while those who thought they could learn and grow were more likely to keep going and achieve their goals.

A growth mindset is an important part of personal development because it helps people achieve their full potential. People are more likely to take on challenges, keep going when things get hard, and achieve their goals when they believe that their skills can be changed and improved with hard work and dedication. A growth mindset also encourages people to love learning and be willing to take risks, which are both important for personal growth and development.

Developing a growth mindset

Developing a growth mindset is not a one-time event but a continuous journey that requires conscious effort and practice. It starts with the belief that abilities can be developed through dedication and hard work. When faced with a challenge or a setback, those with a growth mindset do not give up. Instead, they use the experience as a learning opportunity, figuring out what went wrong and how they can do better next time.

One way to cultivate a growth mindset is to focus on the process rather than the outcome. When we set goals for ourselves, it's easy to get caught up in the end result and forget about the journey. But when we focus on the process, we can appreciate the small steps we take along the way and see each obstacle as a chance to improve. By breaking down our goals into manageable tasks and celebrating our progress, we can build momentum and stay motivated.

Another key aspect of developing a growth mindset is learning to embrace failure. For many, failure is seen as a setback, a mark of inadequacy or incompetence. However, those with a growth mindset view failure as an opportunity to learn and grow. They understand that failure is not the end, but rather a stepping stone towards success. By reframing failure as a chance to learn, we can develop resilience and bounce back from setbacks more quickly.

Understanding Fixed Mindset vs. Growth Mindset

A fixed mindset is the belief that one's abilities and talents are predetermined and cannot be improved upon. Those with a fixed mindset may avoid challenges or give up easily, believing that their effort will not make a difference. They may also be threatened by the success of others, seeing it as a reflection of their own inadequacy. In short, a fixed mindset is limiting and can prevent individuals from reaching their full potential.

On the other hand, a growth mindset is the belief that abilities and talents can be developed through dedication and hard work. Those with a growth mindset embrace challenges and see failure as an opportunity to learn and grow. They understand that setbacks are a natural part of the learning process and are not deterred by them. In short, a growth mindset is empowering and can lead to greater success and achievement.

The differences between a fixed mindset and a growth mindset are significant. Those with a fixed mindset tend to avoid challenges, give up easily, and view failure as a mark of inadequacy. They may also feel threatened by the success of others and believe that their abilities are fixed and cannot be improved upon. On the other hand, those with a growth mindset see challenges as opportunities for growth, embrace failure as a chance to learn, and are motivated by the success of others. They believe that their abilities can be developed through hard work and dedication and are willing to put in the effort required to achieve their goals.

Personal Story: From Fixed to Growth Mindset: How Priya Achieved Success in Her Career

My name is Priya Tiwari, and I'd like to tell you my personal story about how I overcame a fixed mindset to be successful in my career.

Earlier I used to think that my skills were fixed and that success came easily to me because of my natural talents. But when I started working in the field of marketing, I quickly realized that my fixed mindset was holding me back.

I was afraid to take on new challenges and avoided situations where I might fail. I was defensive when people gave me feedback and criticism, and it was hard for me to adapt to new situations or learn new skills. As a result, my career stalled, and I ended up feeling unfulfilled and frustrated.

Once, I decided to attend a class on growth mindset, and it was a turning point in my life. I learned that my skills were not fixed and that I could develop and improve them through work and practice. I started accepting challenges and taking on new projects, even if it meant getting out of my comfort zone.

At first, it was hard, and I had many setbacks and failures. But instead of giving up, I used these things as opportunities to learn and grow. I asked for feedback and criticism, even when it made me uncomfortable, and I used it to improve my skills and abilities.

Over time, my efforts paid off, and I started to see big improvements in my work. I was able to take on bigger challenges and responsibilities, and I felt more confident in my abilities. Today, I have achieved a level of success in my career that I never thought was possible, and I am proud of what I have done.

In conclusion, overcoming a fixed mindset was not easy, but it was a step I had to take to be successful in my career. I was able to overcome my limitations and achieve my full potential by having a growth mindset and focusing on learning and getting better. I hope that my story will encourage others to have a growth mindset and work hard to achieve their dreams.

The Benefits of a Growth Mindset

Those with a growth mindset are more likely to bounce back from setbacks and challenges because they see them as opportunities to learn and improve. They don't give up easily and are willing to put in the effort required to overcome obstacles. This resilience can be particularly valuable during difficult times, such as during a job search, when facing a health crisis, or dealing with personal loss.

When we adopt a growth mindset, we are more open to new ideas and perspectives. We don't see failure as a roadblock, but rather as an opportunity to learn and try new approaches. This flexibility can lead to more innovative thinking and problem-solving.

Also, those with a growth mindset are more likely to set ambitious goals and work towards achieving them. They are not discouraged by setbacks, but rather use them as a stepping stone towards success. This sense of purpose and motivation can lead to greater productivity, satisfaction, and fulfillment in both personal and professional life.

Individuals with a growth mindset are more likely to be open to feedback and are seen to be willing to learn from others. They are also more supportive of the growth and success of others, rather than feeling threatened or envious. Such a mindset leads to stronger, more positive relationships with colleagues, friends, and family members.

Overcoming Obstacles and Achieving Goals with a Growth Mindset

Individuals with a growth mindset understand that overcoming obstacles is an essential part of the learning process and that their efforts can lead to success. This mindset enables them to approach obstacles with a positive attitude, rather than seeing them as insurmountable barriers.

Those with a growth mindset understand that failure is a natural part of the learning process and that they can use it as a learning experience to improve their performance. Rather than giving up when faced with failure, they use it as a motivation to try again, with a new perspective and strategy.

Individuals with a growth mindset understand that they have the power to improve their abilities and that success is a result of hard work and dedication. This belief in oneself can be a powerful motivator, helping them push through obstacles and overcome challenges.

Also, individuals with a growth mindset are seen to be more open to learning from others and are not afraid to ask for help when needed. This mindset helps them identify areas for improvement, which they can then work on to overcome obstacles and achieve their goals.

Individuals with a growth mindset understand that growth and success come from stepping outside of their comfort zone and taking on new challenges. This willingness to try new things helps individuals overcome obstacles and achieve their goals in ways they may never have imagined.

Case study: A Story of Resilience and Persistence

Aisha's story of how she used a growth mindset to get through hard times.

Aisha had been dealing with depression and anxiety for a few months. Her husband died suddenly, leaving her alone to raise their two young children. Aisha felt overwhelmed and didn't know how to cope with her grief and responsibilities.

One day, Aisha was talking to her friend Shahana, who told her about the concept of a growth mindset. She explained how individuals with a growth mindset view challenges as opportunities for growth and learning, and how this attitude can help them overcome obstacles and achieve their goals.

At first, Aisha didn't believe it, but she decided to find out more. She read books and articles about having a growth mindset and went to a workshop on the subject. She realized that she had been stuck in a fixed mindset, in which she thought that her abilities and intelligence were fixed and couldn't change.

Aisha began to practice a growth mindset and took the help of her friend Shahana. She gave herself small goals, like going for a walk or making her kids a healthy meal. She thought of these goals as chances to grow and learn, not as things she had to do just to stay alive.

As Aisha made progress toward her goals, she started to feel better about herself and her life. She realized that she could change her situation and that she could get through her problems if she had a growth mindset.

Aisha started to take more steps on her own to take care of herself and her kids. She started going to a therapist to deal with her grief and anxiety. She also asked for help from people in her community and joined a group for single moms.

Aisha's hard work paid off in the long run. She was able to find a job that she could do from home so she could be with her kids. She also started helping out at the mosque in her neighborhood and got more involved in her community.

Aisha kept having a growth mindset and saw every challenge as a chance to grow and learn. She realized that the best way to get past problems was to keep going with a positive attitude and a willingness to learn and grow.

In short, Aisha's adoption of a growth mindset helped her overcome her problems by fostering a positive attitude toward challenges, encouraging resilience and persistence, promoting openness to feedback, and cultivating flexibility. By having a growth mindset, she was able to learn the skills and attitudes she needed to overcome problems and achieve her full potential, even though she was going through hard times.

Identifying Limiting Beliefs

Limiting beliefs can take many forms and can be difficult to identify as they often become ingrained in our thinking patterns over time.

One common limiting belief is "I'm not good enough." This belief can manifest in a variety of ways, such as feeling inadequate in certain areas, doubting one's abilities, or feeling like a fraud. To identify this belief, individuals may notice that they frequently engage in negative self-talk, discount their achievements, or avoid taking on new challenges due to fear of failure.

Another common limiting belief is "I don't have enough time." This belief can create a fixed mindset around productivity and can prevent individuals from pursuing their goals. To identify this belief, individuals may notice that they frequently feel overwhelmed, procrastinate on important tasks, or prioritize less important activities over their goals.

A third common limiting belief is "I'm too old/young." This belief can create a fixed mindset around age and can prevent individuals from pursuing new opportunities or learning new skills. To identify this belief, individuals may notice that they frequently use age as an excuse for not pursuing their goals or that they feel intimidated by individuals who are either older or younger than them.

Another way to identify limiting beliefs is to pay attention to negative self-talk and inner dialogue. When negative thoughts arise, individuals can ask themselves if these thoughts are helpful or if they are holding them back from achieving their goals. By noticing and challenging negative self-talk, individuals can begin to reframe their thinking patterns and develop a more positive and growth-oriented mindset.

Examples of how limiting beliefs can hold individuals back from developing a growth mindset

1. **"I'm too busy":** This limiting belief can prevent individuals from making time for self-improvement or pursuing their passions. They may believe that their schedule is too full, and that they don't have time to devote to personal growth, rather than recognizing that small steps and consistent effort can lead to significant progress over time.
2. **"I'm not creative":** This limiting belief can prevent individuals from pursuing creative pursuits or trying new things. They may believe that creativity is a fixed trait and that they either have it or they don't, rather than a skill that can be developed with practice and effort.
3. **"I'm not smart enough":** This limiting belief can prevent individuals from pursuing education and learning new skills. They may believe that their intelligence is fixed and cannot be improved, so they may avoid challenges that could help them grow and learn.
4. **"I'm not good with people":** This limiting belief can prevent individuals from developing social skills and building meaningful relationships. They may believe that their social skills are fixed and cannot be improved, which can lead to avoidance of social situations and missed opportunities for growth and connection.
5. **"I'm too old to start something new":** This limiting belief can prevent individuals from pursuing new opportunities or starting a new career. They

may believe that they have missed their chance, and that it's too late to learn new skills or pursue their passions.

Exercise

A worksheet for you to identify and overcome your own limiting beliefs.

Step 1: Identify Your Limiting Beliefs

Spend some time thinking about whether the things you think about yourself and the world are helping you or holding you back. Jot down whatever comes to mind in terms of ideas or beliefs. For starters, consider the following:

- I am not good enough.
- I'll never be successful.
- I am not attractive enough to be liked by others.
- It is too late for me to pursue my dreams.
- I am not smart enough to achieve my goals.
- I am not smart enough to understand complex concepts.
- I am too old/young to do this.
- I don't have enough money to do what I want.

Step 2: Challenge Your Limiting Beliefs

Once you have identified your limiting beliefs, take some time to challenge them. Ask yourself if there is any evidence to support these beliefs or if they are simply assumptions you have made about yourself or the world around you. Consider the following questions:

- Is this belief based on fact or assumption?
- Is there any evidence that contradicts this belief?
- Have I ever accomplished anything that goes against this belief?
- How is this belief limiting me, and what would be possible for me if I didn't believe it?

Take the limiting belief that "I am not good enough to follow my aspirations." as an example. If you doubt this, you may ask yourself "Where do I find the proof for this claim? Have I done anything to disprove this notion? What might I be able to do if I believed in myself, and how has this belief prevented me from doing so thus far?"

Step 3: Reframe Your Limiting Beliefs

Once you have challenged your limiting beliefs, try to reframe them more positively. Consider how you can turn your negative self-talk into positive affirmations. Here are some examples:

- **I am not good enough ->** I am capable of achieving my goals.
- **I will never be successful ->** I am capable of achieving success with hard work and determination.
- **It is too late for me to pursue my dreams ->** By working intelligently and diligently, I can still achieve my dreams.
- **I am not smart enough to achieve my goals ->** I am capable of learning and growing.
- **I am too old/young to do this ->** My age does not define my abilities. I am rightly poised at this age to do this.

Step 4: Take Action

Taking action is the final step in overcoming your limiting beliefs. Here are some steps you can take to turn your re-framed beliefs into reality:

- Set specific, achievable goals that align with your re-framed beliefs.
- Break down your goals into smaller, manageable steps, and focus on making progress rather than achieving perfection.
- Surround yourself with supportive people who believe in your abilities and can encourage you along the way.
- Practice self-compassion and forgiveness, recognizing that setbacks and failures are a natural part of the process.
- Celebrate your successes along the way, no matter how small they may seem.

By following these steps, you can begin to overcome your limiting beliefs and achieve your full potential. Remember to be patient and persistent, and to keep working towards your goals even when it feels challenging. With time and effort, you can transform your beliefs and create the life you truly desire.

Embracing Challenges and Failure

Embracing challenges and viewing failure as a learning opportunity can be challenging, but it is an essential part of developing a growth mindset. Shift your mindset from one of fear and avoidance to one of curiosity and excitement. Instead of viewing challenges as threats or obstacles, approach them with a sense of willingness to learn. This can help you stay motivated in the face of difficulties.

Be kind and understanding towards yourself, even when things don't go as planned. Remember that setbacks and failures are a natural part of the learning process, and treat yourself with the same level of kindness and understanding that you would offer to a loved one. This can help you stay resilient and motivated even when things get tough.

Set realistic goals and work towards them consistently, even when progress is slow or difficult. Seek out support and feedback from others, whether it be from mentors, peers, or coaches. Thus, you can continue to learn and grow from your experiences, and become more resilient.

How to develop resilience and bounce back from setbacks

Resilience is the ability to adapt and recover in the face of adversity, and it can be learned and cultivated over time. One of the key ways to develop resilience is to practice mindfulness and self-awareness. This means paying attention to your thoughts and emotions and learning to manage them in a healthy way. Mindfulness can help you stay present and focused, even in the face of difficult circumstances, and can help you avoid becoming overwhelmed by stress or negative emotions.

Another important aspect of developing resilience is to build a strong support system. This includes cultivating positive relationships with friends, family, and mentors who can offer support and guidance when you need it. It also means seeking out resources and tools that can help you stay motivated and engaged, such as books, podcasts, or online communities.

It is also important to approach setbacks as opportunities for growth and learning. This means reframing setbacks as valuable experiences that can teach you important lessons and help you build resilience over time. Instead of dwelling on the negative aspects of a setback, try to focus on what you can learn from the experience and how you can use that knowledge to move forward in a positive way. By adopting a growth mindset and learning from setbacks, you can build the resilience you need to achieve your goals and reach your full potential.

Personal story: From Failure to Success: The Journey of Rati Malhotra, a Fashion Designer

My name is Rati, and I had always been passionate about fashion design. After completing my fashion design course, I was excited to launch my own label and showcase my creativity to the world. However, the reality of the business world hit me hard when my first collection failed to sell and I was left with a lot of unsold inventory and a huge amount of debt.

At first, I was devastated by the failure of my first collection. I felt like I had let down my family, my friends, and most importantly, myself. I questioned my abilities as a designer and wondered whether I had made a huge mistake in pursuing my dream.

But then, I decided to take a step back and evaluate what had gone wrong. I realized that I had made a mistake by not doing enough market research before launching my collection. I had assumed that my designs would be well-received by everyone, without taking into account the preferences and tastes of my target audience. Additionally, I made some design choices that didn't resonate with my potential customers, which resulted in the failure of my collection.

Instead of giving up on my dream, I decided to learn from my mistakes and make changes to my business plan. I took some time to study the market and understand the latest trends in fashion. I also reached out to potential customers to get feedback on my designs and made changes accordingly. I started small by launching a new collection with a limited number of pieces and used social media to promote my brand.

Despite my initial fears and doubts, my new collection was well-received by my target audience. I started to gain more visibility and recognition as a designer, which led to more business opportunities such as collaborations with other designers and participation in fashion shows.

Over time, my brand grew in popularity and I was able to overcome the setbacks and challenges that I faced along the way. Today, my brand has become a well-known name in the fashion industry, and I have won several awards for my designs. Looking back, I realize that my failure was a learning opportunity that helped me grow as a designer and entrepreneur. It taught me the importance of market research, customer feedback, and the value of resilience and perseverance.

Cultivating a Growth Mindset

It is important to focus on your strengths and skills, rather than your weaknesses and limitations. Celebrate your accomplishments, no matter how small they may be, and use them as a foundation for further growth and development. This can help you develop a positive self-image and build confidence in your abilities.

Embrace learning opportunities and seeking new experiences can help you expand your knowledge and skills, and develop a sense of curiosity and wonder towards the world around you. Instead of fearing new challenges, view them as opportunities for growth and development.

Seek feedback from others and use it to improve yourself. Constructive criticism can be a valuable tool for personal growth and development. Be open to feedback, and use it to identify areas for improvement and develop your skills further.

Rather than relying on innate talent, focus on putting in consistent effort and hard work towards achieving your goals. This can help you stay motivated and persistent, even in the face of challenges and setbacks.

Exercise: A detailed self-reflection exercise for you to evaluate your own mindset:

Step 1: Reflect on Your Current Mindset

Take some time to assess your current beliefs, attitudes, and thought patterns that may be holding you back from achieving your goals and potential. By reflecting on your current mindset, you can identify any fixed mindset tendencies that you may have, such as believing that your abilities are predetermined and cannot be improved upon.

Reflecting on your current mindset also involves being aware of any negative self-talk or limiting beliefs that you may hold about yourself and your abilities. It can help you recognize patterns of thinking that may be hindering your growth and progress. Once you are aware of these patterns, you can start to challenge them and replace them with more positive, growth-oriented thoughts.

Prompts for reflecting on your current mindset:

1. In what situations do you find yourself feeling stuck or unmotivated?
2. How do you typically react to failure or challenges?
3. Are there any limiting beliefs that you hold about yourself or your abilities?
4. How do you approach learning and personal development?
5. Do you tend to focus more on your strengths or your weaknesses?
6. How do you react to feedback, both positive and negative?
7. Are there any areas of your life where you have a fixed mindset instead of a growth mindset?
8. In what ways can you challenge yourself to grow and develop a more positive and growth-oriented mindset?

Answering these questions can help you identify areas where you may need to shift your mindset and work towards cultivating a more positive and growth-oriented perspective.

Step 2: Identify Your Fixed Mindset Tendencies

Identifying your fixed mindset tendencies involves reflecting on the beliefs and attitudes you have about yourself and your abilities. A fixed mindset is characterized by the belief that your abilities and intelligence are fixed traits that cannot be changed or improved.

By identifying your fixed mindset tendencies, you can start to challenge and change these limiting beliefs and attitudes and work towards cultivating a growth mindset. To help you identify this, think of a recent situation where you faced a challenge or setback.

1. What was your initial reaction or thought about the situation?
2. Did you immediately feel discouraged or did you try to problem-solve and find a solution?
3. Reflect on your thoughts and emotions in that situation. Did you feel like your abilities were limited or did you see the challenge as an opportunity for growth and learning?
4. Based on your reflection, what fixed mindset tendencies do you notice in yourself? Do you tend to give up easily, avoid challenges, or believe that your abilities are fixed and cannot be improved?
5. How can you reframe your thinking in this situation to adopt a growth mindset? What steps can you take to turn this setback into an opportunity for growth and learning?

Step 3: Identify Your Growth Mindset Tendencies

Identifying your growth mindset tendencies involves reflecting on your thoughts, actions, and behaviors that reflect a growth-oriented mindset. These tendencies can include embracing challenges, persisting in the face of obstacles, seeing effort as a path to mastery, and learning from criticism and feedback.

Identifying these growth mindset tendencies can help you recognize and reinforce the positive aspects of your mindset, and work towards developing them further. Here is a self-reflection exercise to identify growth mindset tendencies:

1. Think of a recent challenge or setback you faced. Write down your initial thoughts and feelings about the situation.
2. Reflect on how you responded to the challenge or setback. Did you give up easily or did you persist in finding a solution? Did you view the situation as an opportunity to learn and grow, or did you see it as a failure that reflects on your abilities?

3. Identify any growth mindset tendencies you displayed in your response to the challenge or setback. For example, did you:
    a. Embrace the opportunity to learn and grow from the experience?
    b. Focus on the process and effort you put in, rather than just the outcome?
    c. Seek out feedback and use it to improve?
    d. View mistakes and failures as opportunities to learn and improve?
    e. Encourage and support others in their efforts to learn and grow?
4. Reflect on any fixed mindset tendencies you displayed in your response to the challenge or setback. For example, did you:
    a. Give up easily or avoid challenges to protect your ego?
    b. View your abilities as fixed and unchangeable?
    c. Ignore or reject feedback because you didn't want to hear criticism?
    d. Believe that mistakes and failures are proof of your limitations or shortcomings?
    e. Feel threatened or envious of others' successes and achievements?
5. Think about how you can cultivate and strengthen your growth mindset tendencies in the future. For example, you could:
    a. Set goals that challenge you and push you out of your comfort zone.
    b. Embrace mistakes and failures as opportunities to learn and grow.
    c. Seek out feedback and use it to improve your skills and abilities.
    d. Focus on the process and effort you put in, rather than just the outcome.
    e. Surround yourself with people who have a growth mindset and support your efforts to learn and grow.
6. Write down your action plan for cultivating a growth mindset, including specific goals and strategies for overcoming your fixed mindset tendencies.

Step 4: Set Goals for Growth

Setting goals for growth involves identifying specific areas where you want to develop a growth mindset and setting goals that will help you achieve that growth. It requires you to think about where you want to be in the future and what steps you need to take to get there. The goals you set should be challenging but achievable, and they should focus on the process rather than just the outcome.

A self-reflection exercise:

1. Reflect on your current goals: What are your current goals? Are they primarily focused on achievement or personal growth? Do you feel like you are constantly striving for external validation or recognition?
2. Identify areas for growth: Think about areas of your life where you would like to see improvement. These could be related to relationships, career, health, or personal development. What skills or qualities do you want to develop or improve upon?
3. Create SMART goals: Use the SMART framework to set goals for growth. Ensure that your goals are specific, measurable, achievable, relevant, and time-bound. For example, instead of setting a vague goal like 'be more confident,' set a SMART goal like 'give a presentation in front of a group of colleagues within the next month.'
4. Take action: Identify specific steps you can take to work towards your goals. This could involve taking a course, seeking feedback from a mentor, or practicing a new habit daily. Set yourself up for success by breaking down your goals into smaller, manageable steps.

Step 5: Practice Self-reflection

Self-reflection is the process of looking inward and examining one's thoughts, feelings, and actions. It involves taking a step back from the daily routine and reflecting on past experiences, behaviors, and reactions to better understand oneself. Through self-reflection, individuals can identify their strengths, weaknesses, and areas for improvement. It can also help individuals gain clarity on their goals, values, and beliefs, and make decisions that align with them. Practicing self-reflection regularly can also help individuals develop greater self-awareness, empathy, and a more positive outlook on life.

Practicing self-reflection to cultivate a growth mindset:

1. Take a few moments to reflect on your recent accomplishments, challenges, and setbacks. Ask yourself:
    a. How did I respond to these situations?
    b. Did I approach them with a growth-oriented mindset or a fixed mindset?
    c. What did I learn from these experiences?
    d. How can I apply these learnings to future situations?
2. Think about a recent mistake or failure you experienced. Ask yourself:
    a. How did I react to this failure/mistake?

   b. Did I view it as a learning opportunity or a setback?
   c. What did I learn from this experience?
   d. How can I use this experience to grow and improve in the future?
3. Consider your typical reactions to feedback. Ask yourself:
   a. How do I typically react to feedback?
   b. Do I become defensive or open-minded?
   c. How can I learn to view feedback as an opportunity for growth rather than criticism?
4. Reflect on your current mindset. Ask yourself:
   a. Do I have a growth-oriented mindset or a fixed mindset?
   b. In what ways can I work towards cultivating a growth mindset?
   c. What strategies can I use to challenge my fixed mindset thoughts and beliefs?
5. Identify someone in your life who you feel has a growth-oriented mindset. Ask yourself:
   a. What traits and behaviors does this person exhibit?
   b. How can I learn from and emulate their mindset?
   c. In what ways can I surround myself with more growth-minded individuals?

Take the time to reflect on each of these prompts, and consider how you can apply the lessons learned to cultivate a more positive and growth-oriented mindset.

Step 6: Surround Yourself with Growth-Minded Individuals

Surrounding yourself with growth-minded individuals means seeking out people who share your desire for personal growth and development. These individuals can be positive influences on your own mindset and can help motivate and support you as you work towards cultivating a growth-oriented mindset.

It is important to look for people who are supportive, encouraging, open to learning, and excited about new experiences. Spending time with people who have a fixed mindset or who are negative and critical can hold you back from developing a growth mindset. Seek out individuals who challenge you to grow, offer constructive feedback, and inspire you to become your best self.

Being around growth-minded individuals can also provide you with opportunities for learning and development. You can learn from their experiences and perspectives, and they can help you see new possibilities and potential in yourself. Additionally, by surrounding yourself with people who share your values and goals, you can build a supportive network that helps you stay accountable and motivated in your pursuit of growth. A few pointers:

1. Think about the people in your life who have a growth mindset. Who are they? What qualities do they possess that make them growth-minded?
2. Do you actively seek out opportunities to connect with and learn from growth-minded individuals? Why or why not?
3. Consider the people in your life who have a fixed mindset. How do they influence your mindset and beliefs? In what ways do they hold you back or limit your growth?
4. Are there any toxic or negative relationships in your life that are hindering your growth? How can you distance yourself from those individuals or set boundaries to protect your mindset?
5. Reflect on your own behavior and attitudes towards others. Are you a positive influence on those around you, encouraging growth and development? How can you be more intentional about fostering a growth mindset in your interactions with others?
6. Think about the ways in which you can actively seek out and connect with growth-minded individuals. What steps can you take to surround yourself with people who challenge you to grow and support your journey toward cultivating a growth mindset?

Personal Stories and Case Studies

Individuals who have developed a growth mindset and how it has impacted their lives and careers:

1. **Michael Jordan**: Michael Jordan is widely regarded as one of the greatest basketball players of all time. He attributes his success not just to his natural talent but also to his mindset. He once said, "I have missed more than 9,000 shots in my career. I have lost almost 300 games. 26 times, I have been trusted to take the game-winning shot and missed. **I have failed over and over and over again in my life. And that is why I succeed.**" Jordan's growth mindset made him see his failures and setbacks as opportunities for learning and improvement.
2. **Oprah Winfrey**: Oprah Winfrey is a media mogul and philanthropist who has overcome significant adversity in her life, including poverty, abuse, and discrimination. Despite these challenges, she has been able to achieve

tremendous success due in part to her growth mindset. Oprah has said, "**I believe that one of life's greatest risks is never daring to risk**," and has spoken about the importance of viewing challenges as opportunities for growth and learning.

3. **Elon Musk**: Elon Musk is a visionary entrepreneur who has founded several successful companies, including SpaceX and Tesla. Musk's growth mindset has allowed him to take risks and pursue ambitious goals, even in the face of significant obstacles. He has said, "**When something is important enough, you do it even if the odds are not in your favor.**" Musk's willingness to embrace failure and learn from his mistakes has been critical to his success.

The Power of Adopting a Growth Mindset

By viewing challenges as opportunities to learn and improve, individuals with a growth mindset are more likely to take on new projects and push themselves outside of their comfort zones. This can lead to increased creativity, innovation, and productivity in the workplace.

The growth mindset can help individuals develop important skills such as resilience, adaptability, and perseverance. These skills are highly valued by employers and can make individuals stand out in the workplace. By embracing challenges and viewing failure as a learning opportunity, individuals with a growth mindset are better equipped to handle setbacks and overcome obstacles, which can lead to increased confidence and success in their careers.

Individuals with a growth mindset are more likely to seek out feedback and constructive criticism, which can help them identify areas for improvement and continue to grow and develop their skills. This can lead to increased job satisfaction and a sense of purpose in one's career, as well as opportunities for advancement and career growth.

Case Study: The story of Satya Nadella who used a growth mindset to overcome challenges and achieve success

Satya Nadella was born in Hyderabad, India in 1967 and was raised in a family that valued education and hard work. Nadella pursued a degree in electrical engineering and later earned a master's degree in computer science from the University of Wisconsin and an MBA from the University of Chicago.

Nadella joined Microsoft in 1992. In 2013, when Nadella was appointed as the CEO of Microsoft, the company was struggling to keep up with its competitors in the technology industry.

Under Nadella's leadership, Microsoft underwent a massive transformation, shifting its focus to cloud-based services and mobile devices. Nadella's growth mindset played a crucial role in this transformation. He encouraged his team to embrace new ideas and take risks, even if it meant failing.

Nadella's leadership style also emphasized empathy and inclusivity. He understood that the key to success was not just about technical expertise but also about creating an inclusive culture where everyone feels valued and empowered to contribute their ideas. This approach helped to create a more collaborative and innovative environment at Microsoft.

Nadella's growth mindset and leadership style paid off, and under his leadership, Microsoft has regained its position as a leader in the technology industry. In 2018, Microsoft surpassed Apple as the world's most valuable company, a testament to the success of Nadella's growth mindset and leadership style.

Author's Personal Story: "How Shifting to a Growth Mindset Transformed My Life."

As a trainer of the subconscious mind and a motivational speaker, I have seen how a growth mindset can change people's lives. But I didn't always feel this way.

As a child, I was taught to have a fixed mind. I used to think that people were either born with talent and intelligence or they weren't. This way of thinking made me afraid of failing, so I didn't take chances. I never really pushed myself out of my comfort zone in either my personal or professional life.

I didn't realize how limited my fixed mindset was until I started speaking as a motivational speaker. As a business owner, I had to deal with failures and setbacks all the time. I had to take chances and go beyond what I thought I could do. During this time, I realized that my fixed mindset was keeping me from being as good as I could be.

I started to think in a way that would help me grow. I started to accept challenges, look for ways to learn, and put more emphasis on how hard I worked instead of just how smart I was. I started to see failures and setbacks as chances to learn and grow instead of as signs of how talented I was.

This change in my thinking changed my life and career. I started speaking at more difficult events, grew my business, and pushed myself to achieve new heights. I started to see success not as a destination but as a journey that required me to keep learning, growing, and getting better.

As a subconscious mind trainer and motivational speaker, I now help other people make the same shift toward a growth mindset that changed my life. I talk about my own journey and the things that have helped me get where I am now. I encourage other people to take on challenges, look for ways to learn, and focus on their effort rather than just their natural abilities.

As part of my job, I have seen a lot of people change their lives and careers by having a 'growth mindset.' I am thankful for my own journey and the chance to help others make the same change toward a more positive and growth-focused mindset.

Exercises for you

- Reflect on your current mindset and identify whether it is fixed or growth-oriented.
- Challenge a limiting belief you have about yourself and reframe it into a growth-oriented mindset.
- Practice self-compassion and forgiveness when faced with setbacks or failures.

Share your Thoughts

Congratulations on completing Chapter 4: The Growth Mindset Blueprint! I hope you found it to be an inspiring and insightful read. As we come to the end of this chapter, I would like to ask you a question: do you feel inspired to adopt a growth mindset? I hope that the stories, examples, and strategies presented in this chapter have convinced you of the power of a growth mindset, and that you feel motivated to adopt one in your own life.

Speaking of stories, let me share a humorous one with you. A grandfather was deeply steeped in the fixed mindset, convinced that he was always right and resistant to change. One day, he spent hours searching for his dentures, convinced that they must have been stolen. He searched high and low, turning his house upside down, until he finally gave up and decided to call his dentist to order a new set. As he reached for the phonebook, he was surprised to find his dentures tucked inside. Confused, he tried to remember how they ended up there, only to realize that it was his own mistake. With a sheepish grin, he couldn't help but laugh at how his fixed mindset had led him to blame others for his own forgetfulness.

I would love to hear your stories too! If you have had any experiences with adopting a growth mindset, please leave a review and share them with me and other readers. Your personal experiences may inspire someone else to take that leap of faith and challenge their fixed mindset.

To write a review, simply go to Amazon, locate the review section, and leave your thoughts. It's that simple! If you need help with writing a review, don't worry. I have got you covered. First, think about what you liked most about this chapter and how it has helped you. Then, write a few lines expressing your thoughts. Finally, hit submit, and you're done!

As a special incentive for leaving a review, I am offering the 'Author's Draft' of this chapter. It contains extended details and research that may not have made it into this final published version. To claim your copy, simply send an email to sworld.mind@gmail.com after you have submitted your review.

Conclusion

In this chapter, we have explored the concept of the growth mindset and its benefits. We learned that a growth mindset can help us overcome limiting beliefs, embrace challenges, and achieve our goals. We also discussed the importance of identifying and challenging our fixed mindset and the myths surrounding it. By understanding the differences between a fixed and growth mindset, we can cultivate a positive and proactive approach to life that will help us achieve success.

During our exploration, we gained a deeper understanding of how adopting a growth mindset can help us achieve our full potential. We discovered that reframing our mindset not only allows us to move beyond our comfort zones but also enables us to embrace challenges and failures as opportunities for growth and development.

Additionally, we learned about practical strategies that we can apply to our personal growth journey, including learning from mistakes, seeking feedback, and staying motivated. By studying personal stories and case studies, we gained valuable insights and inspiration to help us navigate the ups and downs of our growth journey.

In the next chapter, we will explore the concept of time management and productivity. We will also examine common obstacles to productivity and how to overcome them. By mastering time and boosting productivity, we can achieve more and lead a more fulfilling life.

Wrap up

Congratulations on taking this very important step towards your personal development journey by exploring the concept of a growth mindset in this chapter.

As you may have learned, developing a growth mindset involves recognizing and challenging your limiting beliefs, embracing challenges and failures, and cultivating a mindset that seeks growth and learning.

It is important to understand that developing a growth mindset is not an overnight process. It requires consistent effort and patience. But, every little step you take towards cultivating a growth mindset will help you reach your full potential.

By embracing challenges and failures, you will become stronger and more resilient, and learn valuable skills that can help you overcome obstacles in your personal and professional life.

It is easy to get caught up in wanting to be perfect, but it's important to remember that a growth mindset is about embracing imperfection and learning from our mistakes. Setbacks and failures are not the end of the road, but rather opportunities for growth and learning. Every time you reflect on what went wrong, you will be better equipped to do better next time.

So, keep in mind that progress takes time and effort. A growth mindset requires us to put in the work to improve ourselves, but every effort we make to learn and grow strengthens us. Always be kind to yourself, celebrate your progress, and stay motivated.

Remember that the best version of yourself is waiting to be discovered, and with a growth mindset, you can achieve anything you set your mind to. Keep going, keep learning, and keep growing towards your goal of becoming the best version of yourself. You are more than capable of succeeding!

"If you can't fly, then run. If you can't run, then walk. If you can't walk, then crawl. But whatever you do, keep moving forward."

- Martin Luther King Jr.

❑

CHAPTER 5

Mastering Time and Boosting Productivity

"Procrastination is the thief of time."

– Edward Young

Introduction

Do you ever feel like there aren't enough hours in the day? Are you struggling to manage your time effectively and be productive? In today's fast-paced world, time management and productivity are essential skills that can help you lead a fulfilling life.

In the previous chapter, we discussed the importance of developing a growth mindset that empowers us to learn, grow, and reach our full potential. In this chapter, we will explore how to manage your time effectively, overcome procrastination, boost your productivity, and manage stress.

Time is a precious resource, and how we manage it can have a significant impact on our success and happiness. We will explore the concept of time management and various strategies to help you make the most of your time. We will also discuss how to overcome procrastination, boost your productivity, and manage stress.

Effective time management is not just about being productive, but also about achieving a better work-life balance and having more time for the things that matter to you. We will be sharing practical tips and techniques that you can implement in your daily life to manage your time better and increase your productivity.

As always, we will be using personal stories and case studies to illustrate the concepts and make them relatable to your own life. Are you ready to take control of your time and boost your productivity? So, let's dive into this chapter and learn how to manage your time effectively and be more productive!

Effective time management and productivity

Mastering time management and productivity means making conscious choices about how we spend our time and setting clear goals and priorities. It involves identifying and eliminating time-wasters, such as distractions and procrastination, and using proven strategies to optimize our focus and energy. By doing so, we can achieve more with less effort and create the space for the things that matter most to us.

Effective time management and productivity also require a mindset shift. We need to cultivate habits of discipline, consistency, and perseverance, and learn to say no to things that do not align with our goals and values. We must also learn to delegate, outsource, and automate tasks that are not essential, freeing up our time and energy for the things that truly matter.

The benefits of mastering time management and productivity are numerous. We can create more time for self-care, leisure, and personal growth, improving our overall well-being and satisfaction. We can also increase our efficiency and effectiveness at work, leading to greater success and recognition. Moreover, we can create more meaningful connections with others, as we have more time and energy to invest in our relationships.

How you may develop the skills necessary to manage your time and increase productivity

By developing these skills, you can create more time and space for the things that matter most to you and achieve your goals with greater ease and efficiency.

The first step in mastering time management is to become aware of how you currently spend your time. This means tracking your time and identifying your time-wasters, such as social media, email, or unnecessary meetings. Once you know where your time is going, you can start making conscious choices about how to use it more effectively.

The next step is to set clear goals and priorities. By defining what is important to you and what you want to achieve, you can focus your time and energy on the things that matter most. This means saying no to distractions and other commitments that do not align with your goals and values.

Another key skill in mastering time management is to learn how to plan and organize your time effectively. This means breaking down your goals into smaller, manageable tasks, and creating a schedule or to-do list that helps you stay on track. By planning ahead and staying organized, you can reduce stress and increase your productivity.

You may also learn how to manage your energy levels effectively. This means taking breaks when you need them, getting enough sleep, and prioritizing self-care and other activities that recharge your batteries. By managing your energy levels, you can avoid burnout and stay focused and productive throughout the day.

Last but not the least, it is important to learn how to delegate, outsource, or automate tasks that are not essential. This means identifying the tasks that can be done by someone else or by a machine and freeing up your time and energy for the things that truly matter. By delegating and automating tasks, you can achieve more with less effort.

Understanding Time Management

Time management refers to the process of organizing and planning the usage of your time effectively and efficiently. It involves prioritizing tasks, setting goals, and managing distractions to optimize your productivity and achieve your desired outcomes.

Time management helps us to maximize our productivity and get more done in less time. By prioritizing tasks and focusing our energy on the most important ones, we can achieve our goals more quickly and efficiently. Time management also helps us to reduce stress and increase our overall well-being. When we feel in control of our time, we are less likely to feel overwhelmed or anxious, and we can create more time for the things that bring us joy and fulfillment.

Effective time management also helps us to build self-discipline, which is a key ingredient for personal and professional success. It also helps us to cultivate a mindset of abundance, as we begin to see time as a valuable resource that can be optimized and leveraged for our benefit.

Most importantly time management enables us to create a more balanced and fulfilling life. By managing our time effectively, we create more time for our relationships, hobbies, and personal growth. Through time management we also avoid burnout and create more sustainable, long-term success in our personal and professional lives.

Consequences of poor time management

One of the most significant consequences of poor time management is stress. When we have a lot to do and not enough time to do it, we can become overwhelmed and anxious. This can lead to physical and mental health problems and can even impact our relationships with others. Moreover, when we feel stressed and overwhelmed, we are less productive, which can create a vicious cycle of stress and inefficiency.

When we don't prioritize our time effectively, we can miss out on important opportunities that could help us achieve our goals. For example, if we don't manage our time effectively at work, we may miss out on promotions or career advancement opportunities. Similarly, if we don't manage our time effectively in our personal lives, we may miss out on opportunities to pursue hobbies or spend time with loved ones.

With poor time management we can find ourselves easily distracted by unimportant tasks or activities. This can lead to a lack of focus and a feeling of being overwhelmed, which can ultimately impact our ability to achieve our goals and succeed in our personal and professional lives.

Personal story: Overcoming the Consequences of Poor Time Management

Akash Kumar was a successful businessman, father of two children, and a devoted husband to his wife, Priya. He was always busy with work and was proud of his ability to juggle multiple tasks at once. But as the years went by, he realized that his poor time management was taking a toll on his personal and professional life.

At work, he struggled to meet deadlines and found himself working late nights and weekends to catch up. This meant that he had less time to spend with his family, causing them to feel neglected and unhappy. Let us hear the rest directly from Akash.

It wasn't until my daughter's tenth birthday that I realized how much I had been missing out on. I had promised to take her to the amusement park that weekend, but as usual, work took over, and I had to cancel. Seeing the disappointment in my daughter's eyes broke my heart, and I knew that I needed to make a change. That incident made me reflect on my life, and I realized that I was missing out on so many precious moments with my family.

My poor time management not only affected my personal life but also impacted my work. I was always tired and stressed out, which affected my productivity and my relationships with my colleagues. I found myself always trying to catch up and constantly falling behind schedule.

It wasn't until I started attending workshops and reading books on time management that I realized the value of effective time management. I learned the importance of prioritizing tasks and setting realistic deadlines. I started delegating tasks and saying no to things that weren't important. I began to create a schedule for myself that allowed me to balance work and family time.

Now, I am much more productive at work, and I have much more quality time with my family. I make it a point to have dinner with my wife and daughter every day, and we take regular family vacations. I no longer bring work home with me, and I am able to be fully present with my family.

I have also started to pursue my hobbies again, such as playing the guitar and reading books. These activities help me relax and recharge, which ultimately improves my overall productivity.

Looking back, I wish I had realized the importance of time management earlier. But I am grateful for the wake-up call that my daughter's tears gave me. It's never too late to make a change and prioritize what's truly important in life.

I hope my story serves as a reminder to others that poor time management can have negative consequences in both personal and professional life. With the right mindset and tools, anyone can master their time and boost their productivity to achieve their goals while still enjoying a fulfilling personal life.

Time Management Strategies

Setting priorities is one of the most important things you can do. By figuring out which tasks are the most important and doing them first, people can make sure they achieve their most important goals without getting stuck on less important tasks. A prioritization matrix can help you figure out which tasks are urgent and important, which ones can be given to other people, and which ones can be put off or even thrown out.

Making a schedule is another important way to manage your time. People can plan their day, week, or even month ahead of time with the help of a schedule, making sure they have enough time to do all of their important tasks. It is also important to give yourself enough time for breaks and relaxation, which can help you avoid burnout and get more done.

The Pomodoro Technique is another time management strategy that involves breaking work into intervals of 25 minutes, followed by short breaks. This technique helps to maintain focus and avoid burnout by working in short, focused bursts. It is particularly useful for tasks that require intense concentration, such as writing or studying.

Getting rid of distractions is another important part of managing your time. Social media, phone calls, and emails are all examples of things that can get in the way of work and waste time. By making sure there are no distractions, people can focus on their most important tasks, finish them quickly, and manage their time better.

Prioritization Matrix

A prioritization matrix is a tool that helps one to prioritize tasks and make informed decisions about how to allocate time and resources. It is also known as an Eisenhower Matrix or a 4-quadrant matrix

The matrix involves dividing tasks into four categories based on two dimensions: urgency and importance. Urgent tasks are those that require immediate attention, while important tasks are those that align with your goals and values.

Here is an example of a prioritization matrix:

	Urgent	Not Urgent
Important	Quadrant 1: Do First	Quadrant 2: Schedule
Not Important	Quadrant 3: Delegate	Quadrant 4: Eliminate

Tasks that fall into Quadrant 1 are both urgent and important and should be done first. These are typically high-priority tasks that require immediate attention, such as meeting a deadline or addressing an urgent issue.

Tasks in Quadrant 2 are important but not urgent, and should be scheduled for a later time. These might include long-term goals, strategic planning, or important projects that don't require immediate attention.

Tasks in Quadrant 3 are urgent but not important and can be delegated to others if possible. These might include routine tasks, administrative work, or tasks that can be completed by someone else.

Tasks in Quadrant 4 are neither urgent nor important and can be eliminated altogether. These might include time-wasters, distractions, or low-priority tasks that don't align with your goals and values.

By using a prioritization matrix, you can identify which tasks are most important and allocate your time and resources accordingly.

Using tools like to-do lists and calendars to manage time effectively

A to-do list is one of the best ways to keep track of time. A well-organized list of things to do can help people stay focused and on track all day. To make a good list of things to do, it is important to put tasks in order of importance, break them down into smaller, more manageable steps, and give yourself realistic due dates.

Calendars and planners are also important tools for getting the most out of your time. Using a calendar can help people stay organized, plan ahead, and make sure they don't miss important dates or meetings. When using a calendar, it is important to set aside time for specific tasks and put them in order of how important they are. Making a daily schedule with set times for tasks and breaks can also help people manage their time better and keep them from wasting time on things that aren't important.

Exercise: To Boost Your Productivity

An in-depth time tracking exercise to find time wasters and make you more productive

Step 1: Set a Goal and a Time Frame

It is important to know your goal and how much time you have before you start the exercise. What are you trying to do? Is it to get more done or to have more time for yourself? How long do you want your time to be tracked? Most of the time, one week is a good place to start.

Step 2: Create a Time Log

The next step is to keep track of how you spend your time during the day by making a time log. You can do this with a spreadsheet, a journal, or an app made just for keeping track of time. Each task's time, activity, and length should be recorded in the log.

Step 3: Keep a Week's Worth of Time Logs

Start noting how you spend your time for a week. Make sure to write down everything you do, no matter how small or unimportant it seems. This includes time spent on social networks, watching TV, and doing other fun things. Remember that the point of this activity is to find out how you spend your time now.

Step 4: Look at the Time Log

After a week of keeping track of your time, it is time to look at what you've learned. Find patterns and long-term tendencies. What takes up most of your time? Do you spend a lot of time on things that don't really get you anywhere? Are there any tasks you can get rid of or give to someone else? By looking at your time log, you can see where you can make changes.

Step 5: Make Adjustments

Based on what you've found, it is time to change your schedule. Find out which tasks are most important and put them in order of importance. If there are tasks you can get rid of or give to someone else, do so. Try to spend less time on things that don't help you achieve your goals and more time on things that do.

Step 6: Look Back and Think

Review and think about the changes you've made to your schedule after you've made them. Has your work gotten better? Do you have more time on your hands? If not, what changes can you make to improve how you use your time?

Let's say you are a freelance writer and you want to get more done. You decide to keep track of how you spend your time for a week to see where you can make changes. You make a time log to keep track of what you did during the week. After looking at the data, you realize that you spend a lot of time checking emails and social media. You also realize that you spend too much time doing research.

You decide to change your schedule based on what you've found. You schedule times to check your email and social media, and you limit how long you spend doing these things. You also decide to use more efficient research methods to reduce the time you spend on research. As a result of these changes, you will have more time to focus on writing, which will help you get more done.

Overcoming Procrastination

Procrastination is the tendency to put off or put off doing things. This usually leads to missed deadlines, less work done, and more stress. Individuals delay for different reasons, including fear of failure, lack of desire, diversions, and disorganization. This behavior may be damaging to personal and professional growth and can lead to missed opportunities and unmet ambitions.

To combat procrastination, it is vital to understand the underlying causes and establish effective ways for managing time and enhancing motivation. One strategy to overcome procrastination is to break down major activities into smaller, more manageable pieces and to prioritize them based on urgency and significance. It is also useful to make clear, realistic goals and to build a pattern that includes frequent pauses and rewards for accomplishing chores.

Another helpful method is to minimize distractions, such as social media or email updates, during focused work hours. This can help boost attention and lessen the risk of procrastination. Also, it is necessary to acquire self-discipline and to hold oneself accountable for finishing duties on time. This can be done by sharing objectives and progress with others or by seeking the help of a coach or mentor.

Strategies for overcoming procrastination

It can be hard to break the habit of putting things off, but there are several good ways to do so. One useful approach is to break larger tasks into smaller, more manageable steps. By doing this, you will be less likely to feel overwhelmed and more able to focus on taking one step at a time to move forward. Also, breaking up tasks can help you set goals and deadlines that are more realistic, which can make you less likely to put things off.

Positive self-talk is another good way to help yourself. To do this, you have to change your negative thoughts and beliefs about tasks into ones that are more positive and encouraging. For example, instead of telling yourself, "I'll never be able to finish this project on time," you could tell yourself, "I can take it one step at a time and get closer to finishing this project." By talking to yourself in a positive way, you can get more motivated and feel less stressed and anxious, which can make you put things off.

It can be helpful to figure out what may be causing you to put things off and do something about it. For example, if you have trouble with perfectionism, you might need to work on realizing that tasks don't have to be done perfectly to be successful. Or, if you find that your environment makes it easy for you to get sidetracked, you may need to change your workspace or find ways to stay focused. By addressing these underlying causes, you can better prepare yourself to stop putting things off and better manage your time.

Case study: Overcoming procrastination to complete a challenging project.

Name: Riya Gonzales

Background: Riya is a software developer who works at a tech startup in Bangalore, India. She is passionate about coding and loves her job, but struggles with procrastination when it comes to completing larger projects.

Challenge: Riya was assigned to lead the development of a new software application for the company's biggest client. The project was complex and would require a significant amount of time and effort from the team. Despite her excitement for the project, Riya found herself procrastinating and struggling to make progress.

Solution: Riya decided to use several strategies to overcome her procrastination and successfully complete the project:

1. **Break tasks into smaller steps:** Riya's first plan was to break the project into smaller steps that would be easier to handle. She did this by making a detailed project plan with clear milestones and due dates. This made it possible for her to divide the work into smaller, more manageable tasks, which helped her stay on track and keep from feeling overwhelmed.
2. **Use a timer:** The second strategy that Riya implemented was using a timer. She found that if she worked for 25 minutes straight and then took a 5-minute break, she was able to get more done and stay focused. This method called the *Pomodoro Technique*, helped her stay focused on the task at hand and not let other things distract her.
3. **Get enough sleep and exercise.** Riya also knew it was important to put her health and well-being first. She made sure to get enough sleep and took breaks during the day to work out. By taking care of her body, she was able to keep her energy up and keep her mind on the task at hand for longer.
4. **Ask for help.** Riya asked her co-workers for help. She asked them to help her stay on track and give her feedback on how she was doing. This helped her stay on track and stay motivated, and it also gave her a chance to learn from and get advice from her peers.

Results: With these plans in place, Riya was able to stop putting things off and finish the project on time and on budget. The client and the top leaders of the company liked what her team did, and Riya felt proud and accomplished about her work. She also kept using these strategies in her future projects, which made her a more efficient and productive developer.

Boosting Productivity

One strategy for boosting productivity is delegating tasks to others. This means figuring out which tasks can be given to other people who may be better at them or can do them more quickly. Delegating tasks not only frees up time, but also allows one to focus on tasks that align with their strengths and expertise, leading to higher-quality work.

Focusing on one task at a time is another way to be more productive. Multitasking may seem like a good way to get more done in less time, but it often slows people down and makes their work less good. When people focus on one task at a time, they can give that task their full attention and effort, which leads to better results and faster completion.

Taking breaks is another important way to increase productivity. Even though it might seem counterintuitive to take a break when there are things to do, breaks actually help people re-energize and refocus, which leads to more and better work. Taking short breaks throughout the day can help keep you from getting too tired and boost your motivation to get things done.

Using Technology to Increase Productivity: Productivity Apps and Email Filters

Technology has become an important part of our everyday lives, and it can be a very effective way to get more done. Using productivity apps is one way to use technology to get more done. These apps can help you keep track of your progress, organize your tasks, and set reminders. Trello, Asana, and Todoist are all examples of popular productivity apps. You can download these apps to your computer or mobile device, so you can use them whenever and wherever you want.

Setting up email filters is another way to use technology to get more done. Email can be a big time-waster and distraction, but if you set up filters, you can have your emails automatically put in different folders based on their content or sender. This can help you decide which emails are most important and answer them first. Also, many email clients have features that let you schedule emails to be sent at a later time or date. This can help you keep your inbox organized and reduce distractions.

In addition to productivity apps and email filters, there are many other tools and technologies that can help you be more productive. These include time-tracking apps, project management software, and automation tools. It is important to find the tools that work best for you and your specific goals and needs. By using technology to boost productivity, you can save time and focus your attention on the most important tasks.

Personal story: Shweta Adwani from Jaipur, India, shares how she increased her productivity.

As a business manager, it is my job to keep track of several teams and make sure deadlines are met. But I was always struggling to keep up with the demands of my job, and I often felt like I had too much to do. That was until I found a specific method that helped me get a lot more done in a lot less time.

The strategy I used was based on putting tasks in order of importance. I realized that I was spending a lot of time on tasks that weren't necessarily urgent or important. This meant that I had less time to focus on tasks that were more important. To fix this, I started putting my tasks in order of importance by putting them into three groups: urgent and important, important but not urgent, and not important.

I made sure to do important and urgent tasks first thing in the morning when I was most alert and productive. For tasks that were important but didn't have to be done right away, I set aside specific times during the day to work on them and made sure to give myself a deadline. Lastly, I gave less important tasks to someone else or took them off my list.

In addition to putting things in order of importance, I made sure to take breaks throughout the day to give my mind a rest and a chance to refuel. This meant taking short walks outside, doing stretches, or just sitting still for a few minutes to clear my mind. I found that taking breaks helped me stay focused and get more work done when I got back to it.

By using this strategy, I was able to make a big difference in how much I got done and how well I did. I had more time and energy to focus on the tasks that really mattered, which led to better results for me and my team as a whole.

I learned from this that to be productive, you don't just have to work harder or longer; you also have to work smarter. By putting things in order of importance and taking breaks, I was able to work faster and better, which helped me do a better job as a business manager.

Managing Stress

Effective time management and productivity can help a lot with stress management. When you know how to use your time well, you can finish your tasks on time and avoid the stress of rushing at the last minute. A well-organized schedule can help you decide which tasks are most important, how much time to spend on each, and how much you can handle. This makes sure you have enough time for each task and also makes you feel less overwhelmed and anxious.

Also, being more productive can help you feel less stressed. When you are productive, you can get more done in less time, which means you can get your work done quickly and well. This gives you more time to relax, take care of yourself, and spend time with friends, all of which can help you feel less stressed. Also, when you finish your tasks, you feel good about yourself. This can help you deal with stress and boost your self-esteem.

Good time management can help you find a balance between work and other parts of your life, which is a key part of dealing with stress. When you have a well-balanced life, you can make sure that your personal and professional lives don't get in the way of each other. This can make you feel like you have more control over your life, which can lower your stress. Thus, good time management and productivity can help you deal with stress and live a happier, healthier life.

Exercise can help reduce stress because it releases endorphins, which are natural mood boosters, and lowers the levels of stress hormones like cortisol in the body. Any kind of exercise can help, whether it is a brisk walk, a yoga class, or a workout at the gym. It is important to find an exercise routine that you like and that works with your schedule.

Meditation is another good way to manage stress. Meditation is a way to clear your mind and relax by focusing on a single object or thought. There are many ways to meditate, like guided meditation, mindfulness meditation, and transcendental meditation. Find a way to meditate that works for you and do it on a regular basis to get the most out of it.

Other ways to deal with stress are deep breathing exercises, progressive muscle relaxation, and spending time in nature. To effectively deal with stress and improve your overall health, you need to find the methods that work best for you and add them to your daily routine.

Mindful Breathing Meditation for Stress Reduction

Objective: This exercise aims to reduce stress and increase relaxation through a mindful breathing meditation.

Steps:

1. Find a quiet, comfortable place where you won't be disturbed for 10 to 15 minutes. It is best to choose a location where your phone or other electronic devices won't distract you. Use a meditation cushion or chair to stay in a comfortable position. If not, you can sit on a cushion or a folded blanket on the floor or in a chair with your feet flat on the ground.
2. Once you are in a comfortable position, gently close your eyes and take a deep breath through your nose. Let your belly get as big as it can. Hold your breath for a few seconds, and then let it out slowly through your mouth. As you exhale, let any tension or stress leave your body.
3. Pay attention to the feeling of your breath as it moves in and out of your body. Notice how the air feels cool when you inhale and warm when you exhale. Allow yourself to fully feel the physical sensations of breathing, from the rise and fall of your chest to the movement of air in your nostrils.
4. When your mind begins to wander, gently bring it back to your breath. Don't judge yourself for losing focus. Instead, just acknowledge the thought or distraction and bring your attention back to your breath.

5. As you keep breathing mindfully, check your body for any places where you feel tight or uncomfortable. As you find these spots, imagine sending your breath to that part of your body and letting the tension leave with each exhale. For example, if you feel the tension in your neck and shoulders, imagine sending your breath there and feeling the muscles start to relax and let go.
6. If any thoughts or feelings come up during the practice, acknowledge them without judging them and gently let them go. Then bring your attention back to your breath. Do not dwell on bad thoughts or feelings. Instead, see them as temporary and focus on your breath.
7. Keep breathing mindfully this way for 10–15 minutes. You may find that your mind wanders a lot at first, but with practice, you will get better at staying focused and in the moment.
8. When you are ready to stop, take a deep breath in through your nose, hold it for a few seconds, and then slowly let it out through your mouth. Take a moment to notice how you feel after the practice, and keep this feeling of relaxation and calm with you as you go about your day.

Tips:

1. Do this exercise at the same time every day to make it part of your routine and easier to fit into your life.
2. Set a timer for 10 to 15 minutes so that you won't lose track of time.
3. If you've never meditated before, start with shorter sessions and build up to longer ones as you get used to the technique.
4. You can also make this exercise a part of your daily life by practicing mindful breathing while doing things like walking or washing dishes.

By regularly practicing this mindful breathing meditation exercise, you can reduce stress and increase relaxation, ultimately leading to a more peaceful and balanced life.

Personal Stories and Case Studies

Some examples of people who have learned how to manage their time and get more done and how that has changed their lives and careers

Example 1: Hari Narayan, a software developer, is a good example

Hari is an Indian software developer from Mysore who has trouble keeping up with his work. He was often too busy to finish all of the projects he had to do. This made him feel stressed out and burned out.

Hari started using the Pomodoro method, a way to plan his time, to deal with these problems. This method had him divide his workday into 25-minute chunks with 5-minute breaks in between each. After four breaks, he took a 30-minute break that was longer.

Hari found that this method helped him keep his mind on work and keep himself going all day. It also helped him stay on task because he knew he only had a certain amount of time to do each job. Also, the frequent breaks gave him a chance to rest and refocus, which helped him keep working hard in the long run.

Hari was able to finish his work faster and better because of these changes. This made him less stressed and helped him do a better job. He also had more time for hobbies and his personal life, which helped him find a better balance between work and life. So, he went to work feeling more energized and motivated, and he was able to contribute more to the success of his team.

Example 2: Daisy, who is in charge of marketing

Daisy was in charge of marketing for a well-known company in the Indian state of Kerala. She had trouble keeping track of her time, which often led to long days at work and missed deadlines. She had trouble balancing her personal life with her work responsibilities, which made things even worse.

Daisy decided to use several ways to manage her time to solve these problems. She started by putting her daily tasks in a planner and setting goals that she could achieve. She also started giving some of her tasks to other people on her team. This gave her more time to work on important projects.

Daisy also tried to keep herself from getting too distracted at work. She turned off her phone's alerts and used social media less, so she could concentrate on her work. She also set limits with her colleagues and clients, letting them know when she could work and when she needed time to herself.

Daisy was able to be much more productive and feel less stressed after making these changes. She started getting her work done faster, so she could leave the office on time and have more time for herself. Her work performance also got better, and she was moved up to the position of a senior marketing manager.

The Power of Time Management and Productivity

Effective time management and productivity are key components of both personal and professional success. To manage your time well, you need to be able to balance your many responsibilities and commitments. This will help you achieve your goals and be successful. When you manage your time well, you can focus on the most important tasks and set your goals in order of importance. This allows you to be more productive, efficient, and effective in your personal and professional lives.

With good time management and productivity, you can be successful in your personal and professional lives. By managing your time well, you can get more done in less time, which can lead to more opportunities and successes. Better productivity can also give you more confidence and a greater sense of accomplishment, which can help improve your overall happiness and well-being. When you know how to manage your time and work well, you can take control of your life and achieve your goals.

Effective time management and productivity can also contribute to your professional success. When you know how to manage your time well, you can finish tasks on time, meet deadlines, and go above and beyond. This can get you noticed by your colleagues and bosses, and it can even lead to career advancement and chances to grow as a person and professional. By focusing on productivity and time management, you can improve your performance, increase your value as an employee or business owner, and achieve the success you want.

Author's Personal Story: "How Effective Time Management and Productivity Changed My Life"

I have always been a big believer in the power of time management and productivity, and it had a big impact on my own life and career. As a subconscious mind trainer and motivational speaker, I have seen how effective time management can help people achieve their goals and find success.

Early on in my career, I had trouble managing my time well. I would often put off doing important things, which caused me to miss deadlines and feel a lot of unnecessary stress. I knew I needed to make a change, so I started to look into different ways to manage my time.

I started by setting specific goals for myself and breaking them down into smaller, more manageable tasks. I also started to use tools like calendars and to-do lists to help me stay organized and on track. By making these changes, I was able to work more quickly and efficiently, and I was able to get more done in less time.

Over time, I began to see the benefits of better time management in all parts of my life. I was able to spend more time with my family, take on new and challenging projects, and even get back to hobbies and interests that I had put on hold for years.

As my career as a motivational speaker and subconscious mind trainer took off, I realized that managing my time was more important than ever. I had to be able to balance speaking engagements, client meetings, and travel with time to work on my own projects.

By staying organized, setting clear goals, and using my time wisely, I was able to achieve my professional goals and build a successful career. Even though there were problems along the way, I truly believe that being able to manage my time well was a key part of my success.

Today, as a trainer and speaker, I often talk to people about my own experiences with time management and productivity and encourage them to use similar methods in their own lives. Because I know from experience that if you can manage your time well, you can do anything you set your mind to.

Exercises for you

- ❖ Track your time for a week and identify where you are spending your time.
- ❖ Create a prioritized to-do list for each day.
- ❖ Implement a time-management technique, such as the Pomodoro Technique, to increase productivity.

Share your Thoughts

Congratulations! You have made it to the end of the chapter well in time. Do you feel like you have gained control over your time and mastered productivity by now? If not, don't worry, there is always tomorrow. And the day after that. And the day after that.

One productivity tip that has worked wonders for me is the Pomodoro technique. It is simple: work for 25 minutes, take a 5-minute break, then repeat. It is like a game, and it keeps me motivated.

Now it is your turn to share your own productivity hacks! Leave a review and let us know what works for you. Who knows, your tip might just help someone else manage their time better.

Writing a review is easy - just head over to Amazon, find this book, and click on the 'Write a Customer Review' button. Don't worry if you are not a writer or if you are not sure what to say. Just share your thoughts honestly and authentically. Every review helps, and I appreciate them all.

As a thank-you for taking the time to leave a review, I would like to offer you the 'Author's Draft' of this chapter. It contains a lot of extended details and research on this chapter. Simply email us the details at sworld.mind@gmail.com and we will send it over to you. Thank you for your support!

Conclusion

In this chapter, we have discussed the importance of time management and productivity, and how they are closely related to personal development. We explored different strategies and tools that can be used to manage time effectively, overcome procrastination, and boost productivity. We also discussed the negative effects of poor time management, such as stress and missed opportunities, and how to manage them.

To begin mastering time and boosting productivity, it is essential to first understand the concept of time management and its significance. By implementing time management strategies, such as setting goals, prioritizing tasks, and minimizing distractions, one can efficiently manage their time and improve their productivity. Overcoming procrastination is also crucial in achieving our goals and reaching our full potential.

To boost productivity, it is essential to manage our stress levels, as high levels of stress can have a negative impact on our mental and physical health. By identifying the sources of stress and practicing stress management techniques such as meditation, exercise, and time management, we can improve our productivity. Personal development is a continuous journey, and mastering time management and boosting productivity is a critical part of this journey.

Wrap up

Once again, congratulations on completing this chapter on mastering time and boosting productivity! Remember that personal development is not a one-time achievement, but a lifelong journey that requires continuous effort and commitment. Along the way, you may face setbacks or challenges, but do not be discouraged. Use these as opportunities to learn and grow, and continue to move forward with a positive attitude.

It is crucial to understand that time management is not just about working harder, but about working smarter. It involves balancing your personal and professional goals to ensure a healthy, fulfilling life. With effective time management, you can achieve a balance that allows you to excel in both areas without sacrificing one for the other.

Progress is not always linear, and it's normal to face setbacks or challenges along the way. But don't give up. Keep pushing yourself, and remember that every small step you take towards your goals is an accomplishment. Believe in yourself, and never stop striving for excellence.

As you continue on your journey of personal development, I encourage you to set clear goals and prioritize your tasks. Identify the sources of stress in your life and practice stress management techniques. Embrace a growth mindset, and surround yourself with supportive people who inspire and motivate you. With the right mindset and tools, you can turn your dreams into a reality.

Remember, time is a precious resource, and it is up to us to make the most of it. With the strategies discussed in this chapter, you can take control of your time and become more productive, successful, and fulfilled. Keep learning, growing, and taking action towards your goals, and you will achieve the success you desire. Always remember to celebrate your successes, no matter how small they may be, and use them as motivation to keep moving forward.

I wish you all the best on your journey of personal development. You have the potential to achieve great things, and I believe in you. Keep working hard, stay focused, and never give up on your dreams.

"The bad news is time flies. The good news is you are the pilot."

- Michael Altshuler

❑

CHAPTER 6

Positive Habits for Success

"We are what we repeatedly do. Excellence, then, is not an act, but a habit."

– Aristotle

Introduction

Have you ever tried to break a bad habit or build a good one, only to find yourself back where you started? Habits can be powerful forces in our lives, shaping our behavior and influencing our success. In fact, many of the things we do each day are habits that we have developed over time. But what if you could take control of your habits and create positive ones that lead you towards your goals? That's exactly what this chapter is all about: building positive habits.

In the previous chapter, we discussed the importance of time management and productivity, and how to make the most of your time to achieve your goals. In this chapter, we will explore the nature of habits and how they influence our daily lives. We will also look at strategies for building positive habits, overcoming obstacles to habit-building, and maintaining positive habits over the long term. By the end of this chapter, you will have the tools and techniques you need to establish healthy habits that can help you achieve personal and professional success.

So, whether you're looking to adopt a healthier lifestyle, build better relationships, or advance your career, this chapter is for you. Let's get started on building positive habits that will transform your life.

Importance of habits

Have you heard the phrase "you are what you repeatedly do"? It highlights the importance of habits in shaping our lives. Habits are behaviors that are ingrained in our daily routines, often without conscious effort or thought. They are the building blocks of our lives, shaping our character, beliefs, and actions. Whether it's brushing your teeth every morning, hitting the gym before work, or eating healthy, habits are critical to achieving success.

Many successful people attribute their achievements to their positive habits. Habits are powerful tools for achieving our goals because they are automatic, and once established, they require very little effort to maintain. They help us stay focused, motivated, and on track, especially during challenging times.

Positive habits have a significant impact on our personal and professional lives. For instance, waking up early and practicing mindfulness can help us start the day on a positive note, reduce stress and anxiety, and increase our productivity. On the other hand, negative habits like procrastination, laziness, and negative self-talk can hinder our progress, derail our plans, and negatively impact our mental health.

When we cultivate positive habits, we create a ripple effect that spreads across our lives. Our health, relationships, finances, and career all improve. They assist us to become the best version of ourselves. By making small, consistent changes in our habits, we can achieve significant results over time.

Understanding Habits

Habits are behaviors that are ingrained in our daily routines, often without conscious effort or thought. They are automatic responses to specific situations, stimuli, or triggers. Habits can be positive or negative, and they have a significant impact on our daily lives.

Positive habits, such as regular exercise, healthy eating, and practicing gratitude, can enhance our physical and mental well-being. They can boost our energy levels, reduce stress and anxiety, and improve our mood and outlook on life. In contrast, negative habits, such as procrastination, smoking, or overeating, can be detrimental to our health, relationships, and career prospects.

Habits are formed through a process called habituation, which involves repeated actions and a reward system. When we engage in a behavior that brings pleasure or rewards, our brain releases dopamine, a neurotransmitter that creates a pleasurable sensation. This dopamine release reinforces the behavior, making it more likely that we will repeat it in the future.

Over time, the behavior becomes automatic, and the brain associates it with the trigger or cue that initiated the behavior. For example, if you feel stressed and automatically reach for a cigarette, the stress becomes the trigger for the smoking habit. As the habit becomes ingrained, it becomes more challenging to change.

Habits can be difficult to change because they are deeply ingrained in our subconscious mind. Changing a habit requires breaking the automatic response pattern, which can be challenging without conscious effort and deliberate action. Additionally, habits are often associated with rewards or pleasure, which makes it harder to give them up.

However, changing a habit is not impossible. It requires a conscious effort and a willingness to break the cycle of automatic behavior. The key is to identify the trigger or cue that initiates the habit and replace it with a new, positive behavior. By consistently practicing the new behavior, we can create a new habit and eventually override the old one.

Personal story: Juwaria shares how she overcame one of her negative habits and replaced it with a positive one.

I had a hard time getting things done on time for as long as I could remember. Even though I tried not to, I often put off important tasks until the last minute. This made me feel stressed, overwhelmed, and angry with myself. I knew that this habit was keeping me from achieving my personal and professional goals, but I didn't know how to break it.

I finally said, "Enough is enough," one day. I promised myself that I would stop putting things off and replace them with a positive habit that would help me achieve my goals. I started by reading up on the psychology of habits, hoping to figure out why I was so bad at putting things off.

I learned from what I read that habits are made up of cues, routines, and rewards. I realized that my tendency to put things off until the last minute was triggered by certain cues, like feeling overwhelmed or unsure about a task, and that I had made it a habit to put things off until the last minute. I realized that the reward was the short-term relief I felt when I finally finished the task, even if I did it under pressure.

With this knowledge in mind, I decided to change my negative habit into a good one. I had heard that mindfulness meditation could help reduce stress and make it easier to concentrate, so I decided to give it a try. I liked Grandmaster Avadhut sir's guided meditation, so I decided to do it for at least 20 minutes every day.

At first, I found it difficult to sit still and silence my mind. Various thoughts would just come and go, and I would feel restless and want to move about. But I didn't give up. I told myself over and over that change takes time and effort. Over time, I found that it became easier and more natural for me to meditate. I started looking forward to my daily meditation because it helped me slow down, think deeper, and connect with myself.

As I kept up with my regular meditation, I noticed that my ability to deal with stress and concentrate on my work got a lot better. I noticed that I didn't put things off as much as I used to and that I had a new sense of motivation and purpose in my life.

My meditation practice wasn't always easy to keep up with, especially on days when I was busy or stressed out. But I made sure to put it at the top of my list because I knew it would help me achieve my goals and feel better. Over time, meditation became an important part of my daily routine, and I started to see positive changes in my relationships, my work, and my overall outlook on life.

When I look back, I am proud of the positive habits I have formed. Getting rid of my old habits and making new ones wasn't easy, but it was well worth the trouble. I still meditate every day, and I have even started to look into other healthy habits, like getting regular exercise and eating well. By replacing my negative habits with good ones, I have been able to achieve my full potential and live a happier, healthier, and more fulfilling life.

Strategies for Building Positive Habits

One of the most effective strategies for building positive habits is to start small. Instead of trying to change everything at once, focus on one small change that you can commit to every day. For example, if you want to start exercising, commit to doing ten minutes of physical activity each day. As you become comfortable with the habit, you can gradually increase the duration or intensity.

Another strategy is to set achievable goals. Setting goals that are too lofty or unrealistic can lead to frustration and discouragement, making it harder to stick to the habit. By setting achievable goals, we create a sense of accomplishment and build confidence, making it easier to stay motivated.

Tracking progress is also a powerful strategy for building positive habits. By keeping track of our progress, we can see how far we've come and identify areas where we need to improve. This can be done through a habit tracker, journaling, or other methods of record-keeping.

Habit loops

A habit loop is a simple yet powerful tool that can help you establish new habits. It involves three components: the cue, the routine, and the reward.

The cue is the trigger or prompt that initiates the habit. It could be a specific time of day, a particular location, or a particular emotion. For example, if you want to establish a habit of going for a run every morning, your cue could be setting your alarm for a specific time each day.

The routine is the behavior that you want to turn into a habit. In this case, the routine would be going for a run every morning.

The reward is the positive outcome that you associate with the behavior. In this case, the reward could be the endorphin rush and sense of accomplishment that comes from completing the run.

To create a habit loop, you need to follow a simple process:

1. Identify the habit you want to establish: Start by identifying the habit you want to establish. Be specific about what you want to achieve and why it's important to you.
2. Identify the cue: Once you've identified the habit, identify the cue that will prompt you to take action. It could be a specific time of day, a location, or an emotion.
3. Establish the routine: Next, establish the routine that you want to turn into a habit. Make it simple and achievable, and break it down into small steps if necessary.
4. Identify the reward: Finally, identify the reward that you will associate with the behavior. This could be a physical reward, such as a healthy snack, or an emotional reward, such as a sense of accomplishment.

For example, let us say you want to establish a habit of reading for 30 minutes every night before bed. Here's how you can create a habit loop:

1. Identify the habit: Reading for 30 minutes every night before bed.
2. Identify the cue: Setting an alarm on your phone for a specific time each night, or setting a reminder on your calendar.
3. Establish the routine: Set aside 30 minutes before bed each night to read. Find a comfortable and quiet spot, turn off distractions like your phone or TV, and focus solely on reading.
4. Identify the reward: The reward could be the sense of accomplishment that comes from completing your reading for the night, or the feeling of relaxation that comes from getting lost in a good book.

Once you've created your habit loop, the key is to repeat the behavior consistently. By consistently following the same cue, routine, and reward, you will start to establish the habit and make it automatic.

It is also important to track your progress and adjust your habit loop as needed. If you find that the routine is too challenging or the reward isn't motivating enough, make adjustments to the habit loop until you find a combination that works for you.

Breaking a negative habit

In order to develop positive habits for success, it is important to first identify and get rid of any negative habits that may be holding us back. The negative habits are often hardwired into our brains and can be difficult to break. However, it is not impossible to change negative habits into positive ones. One way of doing this is by interrupting the habit loop.

The first step is to identify the cue that triggers the negative habit. For example, if you have a habit of eating unhealthy snacks in the afternoon, the cue may be a feeling of boredom or stress. Once you have identified the cue, you can work on replacing the routine with a positive habit. Instead of reaching for a packet of chips, you could go for a walk, do some stretches, or call a friend.

Then reward yourself for completing the positive habit. This reward should be something that gives you a sense of accomplishment or satisfaction, such as a few minutes of meditation or listening to your favorite music. By creating a new habit loop with a positive routine and reward, you can replace the negative habit with a healthier one.

Breaking free from a negative habit takes time and effort. You might slip up and fall back into old behaviors, but that's okay. The key is to keep trying and to focus on the progress you have made. With consistency and commitment you can certainly get rid of each of your negative habits.

Exercise: A Habit Tracking Plan for You

Step 1: Identify Current Habits

Make a list of your current habits. It can be helpful to track your daily routine for a week or two to get a full picture of your habits. Some examples of habits might include:

- Drinking multiple cups of coffee each day
- Snacking on unhealthy foods between meals
- Reading before bed

- ❖ Oversleeping
- ❖ Spending too much time on social media
- ❖ Meditating in the morning
- ❖ Skipping workouts
- ❖ Biting nails
- ❖ Procrastinating
- ❖ Skipping breakfast
- ❖ Exercising daily
- ❖ Drinking plenty of water

Step 2: Evaluate Each Habit

Once you have your list of habits, evaluate the impact of each one on your life. Consider how each habit affects your physical health, mental health, relationships, and productivity. For each of the habit, ask yourself questions such as:

1. How does this impact my well-being and happiness?
2. What are the long-term consequences of this habit?
3. Am I able to control this habit or does it control me?
4. How does this affect my relationships with others?
5. What is the cost of this habit?
6. What is the contribution of cultivating this habit, to take me to where I want to be in my life?
7. Does this habit benefit or harm my physical, mental, social, and spiritual health?
8. Does this habit align with my values and goals?
9. How would my life be different if I didn't have this habit?
10. Am I willing to make changes to this habit to improve my life?

    Make notes on each habit to reflect on its effects on your life.

Step 3: Set Goals for Positive Habits

Select one or two negative habits you want to break and set a specific, measurable, achievable, relevant, and time-bound (SMART) goal for changing your chosen habit. For example, "I will reduce my caffeine intake to one cup of coffee per day by the end of the month." Make sure your goal is realistic and something you can commit to.

Step 4: Track Your Progress

Creating a habit tracker to monitor your progress can be a useful tool for developing positive habits. It is important to hold yourself accountable in order to ensure that you are making progress toward your goals. You can use a simple checklist or a more detailed habit-tracking app to keep track of your progress. The habit tracker will allow you to see how far you have come and help you identify areas where you need to focus more.

Celebrating your successes along the way is important because it will motivate you to continue working towards your goals. At the same time, it is equally important to not get discouraged if you slip up. Remember that building positive habits is a journey, and it takes time and effort to see results. Focus on progress rather than perfection, and keep pushing forward.

Step 5: Reflect and Adjust

At the end of each week or month, reflect on your progress. If you find that you are struggling to meet your goal, don't give up. Re-evaluate your approach and adjust as needed. Maybe you need to break your goal down into smaller steps or find a new strategy for overcoming challenges. Celebrate your successes and identify areas that need improvement.

Step 6: Repeat

Once you have successfully modified and altered one habit, it is imperative to continue with another habit you want to transform and repeat the entire process. By doing so, you will establish a pattern of beneficial habits that will contribute to the realization of your aspirations and enhance your overall quality of life. It is essential to understand that it is a continuous process, and persistence and dedication are necessary to establish lasting and positive change. By adopting this approach, you will gradually create a healthy and productive lifestyle that will lead to a more fulfilling and prosperous life.

Overcoming Obstacles to Building Positive Habits

One of the most common obstacles to building positive habits is a lack of motivation. It is easy to feel overwhelmed by the idea of making significant changes in our lives, and this can lead to procrastination or giving up altogether. To overcome this obstacle, it is essential to identify the reasons behind your lack of motivation and find ways to reignite your passion for personal growth.

Our environment plays a significant role in shaping our habits. Certain environmental triggers can make it difficult to build positive habits, such as being surrounded by negative influences or living in a cluttered space. To overcome these obstacles, it is crucial to identify and eliminate the triggers that are holding you back from developing positive habits.

One effective strategy for overcoming obstacles to building positive habits is finding an accountability partner. This can be a friend, family member, or colleague who shares your goals and is willing to support you in your journey. By regularly checking in with your accountability partner, you can stay motivated and focused on your goals, making it easier to build positive habits.

Another essential strategy for overcoming obstacles to building positive habits is adjusting your environment. This can involve making changes to your physical surroundings, such as decluttering your workspace or creating a dedicated space for relaxation and reflection. Additionally, it can involve surrounding yourself with positive influences, such as joining a support group or spending time with people who share your goals and values.

Personal Story - Overcoming Obstacles

Meet Raj, a software engineer from Mumbai who struggled to build positive habits. But with determination and the right strategies, Raj was able to overcome obstacles and build a successful life. In this personal story, Raj shares his journey and the lessons he learned.

I've always been a hard worker, but I struggled with building positive habits. At times, I felt like I was stuck in a rut, and I wasn't making progress towards my personal or professional goals.

One of the biggest obstacles I faced was a lack of motivation. I would start off strong with a new habit, but after a few days, I would lose interest and fall back into my old ways. It was frustrating and demotivating, and I felt like giving up.

But I didn't give up. Instead, I started exploring different strategies for building positive habits. I read books, watched videos, and talked to people who had successfully built positive habits in their own lives. I realized that starting small was the key. I picked one habit that I wanted to build and focused on that, rather than trying to change everything at once.

I also found that having an accountability partner was helpful. I told my best friend about my goals, and she held me accountable for sticking to my habits. Whenever I felt like giving up, she would encourage me and remind me why I started in the first place.

Another obstacle I faced was environmental triggers. I realized that my environment was not conducive to building positive habits. For example, I would often stay up late watching TV or playing games, which made it hard for me to wake up early and exercise. So, I adjusted my environment. I started going to bed earlier, and I removed distractions like my TV and gaming console from my bedroom.

These strategies worked. I started small by building one habit at a time, and I had my friend to hold me accountable. I adjusted my environment to make it easier for me to stick to my habits. Over time, I built several positive habits, like waking up early, exercising, and reading every day.

Building positive habits was not easy, but it was worth it. Today, I feel more confident and in control of my life. I'm happier, healthier, and more productive than ever before. And I know that I can continue to build positive habits, one small step at a time.

Maintaining Positive Habits

Once we have successfully established a positive habit, it is important to continue practicing it to reap its benefits. However, it is quite easy to fall back into old, negative habits and undo all our hard work.

One way to avoid relapse is to continually remind ourselves of the reasons why we started building positive habits in the first place. This could involve revisiting our goals, reflecting on the positive impact the habit has had on our lives, or even visualizing a future where we have successfully achieved our desired outcome.

Another way to avoid relapse is to track our progress regularly. When we see tangible evidence of our progress, it can motivate us to continue with our positive habits. Tracking can be as simple as marking off days on a calendar or using a habit-tracking app on our phone.

It is essential to acknowledge that setbacks and relapses are a part of the process. Instead of beating ourselves up over a relapse, we can use it as an opportunity to learn and grow. We can reflect on what led to the relapse and make adjustments to our habits and environment accordingly.

Creating a plan for maintaining positive habits and addressing setbacks

Creating a plan for maintaining positive habits is just as important as building those habits in the first place. Without a plan in place, it can be easy to slip back into old habits and lose all the progress that has been made.

The first step in creating a maintenance plan is to identify the positive habits that need to be maintained. This could include things like daily exercise, meditation, healthy eating habits, or any other positive habit that has been developed.

Once these habits have been identified, it is important to set realistic goals for maintaining them. This might mean setting a specific number of days per week to engage in the habit or setting a specific amount of time each day to devote to it.

It is also important to anticipate setbacks and create a plan for addressing them. Setbacks can come in many forms, such as a busy schedule, unexpected events, or lack of motivation. By anticipating these setbacks and creating a plan to address them, it becomes easier to stay on track.

One strategy for addressing setbacks is to have a backup plan in place. For example, if daily exercise is a positive habit that needs to be maintained, but a busy schedule makes it difficult to find time for it, having a backup plan such as a quick 10-minute workout routine can help ensure that the habit is still maintained even in the face of setbacks.

Case Study: A Pediatrician's Journey through Unexpected Challenges

Dr. Lakshmi Narayana Murthy has been working as a pediatrician for over 15 years and has a lot of experience. Dr. Lakshmi has been a doctor for a long time, and she has always been committed to giving her patients the best care possible. Dr. Lakshmi has always shown a strong dedication to her work. Because of this, she has a well-deserved reputation as a respected and admired healthcare professional.

Even though she has a busy schedule, Dr. Lakshmi has always made sure to put her physical and mental health first. One of the ways she does this is by exercising regularly, which is a positive habit she has worked hard to form over the years. Dr. Lakshmi has been able to keep her body in shape and her mind clear by working out regularly. This has helped her do her job as well as she can.

During the COVID-19 pandemic, however, Dr. Lakshmi was overwhelmed by problems that made it hard for her to keep up her positive habit of exercising. She worked long hours, sometimes up to 12 hours a day, and was often too tired to work out. Also, gyms were closed, which made it hard to find a good place to work out. Dr. Lakshmi was determined to keep up her positive habit of exercising despite these problems. She knew that exercise was good for her mental health as well as her physical health, especially during the stressful times of the pandemic.

Dr. Lakshmi had to be smart and creative to deal with the problems she was facing. She started by changing the way she worked out to fit her busy schedule.

Before she went to work, she would get up early and do a quick 20-minute workout at home. She also started taking short walks outside during the day. This helped her get some exercise and fresh air, and it gave her a much-needed break from her work.

Dr. Lakshmi started looking into other ways to work out because gyms were closing because of lockdowns. She found online exercise classes and started following an instructor who specialized in easy-to-follow workouts that could be done at home without any special equipment. Dr. Lakshmi also started doing yoga. This helped her stay physically fit and gave her much-needed mental relaxation during the stressful times of the pandemic.

One of Dr. Lakshmi's biggest problems was staying motivated and on task, especially when she was tired from work. To deal with this, she found a close friend who was also trying to keep up positive habits during the pandemic. This gave her someone to hold her accountable. They would often check in on each other and encourage each other to keep going.

Dr. Lakshmi's hard work paid off, and she was able to keep up her healthy habit of exercising even though she ran into some unexpected problems during the pandemic. She improved not only her physical health but also her mental health, which helped her handle the stress of her job as a pediatrician better. She learned from her past that keeping positive habits requires creativity, resourcefulness, and discipline, especially when unexpected problems come up. Dr. Lakshmi was able to keep up her positive habit of exercising and improve her overall health by making changes to her routine, looking into other options, and finding someone to hold her accountable.

Building Habits for Personal and Professional Success

People's personal success often depends on how well they can manage their time and keep up positive habits. Positive habits like working out regularly, eating well, and getting enough rest helps boost energy, lower stress, and improve overall health. These habits can help you think more clearly and stay focused, which can make you more productive and better at managing your time. Positive habits also help build self-confidence and self-esteem, which are important for personal growth and success.

In professional life, positive habits can make a big difference in how well you do in your job. Getting into positive habits like good communication, managing your time well, and always learning can make you more productive, improve your relationships with co-workers and clients, and give you more chances to move up. People can build a strong personal bond and grow their professional network through positive habits like networking.

Finding habits that can help you achieve your personal and professional goals takes planning and thought. Here are some ways to find out if you have any of these habits:

First, write down your personal and career goals. Start by being clear about both your personal and professional goals. Think about what you want to achieve in different areas of your life, such as your health, career, relationships, and personal growth. For example, if you want to improve your health, you might try to work out regularly, eat a balanced diet, and get enough sleep. If you want to move up in your career, you might try to get better at communicating, build your network, and get more done.

Once you know what your goals are, think about the habits that will help you achieve them. For example, if your goal is to work out every day, you could make it a habit to walk or run every morning or go to a yoga class after work. If you want to improve your communication skills, you could make it a habit to listen carefully to other people, practice public speaking, or ask your colleagues for feedback.

When making a list of habits, it is important to put them in order of importance and feasibility. Start with just one or two habits that you can realistically do every day. Once you've made these habits a part of your life, you can add more as you get used to them.

It is also important to keep yourself going by keeping track of your progress often. You can keep track of your daily habits and track your progress with a habit tracker or a journal. No matter how small, you should celebrate your small wins along the way.

A habit prioritization exercise to help you identify habits that are most important for your personal and professional success.

Step 1:

Set your goals. Finding out what your personal and professional goals are, is the first step to prioritizing the habits that will help you succeed.

First, take some time to think about what you want to achieve in your personal and professional life. This could be done by brainstorming and writing down your ideas in a notebook or by using a goal-setting app to keep track of your ideas.

For your personal goals, think about what parts of your life you want to improve. Do you want to improve your health and fitness, make more friends, or learn a new hobby? Make a list of these goals and rank them in order of importance to you. When it comes to your professional goals, think about what you want to do in your career. Do you want to move up to a higher position, learn new skills, or become known as an expert in your field? Make a list of these goals and rank them based on your long-term career goals.

By taking the time to write down your goals, you will have a clearer picture of what you want to achieve and what habits you need to form to get there. This will help you put your habits in order of importance and focus your energy on the ones that are most important for your personal and professional success.

Step 2:

Make positive habits. Once you know what your personal and professional goals are, the next step is to think of habits that could help you achieve each of them. It is important to think broadly and creatively during this step, as there may be many different habits that could help you succeed.

For example, if your personal goal is to read more books, you could make it a habit to read for 30 minutes every night before bed or set aside time on the weekends to read. If your professional goal is to learn a new skill, you could make it a habit to take online courses or go to workshops related to that skill.

It is important to focus on habits that are specific, measurable, and attainable. For example, instead of setting a goal to exercise more generally, it is better to make it a habit to exercise for a certain amount of time each day or week. In the same way, instead of setting a goal to network more, it is more effective to make it a habit to reach out to a certain number of new contacts each week.

During this step, you can also talk to people who have achieved similar goals or look for books, podcasts, or online forums to get ideas for habits that could help you achieve your goals.

Step 3:

Order your habits. After making a list of habits, it is important to rank them in order of importance so you know which ones to work on first. This step will help you figure out the habits that will have the biggest effect on your personal and professional goals.

To start ranking your habits, start with the most important one and work your way down the list. Consider asking yourself a few questions to help with the process. For example, ask yourself which habit will help you achieve your goal the most. Which habit is easiest to start, and which one will require the most work to keep up with?

Answering these questions can help you get clear on the habits that are most important to you and will have the biggest effect on helping you achieve your goals. You may find that some habits are more important than others, and ranking them can help you stay focused on what really matters.

Step 4:

Make an action plan. Once you've found the top three habits that can help you achieve your personal and professional goals, you need to make a plan to put them into action. To do this, break each habit into specific steps you can take to make it a part of your routine.

For example, if your top habit is to eat healthy food, you might make an action plan that includes specific steps like meal planning, grocery shopping, and making healthy meals in advance. You could also set aside a day each week to prepare meals, buy some kitchen tools to make meal preparation easier, and find healthy recipes that you enjoy.

In the same way, if your top habit is to network more, your action plan could include going to industry events, joining a professional group, and reaching out to new contacts on LinkedIn. You could also schedule time each week to follow up with new contacts, make an introduction for yourself, and work on your networking skills.

Remember to make your action plan realistic and feasible. Set goals you can achieve and break down each habit into smaller goals to make them easier to handle. Make sure to keep track of your progress and celebrate small victories along the way. By doing so, you can stay motivated and committed to achieving your personal and professional goals.

Step 5:

Review and make changes After putting your action plans into place, it is important to keep track of your progress and change your habits and plans as needed. This step helps you make sure you are staying on track with your goals and making the changes you need to keep making progress. Keeping a journal or log of your habits is one way to look back on them. Write down your progress and any problems you may have had. Use this information to make changes and create a plan for moving forward.

If you find that a habit is not working for you, don't be afraid to change it. For example, if you find it hard to go to the gym before work, you might want to change your workout time to the evenings or weekends. If you are not seeing results from a certain habit, try a different approach or talk to a professional in that field. Recognize the progress you've made and use that as motivation to keep building positive habits that will help you succeed in your personal and professional life.

Remember that building positive habits takes time and work, but the rewards can be big in both your personal and professional life.

Motivation

Some examples of individuals who have successfully built positive habits and achieved personal and professional success:

1. **Malala Yousafzai:** The Nobel Prize laureate and activist has built a reputation as a fearless advocate for girls' education. She credits her success to habits such as staying positive in the face of adversity, prioritizing her education, and practicing self-reflection and self-care.
2. **Sheryl Sandberg:** The COO of Facebook is known for her dedication to maintaining a healthy work-life balance. She makes a habit of leaving work at a reasonable hour to spend time with her family, and she also encourages employees to do the same. This has contributed to her personal success as well as the success of the company she works for.

These individuals show how important positive habits are for both personal and professional success. By doing things like setting goals, focusing, being disciplined, taking care of themselves, and learning new things all the time, they have done amazing things and inspired others to do the same.

Positive habits lead to long-term behavior change.

By intentionally cultivating positive habits, we create a consistent pattern of behavior that becomes deeply ingrained in our subconscious mind. This can lead to lasting changes in our thoughts, feelings, and actions, making it easier to maintain our desired behaviors over time.

When we develop positive habits, we create a sense of routine and structure in our lives, which can help us stay focused and motivated. Positive habits also help us to develop self-discipline, which can be applied to other areas of our lives as well. By consistently engaging in positive behaviors, we create a positive feedback loop that reinforces our motivation and helps us stay committed to our goals.

Building positive habits helps us to replace negative behaviors with positive ones. Over time, these positive habits become our default mode of operation, leading to long-term behavior change. By focusing on positive habits, we can transform our lives, create new opportunities, and achieve our full potential.

Author's Personal Journey of Building Positive Habits and Overcoming Negative Ones

When I think back on my journey, I can clearly remember the frustration and disappointment that came with my negative habits. But I also remember the hope and determination I felt when I realized I had the power to change.

Building positive habits isn't easy, but it is definitely worth the effort. It all starts with figuring out the habits that are holding us back and making goals that fit with our vision for the future. We don't have to start with big changes. Instead, we can take small steps toward our goals every day.

I found that being consistent is the key to making positive habits stick. Our daily actions, no matter how small, are what lead to big changes over time. And when we start to see the results of our work, it becomes easier to stay motivated and keep going.

Creative visualization exercises helped me re-program my subconscious mind, which was one of the most helpful tools I used. By picturing myself achieving my goals and living the life I wanted, I was able to create a strong mental picture that kept me focused and motivated even when things got hard.

Thanks to my hard work, the positive habits I have built up have now become second nature. The negative habits that used to get in the way of my progress and success are now a thing of the past. I have come to realize that building positive habits is not a one-time thing but a journey of self-improvement and growth. Achieving your full potential takes unwavering determination, resilience, and a commitment to personal growth, but the reward is worth every effort.

If you are struggling with negative habits, I want to give you some hope: It is never too late to change. Believe in yourself and take small steps towards your goals. Remember that with patience, consistency, and self-discipline, you can build the positive habits that will lead to a brighter future.

Exercises for you

- Identify a positive habit you want to develop and create a plan to implement it.
- Use habit stacking to build new positive habits into your existing routine.
- Identify a negative habit you want to overcome and create a plan to overcome it with a positive replacement habit.

Share your Thoughts

We have come to the end of Chapter 6, and I hope you are feeling motivated to adopt new positive habits in your life. Positive habits are essential for success, and by developing them, we can achieve our dreams and lead a fulfilling life.

Now, let me ask you, do you feel motivated to adopt new positive habits after reading this chapter? I hope so! Remember, it takes time and effort to develop new habits, but with persistence and dedication, you can do it!

Speaking of habits, let me share a funny story with you. Once upon a time, there was a man named Bob who had a bad habit of biting his nails. He tried everything to break the habit - nail polish, fidget toys, snapping a rubber band on his wrist - but nothing worked.

One day, Bob went to the doctor and told him about his problem. The doctor looked at Bob's nails and said, "Well, Bob, I have some good news and some bad news. The good news is, I know how to cure your nail-biting habit. The bad news is, it involves amputating your fingers." Bob was horrified and quickly declined the doctor's solution. The doctor laughed and said, "Just kidding, Bob. You will have to find another way to break the habit. Maybe try wearing spicy gloves – that will teach you to keep your fingers out of your mouth!" Bob left the doctor's office feeling silly, but determined to find a way to break his habit once and for all.

Now, I encourage you to share your own positive habits and goals with us by leaving a review. Your feedback will help us understand how we can better serve you in your personal development journey. To write a review, simply go to Amazon, and leave a review. Don't worry if you're not sure how to write a review. I have got you covered.

First, think about what you liked about this chapter and how it helped you. Then, share your thoughts in a few sentences. Remember to mention your takeaway from this chapter, and how you plan to adopt it in your life.

And as a token of our appreciation, we would like to offer you the 'Author's Draft' of this chapter. It contains extended details and research on the chapter that may not have made it into the final published version. After writing the review, simply inform our office at sworld.mind@gmail.com, and we will send it over to you.

Conclusion

In this chapter, we explored the power of habits in shaping our lives and discussed effective strategies for building positive habits and overcoming negative ones. We also examined common obstacles to building positive habits, and how to address them through finding accountability partners and adjusting our environments. Additionally, we discussed the importance of maintaining positive habits and how to avoid relapse.

By understanding the habit loop and using strategies such as creating implementation intentions, tracking progress, and celebrating successes, we can build positive habits that lead to personal and professional success. We must also be mindful of common obstacles such as lack of motivation and environmental triggers, and take steps to overcome them.

It is important to remember that building positive habits is a continuous process, and setbacks will inevitably occur. However, by creating a plan for maintaining positive habits and addressing setbacks, we can stay on track and continue to make progress towards our goals.

I encourage you to continue applying these strategies to build positive habits that lead to a more fulfilling life. Remember, your habits shape your destiny, and by taking control of them, you can create the life you want.

Wrap up

Congratulations on taking this important step towards personal development by reading this chapter. By investing time and effort in building positive habits, you are investing in yourself and your future.

I want to encourage you to continue building positive habits in your life. It may not always be easy, but the rewards are worth it. With each positive habit you develop, you are taking a step closer towards your goals and creating a better future for yourself.

Remember that building positive habits is a journey, not a destination. Celebrate your successes along the way, but don't let setbacks discourage you. Keep pushing forward and striving to be the best version of yourself.

I also want to remind you that you are not alone in this journey. Reach out to friends, family, or a mentor for support and accountability. And always remember to be kind and patient with yourself as you work towards your goals.

So keep building those positive habits and watch as your life transforms before your very eyes. The power is in your hands, so let's get started!

"Your net worth to the world is usually determined by what remains after your negative habits are subtracted from your good ones."

- Benjamin Franklin

❑

CHAPTER 7

The Art of Effective Communication

"The most important thing in communication is hearing what isn't said."
– Peter Drucker

Introduction

Are you tired of feeling like your message is not getting through? Are you struggling to communicate effectively with your loved ones or colleagues? Communication is an essential part of our daily lives, and the way we communicate can have a significant impact on our personal and professional success.

In the previous chapter, we talked about the importance of building positive habits and the strategies to cultivate them. In this chapter, we will be focusing on a fundamental skill that is essential for success in every aspect of life - Effective Communication.

Communication is the cornerstone of human interaction, and it is vital to develop good communication skills to succeed in personal and professional relationships. In this chapter, we will discuss the various forms of communication, including verbal, nonverbal, and written, and how you can effectively use them to convey your message.

We will also delve into the importance of communication in relationships and the workplace, and how to handle difficult conversations with ease. We will discuss cross-cultural communication, and the challenges that come with it, and strategies to overcome them.

Through personal stories and case studies, you will learn how effective communication can transform your life, both professionally and personally. So, let's dive in and learn the art of effective communication!

Importance of effective communication

Effective communication is the key to building strong relations, expressing ideas, and conveying thoughts and emotions. Communication is not limited to just speaking, but also involves listening, understanding, and responding.

Effective communication plays a vital role in personal relationships, including friendships, romantic relationships, and family relationships. When we communicate effectively, we can express our feelings, thoughts, and emotions clearly and understand those of others. It helps in resolving conflicts, building trust, and strengthening the bond between individuals. Effective communication also plays a crucial role in maintaining healthy relationships, as it helps in addressing issues and concerns before they escalate into larger problems.

In professional relationships, effective communication is even more critical. In the workplace, communication helps in conveying ideas and thoughts, making presentations, conducting meetings, and providing feedback. It is also essential for networking and building professional relationships with colleagues, clients, and partners. A lack of communication or ineffective communication can lead to misunderstandings, conflicts, and missed opportunities.

Do note that effective communication is not limited to just speaking fluently or expressing oneself clearly. It goes beyond that and encompasses active listening, understanding others' perspectives, and responding appropriately. Active listening is a crucial element of effective communication, as it allows us to comprehend the speaker's viewpoint and react accordingly. Additionally, it fosters a sense of connection and trust between individuals, which is vital for building strong relationships. By actively listening, we demonstrate our willingness to understand the other person and establish a meaningful dialogue that facilitates productive communication.

Verbal Communication

The importance of clarity and tone

When it comes to effective verbal communication, two crucial elements that should not be overlooked are clarity and tone. Clarity refers to the ability to express oneself in a manner that is easily understood by the listener. It involves using simple and concise language, avoiding jargon and technical terms, and organizing one's thoughts in a logical sequence. Clarity ensures that the listener can comprehend the message being conveyed without any confusion or ambiguity.

On the other hand, tone refers to the emotional inflection and emphasis that one uses while speaking. It includes the pitch, volume, speed, and intonation of one's voice. Tone plays a significant role in how the listener interprets and perceives the message being conveyed. It sets the mood and creates a particular atmosphere that can either facilitate or hinder effective communication.

The importance of clarity and tone in verbal communication cannot be overstated, particularly in professional settings. For example, in a business meeting, using complex technical terms or industry jargon may make it difficult for non-experts to understand the message. Similarly, using an aggressive or condescending tone can lead to misunderstandings, conflicts, and damaged relationships.

In personal relationships, clarity and tone are equally important. For instance, when having a difficult conversation with a loved one, using a calm and empathetic tone can help defuse the situation and ensure that both parties feel heard and understood. Conversely, using a harsh or dismissive tone can escalate the situation and cause hurt feelings and resentment.

Active listening & "I" statements

Active listening is a technique that involves focusing on the speaker's words, observing their body language, and demonstrating an understanding of the message. Active listening requires the listener to be fully present, attentive, and engaged in the conversation. By actively listening, we can gain a deeper understanding of the other person's perspective and respond in a manner that reflects that understanding.

For instance, suppose you are in a conversation with a friend who is upset about a recent argument with their partner. Active listening would involve paying attention to their words, observing their body language, and asking questions to clarify their point of view. You could say, "It sounds like you are feeling hurt and frustrated by what happened. Can you tell me more about how you're feeling?" This response demonstrates that you are actively listening and seeking to understand their perspective.

Another essential technique is using 'I' statements instead of 'you' statements. Using 'you' statements can come across as accusatory and defensive, and can often escalate conflicts. In contrast, using 'I' statements reflects ownership of one's feelings and can lead to more productive conversations.

For instance, suppose you are having a conversation with a coworker who has been consistently late to meetings. Instead of saying, "You are always late, and it's causing problems," you could say, "I feel frustrated when meetings start late because it affects our team's productivity." This response demonstrates that you are taking ownership of your feelings and encourages the other person to respond without feeling attacked.

Using "I" statements can also be effective in personal relationships. For example, instead of saying, "You never help me with the chores," you could say, "I feel overwhelmed when I have to do all the chores myself." This response demonstrates that you are taking ownership of your feelings and encourages the other person to respond in a way that reflects empathy and understanding.

Empathy & No Jargon

Empathy is an essential component of effective communication, as it allows us to understand and connect with others on a deeper level. When we demonstrate empathy, we show that we care about others and are willing to see things from their perspective. This can help to build stronger connections and foster mutual understanding and respect. By putting ourselves in someone else's shoes and considering their feelings and perspectives, we can better understand where they are coming from and respond in a way that reflects understanding and compassion. Whether in personal or professional relationships, empathy is a valuable tool for building trust, resolving conflicts, and fostering positive connections.

Avoiding the use of jargon is equally important in effective communication. Jargon refers to specialized terminology that is specific to a particular field or profession. Using jargon in everyday conversations can create a barrier to understanding and may cause others to feel excluded or disengaged from the conversation. In personal and professional relationships, it is important to communicate in a way that is clear and accessible to all parties involved. By using plain language and avoiding the use of jargon, we can ensure that our message is understood and that we are able to connect with others on a deeper level. This can help to build stronger relationships and foster mutual understanding and respect, ultimately leading to more positive and productive interactions.

Exercise: A role-playing exercise to help you practice effective verbal communication skills.

Role-playing exercises can be a great way to improve your ability to communicate with words. Here's a practice to get you going. In this role-playing game, you will need help from a friend.

Objective: To practice using 'I' statements and active listening in a conflict resolution scenario.

Example 1

Scenario: You are a customer service representative and a customer has called to complain about a product that they purchased. The customer is angry and frustrated because the product did not work as expected and they feel that they wasted their money.

Instructions: Your friend will play the role of the customer and you will be playing the role of the customer service representative (CSR).

1. The CSR (you) should start the conversation by self-introduction. Then ask the customer to explain the problem.
2. The customer should express their frustration and anger using assertive language and tone.
3. The CSR should listen actively and respond with empathy, acknowledging the customer's feelings and concerns.
4. The CSR should then use 'I' statements to express their own understanding of the problem and offer possible solutions.
5. The customer should continue to express their feelings and concerns, and the CSR should continue to listen actively and respond with empathy.
6. The CSR should work with the customer to find a mutually agreeable solution to the problem.

Example dialogue

Customer: "I am so angry and frustrated right now. I spent my hard-earned money on this product and it doesn't even work!"

CSR: "I understand that this must be frustrating for you. I am sorry that the product didn't work as expected. Let's work together to find a solution to this problem."

Customer: "I feel like I wasted my money on this product. I don't even want it anymore."

CSR: "I hear that you feel like your money was wasted. If you are open to it, we could offer you a replacement product or a refund."

Customer: "I guess a refund would be okay, but I still feel frustrated that I wasted my time and energy on this product."

CSR: "I understand that this has been a frustrating experience for you. I appreciate your feedback and I will pass it along to our product development team. In the meantime, let's process that refund for you right away."

Example 2

Scenario: You are a manager and an employee has come to you with a complaint about a co-worker.

Example dialogue

Employee: "I am having a problem with my co-worker. He's always interrupting me when I am trying to work and it is really distracting."

Manager: "I can understand why that would be frustrating. Have you tried talking to him about it?"

Employee: "Yeah, but he just brushes me off and keeps doing it anyway."

Manager: "I am sorry to hear that. I have had similar experiences in the past, and I know how challenging it can be to work with someone who's not being considerate. What if we came up with some strategies together to help you communicate your needs more effectively?"

Employee: "That sounds like a good idea. What do you suggest?"

Manager: "Well, one option might be to schedule regular check-ins with your co-worker to discuss any issues that come up. That way, he'll know that you are serious about finding a solution and you will have a designated time to bring up any concerns. Another option might be to ask him to use a certain signal or gesture to let you know when he wants to talk, so that you can finish your current task first. What do you think?"

Employee: "I like the idea of scheduling check-ins. I think that could work well. Thanks for your help."

Nonverbal Communication

Nonverbal communication refers to the transmission of information through means other than words, such as body language, facial expressions, and tone of voice. In many cases, nonverbal communication can be even more powerful than verbal communication, as it can convey emotions and attitudes in a way that words alone cannot.

Body language is one of the most important forms of nonverbal communication. It includes gestures, posture, and other physical movements that can communicate our feelings and attitudes towards others. For example, crossing one's arms can be seen as a defensive posture, indicating that a person may be closed off or unwilling to engage in a conversation. On the other hand, maintaining an open posture, such as facing someone directly and maintaining eye contact, can convey a sense of openness and willingness to engage.

Facial expressions are another important form of nonverbal communication. Our facial expressions can convey a wide range of emotions, from happiness and joy to anger and frustration. For example, a smile can indicate that we are happy or pleased, while a frown can indicate that we are upset or unhappy. By paying attention to the facial expressions of others, we can often gain insights into their emotional state and respond in a way that is appropriate.

In personal and professional relationships, it is important to be aware of the impact of nonverbal communication. By paying attention to our own body language and facial expressions, as well as those of others, we can communicate more effectively and build stronger connections with those around us. Whether in a job interview, a first date, or a business meeting, nonverbal communication can play a crucial role in shaping how others perceive us and how we interact with them.

Interpreting nonverbal cues

To interpret nonverbal cues, it is important to pay attention to the other person's body language. Body posture, gestures, and movements can all provide valuable insights into the other person's thoughts and emotions. For example, if the person is leaning forward and making eye contact, they may be interested and engaged in the conversation. On the other hand, if they are leaning away or crossing their arms, they may be defensive or disengaged.

Facial expressions are another important aspect of nonverbal communication. The face is often referred to as the 'window to the soul', as it can reveal a lot about a person's emotional state. A smile can indicate happiness or friendliness, while a frown can indicate sadness or frustration. It is important to pay attention to these cues, as they can help us understand the other person's emotional state and adjust our communication accordingly.

By being aware of our own body language and facial expressions, we can ensure that our message is being conveyed effectively. For example, maintaining eye contact and an open posture can convey confidence and sincerity. On the other hand, avoiding eye contact or fidgeting can convey nervousness or discomfort.

To further illustrate the importance of paying attention to nonverbal cues in communication, let's consider a few scenarios. Imagine you are in a job interview, and the interviewer is leaning forward with their hands clasped in front of them and maintaining eye contact. These are all positive nonverbal cues that indicate they are interested and engaged in the conversation. In this case, you may want to reciprocate by leaning forward as well and maintaining good eye contact to show that you are equally invested in the conversation.

Now, imagine that you are having a conversation with a friend who is slouching and avoiding eye contact. These nonverbal cues may indicate that they are feeling sad or disengaged. In this situation, it may be helpful to ask them directly how they are feeling or if there is anything you can do to support them. By using your knowledge of nonverbal cues and adjusting your communication accordingly, you can deepen your connection with the other person and foster a more positive relationship.

Case Study: The Importance of Nonverbal Cues in Communication

Rahul and Manish had been working together at a software company for several months. They were assigned to work on a new project that required a lot of collaboration and coordination between them. One day, Rahul was discussing an important aspect of the project with Manish during a team meeting. While Rahul was speaking, Manish crossed his arms and looked away from Rahul, which Rahul interpreted as disinterest and disagreement. As a result, Rahul became defensive and felt that Manish was not taking his ideas seriously.

After the meeting, Rahul approached Manish to discuss their differences. However, Manish was confused and had no idea what Rahul was talking about. Manish explained that he was not aware that he was sending any negative cues and that he was simply trying to get comfortable in his seat. He added that he had no intention of being disrespectful or disinterested in Rahul's ideas.

This miscommunication highlighted the importance of paying attention to nonverbal cues and avoiding making assumptions based on them. In this case, Rahul's interpretation of Manish's nonverbal cues was incorrect, which led to a misunderstanding between them. The situation could have been avoided if Rahul had asked Manish about his behavior and intentions rather than making assumptions based on nonverbal cues.

This scenario shows that nonverbal cues can significantly impact communication. Body language and facial expressions can convey different meanings and emotions. However, people often interpret nonverbal cues based on their own experiences, beliefs, and cultural backgrounds, which can lead to misunderstandings.

Effective communication requires not only understanding nonverbal cues but also being aware of our own nonverbal communication. By being mindful of our body language and facial expressions, we can ensure that our message is being conveyed effectively. It is important to maintain eye contact, keep an open posture, and avoid fidgeting, as these can convey confidence and sincerity.

Written Communication

Effective written communication involves communicating ideas, thoughts, and information in a clear, concise, and compelling manner. One of the essential techniques for effective written communication is organization. The information should be presented in a logical order that flows smoothly from one idea to the next. Each paragraph should have a clear topic sentence and supporting details that provide clarity and coherence to the message. Using headings and subheadings can also help to organize the information and make it easier to read and understand.

Another essential technique for effective written communication is tone. Tone refers to the attitude, mood, or emotion conveyed in writing. The tone should be appropriate for the audience and the message being conveyed. A professional tone is usually appropriate for business communication, while a friendly or personal tone may be more appropriate for informal communication. The tone should also be consistent throughout the message to avoid confusion and mixed signals.

Also, effective written communication requires the use of proper grammar, punctuation, and spelling. These elements are crucial for ensuring that the message is clear and easy to understand. Incorrect grammar, punctuation, or spelling can lead to confusion, misinterpretation, and a lack of credibility. Proofreading and editing are critical steps in ensuring that the message is error-free and of high quality.

Tailored written communication

Tailoring your message to your audience and purpose can make a huge difference in how well it is received and understood. To effectively tailor your writing, you must first identify who your audience is and what your purpose is.

Identifying your audience is the first step in tailoring your written communication. This involves considering who your readers are, what they already know about the topic, and what their interests and needs are. For example, if you are writing a report for your boss, you may want to focus on the financial implications of a decision, whereas if you are writing a blog post for a general audience, you may want to focus on the practical applications of the decision.

Once you have identified your audience, you must also consider your purpose. Are you trying to inform, persuade, or entertain? Your purpose will affect the tone, language, and structure of your writing. For example, if your purpose is to persuade, you may want to use strong, persuasive language and include evidence to support your argument. On the other hand, if your purpose is to inform, you may want to use clear, concise language and organize your information in a logical way.

It is important to consider the medium of your written communication as well. Are you writing an email, a report, a blog post, or a social media post? Each medium has its own conventions and expectations, and you should tailor your writing accordingly. For example, an email may require a more conversational tone and shorter paragraphs, while a report may require a more formal tone and a structured outline.

Exercise: A writing exercise to help readers practice effective written communication.

For this exercise, first think of a situation where you need to write something, like an email to a co-worker or a letter to a potential employer. Now,

1. Find out who you are communicating to and why you are communicating with them. Think about what they want, what they are interested in, and what they expect, and how you can make your message fit those needs.
2. Make a plan for your message that focuses on the main points you want to get across. Think about the most important things you want to say and how you want to say them.
3. Write a draft of your message using the techniques discussed earlier, such as clear organization, active voice, appropriate tone, and formatting.
4. To make your speech more effective, edit and revise it. Make sure there are no spelling or grammar mistakes, that the message is clear and to the point, and that the tone is appropriate for your audience and purpose.
5. After you've edited and revised your message, ask a trusted co-worker or friend for feedback. Think about their ideas and use them as needed.
6. Send your message to your intended recipient after making any final edits.

Here's an illustration

Suppose you are a manager at a company and need to send an email to your team about a change in company policy. Your goal is to make sure that everyone on the team is aware of the new policy and wants to follow it.

Follow these steps to practice effective written communication:

1. Find out who you are talking to. In this case, it is your team. Think about how much they know about the policy and how it could affect them. Consider their values and issues, and consider how you can address them in your message.

2. Define your goal: Your goal is to let your team know about the new policy and encourage them to follow it. Make sure you understand the policy well enough so that you can effectively explain it to others.
3. Think about the tone you want your message to have. You should be firm but also positive and encouraging. Use 'you' statements to make the message more engaging and personal.
4. Organize your message: Choose a clear structure for your message. You could start with a short introduction, then explain the policy and why it is important, and end with a call to action or some kind of encouragement.
5. Use the right formatting: use a font that is easy to read and the right size font. Use headings and bullet points to break up the text and make it easier to read.
6. Before sending your message, make sure to proofread it for mistakes and clarity. Ask someone else to read it over for feedback and suggestions.

Here's an example of how the email might look

Subject: New Company Policy

Dear Team,

I hope this email finds you all in good health. I wanted to take a moment to let you know about a new policy that will take effect next month. The policy is meant to help us improve our customer service and make sure we're meeting the needs of our clients.

According to the new policy, we must answer customer inquiries within 24 hours. This implies that any inquiries made during business hours must receive a response by the end of the following business day. All team members, regardless of their position or department, will be subject to this policy.

I know that this might mean we have to change how we work, but I am sure we can all meet the challenge. We can build stronger relationships with our clients and stand out from our rivals by offering them great customer service.

If you have any questions or concerns about the new policy, please don't be afraid to get in touch with me or our HR department. I value your cooperation and commitment to our clients.

Best Regards,

[Your Name]

Communication in Relationships

In personal relationships, communication is essential for expressing emotions, resolving conflicts, and establishing boundaries. Good communication in personal relationships involves listening actively and empathetically, expressing thoughts and feelings clearly and honestly, and practicing active problem-solving skills.

In a professional setting, good communication skills help to establish clear expectations, avoid misunderstandings, and ensure that everyone is on the same page. Effective communication also helps to create a positive work environment and promote collaboration and productivity. Good communication in the workplace involves listening carefully, speaking clearly and concisely, and adopting communication style to fit the needs of different audiences.

However, poor communication can lead to a breakdown in relationships, both personal and professional. Misunderstandings, unspoken expectations, and unresolved conflicts can all lead to damaged relationships. In personal relationships, poor communication can lead to hurt feelings, resentment, and a breakdown of trust. In professional relationships, poor communication can result in missed deadlines, conflicts, and decreased productivity. Therefore, it is crucial to recognize the impact of communication on relationships and develop effective communication skills to build and maintain healthy relationships.

How to handle conflict and disagreement through effective communication

Effective communication allows individuals to express their concerns, understand others' perspectives, and find mutually agreeable solutions. When disagreements arise, it is important to approach the situation with a calm and open mindset. This can be done by actively listening to the other person, acknowledging their point of view, and avoiding blame or defensiveness.

Another important aspect of handling conflict through effective communication is to use 'I' statements instead of 'you' statements. This means expressing your own feelings and thoughts rather than placing blame or accusing the other person. For example, instead of saying 'You are not listening to me', you can say 'I feel like my ideas aren't being heard.' This approach can help avoid escalating the conflict and allow both parties to focus on finding a solution rather than getting defensive.

Finally, it is important to be willing to compromise and find a middle ground. Effective communication involves being open to new ideas and perspectives and being willing to find a solution that works for both parties. This may involve brainstorming ideas, negotiating a compromise, or finding a new approach altogether. By working together to find a solution, conflicts can be resolved in a way that strengthens relationships rather than damaging them.

How I Improved Communication in a Challenging Relationship

Hi, my name is Ritu. As a child, I was very shy and introverted. I would often keep my thoughts and feelings to myself, even when it came to my family. This habit carried over into my adult life, and it began to cause problems in my relationship with my partner, Rohit.

Rohit and I had been together for a few years, and although we loved each other, we struggled with communication. I found it difficult to express myself, and he found it frustrating when I would shut down or become defensive during difficult conversations.

One day, after a particularly heated argument, I realized that something needed to change. I knew that I needed to work on my communication skills if we were going to have a healthy and fulfilling relationship. So, I made a conscious effort to start opening up and sharing my thoughts and feelings with Rohit.

At first, it was uncomfortable and difficult. I had to push past my natural tendencies and force myself to speak up. But, over time, I began to feel more comfortable and confident in expressing myself. I also started to notice a positive shift in our relationship. Rohit seemed more understanding and patient with me, and we were able to work through conflicts without getting defensive or angry.

Today, our relationship is stronger than ever, and I know that it is because of the effort we both put into effective communication. I have learned that being vulnerable and honest is essential for building trust and intimacy in any relationship.

Communication in the Workplace

In the workplace, effective communication is essential for achieving tasks efficiently and ensuring that everyone is working towards the same goals. This means being clear, concise, and mindful of your tone. It also requires actively listening to others, using appropriate communication channels, responding promptly, using positive language, and respecting diversity. Additionally, effective workplace communication involves following up with others, minimizing distractions, and being open to feedback.

To succeed in the workplace, it is crucial to have strong communication skills. This involves expressing oneself clearly, actively listening, and understanding others' perspectives. These skills help to build strong relationships with colleagues, managers, and clients, leading to better teamwork, increased productivity, and improved job satisfaction. Effective communication requires being clear, concise, mindful of tone, using appropriate channels, responding promptly, using positive language, and respecting diversity.

When communicating in various workplace scenarios, there are specific strategies that should be employed. When communicating with seniors, it is important to be respectful and professional, listening carefully to their feedback and suggestions. For juniors, it is important to be clear and patient, providing clear instructions and guidance. Coworkers require collaboration and inclusivity, and clients need responsiveness and proactivity. Establishing clear expectations, following up promptly, and creating a welcoming environment for feedback and questions are all critical components of effective communication in the workplace. Good communication with clients can lead to stronger relationships and increased business opportunities.

Giving and receiving feedback effectively

Feedback is an important part of personal and professional growth. It allows individuals to identify areas for improvement and take necessary steps to enhance their skills and performance. However, giving and receiving feedback can be challenging, and if not done effectively, can result in negative outcomes. Here, we will discuss how to give and receive feedback effectively.

When giving feedback, it is important to be specific and constructive. Feedback should be based on observable behaviors and should not be a personal attack. It is also important to provide feedback in a timely manner and to communicate it in a respectful and empathetic manner. The goal of feedback is to help the individual improve, so it is important to provide suggestions for improvement and to offer support and resources if needed.

When receiving feedback, it is important to listen actively and without defensiveness. It can be difficult to hear criticism, but it is important to understand that feedback is not a personal attack. It is an opportunity to learn and grow. It is also important to ask questions for clarification and to express appreciation for the feedback. If the feedback is difficult to hear, it can be helpful to take a break before responding.

Example of giving feedback:

Let us say you are a manager and you want to give an employee feedback on their presentation skills. Here's an example of how you could provide a constructive feedback:

1. Begin with a positive thought: “Overall, I think you did a good job with your presentation. You came across as confident and knowledgeable.”
2. Give detailed feedback: “But I did notice that you spoke quite quickly, which made it sometimes hard to understand what you were saying. Also, there was a lot of text on your slides, which made them look a little cluttered.”
3. Make suggestions for improvement: “To get better at giving presentations, you could try practicing speaking more slowly and putting more pictures and less text on your slides. This will help your audience understand and remember your message.”

Example of receiving feedback

Let’s say you are an employee, and your manager gives you feedback on a recent project. Here’s an example of how you could effectively receive feedback:

1. Do ‘active listening’: Don’t interrupt or get angry when your manager gives you feedback. Before responding, make sure you understand what they are saying.
2. Request clarification. If there is anything unclear about the feedback, ask your manager to explain it. This shows you are interested and want to get better.
3. Thank your manager for taking the time to give you feedback. This shows that you value their input and are willing to learn and grow.
4. Take some time to consider what you heard and how you can use it after the feedback session. Make a plan to fix any problems, and ask for help or resources if you need them.

Case Study: An Example of a Successful Communication Strategy Used in the Workplace

The company formerly known as Comdrome International, a global technology corporation that offers a variety of products and services such as software development, cloud computing, and cyber security solutions, was struggling to maintain effective communication among its departments, resulting in project delays, deadline confusion, and even team conflicts. Senior management recognized the need for a communication plan to guarantee that everyone was on the same page and that all information was being presented correctly.

The first thing the management did was figure out what the main communication problems were and where they needed to be fixed. They polled and talked to employees from different departments to find out why there were communication problems. The management found the following problems after looking at the data:

1. Roles and responsibilities were not made clear.
2. Inadequate information sharing between departments
3. Communication channels and techniques that are inconsistent
4. Poor listening skills among employees

Based on the communication problems that were found, the management team came up with a comprehensive communication strategy to deal with the problems and improve communication throughout the organization.

The plan included the following steps

1. Role Clarity: The management team gave each employee a clear job description and duties, outlining their roles and responsibilities within the company. This step helped employees understand what was expected of them and cut down on confusion.
2. Information Sharing: The management team set up regular channels and methods of communication to make sure that information was shared well between departments. They made a central platform where all employees could get the information they needed about project deadlines, objectives, and expectations.
3. Consistent Communication Channels and Methods: The management team streamlined communication channels, providing consistent channels and methods of communication. To make sure that everyone on the team was on the same page, they suggested using a standard communication platform, like email and instant messaging.
4. Listening Skills: The management team set up training programs to help employees improve their listening skills. Active listening, empathy, and constructive criticism were all covered in this training.

As a result of these initiatives, the organization's communication processes have significantly improved, employee engagement increased, and project delays and conflicts decreased. The organization became more productive, and teams worked together better, which led to better results.

To maintain these improvements, the management team kept an eye on the communication processes and asked employees for feedback on a regular basis. To make sure the communication strategy remained relevant to the changing needs of the organization, they reviewed it annually.

In conclusion, the organization was able to overcome its communication problems and create a good environment for teamwork and collaboration thanks to the implementation of a thorough communication strategy. The strategy not only led to better communication inside the company but also to a more productive and invested workforce, all of which contributed to the success of the organization.

Cross-Cultural Communication

One of the primary challenges of cross-cultural communication is the language barrier. Even when people are proficient in a shared language like English, differences in accents, dialects, and idioms can lead to misunderstandings. Moreover, language is not only a tool for communication but also a reflection of culture, so it is important to be aware of cultural nuances in language usage.

Another challenge is differences in communication styles. Some cultures place a high value on direct communication and assertiveness, while others prioritize indirect communication and harmony. These differences can lead to misunderstandings and conflict if not properly understood and addressed.

Cultural differences in nonverbal communication can also pose a challenge. Gestures, facial expressions, and body language can vary widely across cultures and can be misinterpreted if not understood in context.

Stereotyping and bias can also impede cross-cultural communication. Preconceived notions about other cultures can lead to assumptions and misunderstandings that can damage relationships and hinder collaboration.

Effective strategies for communicating across cultures

One of the most important strategies for effective cross-cultural communication is to develop cultural awareness. This involves understanding and respecting different cultural norms, beliefs, and customs. For instance, in some cultures, it may be considered impolite to look someone in the eye, while in other cultures, eye contact is a sign of respect. By developing cultural awareness, we can avoid misunderstandings and show respect for different cultures.

Another effective strategy for cross-cultural communication is to use simple and clear language. When communicating with people from different cultures, it is important to avoid using jargon, idioms, or slang, as they may not be familiar with these terms. Instead, we should use simple and straightforward language, and avoid using complex sentence structures or technical terms.

When communicating with people from different cultures, we should also be aware of nonverbal cues, such as facial expressions and body language, as these can vary across cultures.

It is important to be patient and flexible when communicating across cultures. Different cultures have different communication styles and may take longer to establish rapport or build relationships. By being patient and flexible, we can build trust and respect, and communicate effectively with people from diverse cultural backgrounds.

For example, imagine you are a manager of a team that includes people from different cultural backgrounds. To communicate effectively with your team members, you may start by learning about their cultures and customs. You may also avoid using complex language or jargon, and focus on using simple and clear language. You may also practice active listening and ask questions to ensure that you understand their perspectives. By showing patience and flexibility, you can establish a positive and respectful relationship with your team members and achieve better results.

Personal story of Dilip Sen - Navigating Cross Cultural Communication

As a marketing professional, I had always been comfortable communicating with people from different backgrounds, but when I was asked to lead a campaign for a new product launch in Japan, I realized I had a lot to learn about cross-cultural communication.

I knew that being polite and showing respect are very important in Japanese culture and that being direct isn't always appreciated. In light of this, I spent some time learning about Japanese cultural norms and communication techniques. I also asked a colleague for help because he knew a lot about Japanese culture and could give me some good advice.

When I arrived in Japan, I made sure to respect the culture by bowing to my colleagues and using honorific titles when addressing them. I also made sure to pay close attention to what they were saying and to think about their point of view before responding.

I tried to speak slowly and clearly in meetings, and I avoided using idioms that might be hard for my colleagues to understand. I also used pictures to help get my point across and make sure it was clear and to the point.

Throughout the campaign, I made sure to keep in close contact with my colleagues in Japan by checking in often and giving them regular updates. I also tried to build personal relationships with them by inviting them to dinner and drinks outside of work.

In the end, the campaign was a huge success, and I think that my efforts to communicate well across cultures were a big part of that. I came away from the experience with a newfound appreciation for the importance of cross-cultural communication and a deeper understanding of the value of cultural awareness and sensitivity in today's globalized world.

Personal Stories and Case Studies

Examples of people who have improved their communication skills and achieved both personal and professional success

1. Mira De, a sales representative, had trouble explaining to potential clients the advantages of her company's products. She knew where she was weak and worked to improve her communication skills by going to workshops, reading books about communication, and asking her colleagues for feedback. As a result, she was able to close more deals and increase her sales, which led to a promotion to a higher sales position within the company.
2. Project manager Jiv Sharma had trouble getting his team members to understand him. He realized that his instructions weren't clear and that he wasn't paying attention to what his team members had to say. He decided to take a communication course and work on his active listening skills, which helped him understand his team's concerns better. He also started giving clear instructions, which helped the team perform better and finish the project on time.

Case Study: The story of Herb Cohen, a successful negotiator

An example of a successful negotiator who used effective communication to build strong relationships and achieve successful deals is Herb Cohen, a renowned negotiation expert, and author.

Cohen is known for his ability to use effective communication and relationship-building techniques to negotiate successful deals. He has worked with a wide range of clients, including business leaders, politicians, and even the FBI.

One of Cohen's key strategies is to focus on building trust and rapport with the other party. He believes that by establishing a strong relationship with the other person, it becomes easier to reach a successful agreement.

Cohen is also a big believer in active listening and understanding the other person's perspective. He encourages negotiators to ask questions and really listen to the other person's answers, in order to gain a deeper understanding of their needs and motivations.

Cohen's effective communication and relationship-building techniques have helped him to achieve successful deals in a wide range of industries. He has been called in to negotiate everything from business deals to hostage situations.

Effective communication can lead to improved relationship and career success

Strong communication skills are essential in building healthy relationships with friends, family, colleagues, and clients. When you communicate effectively, you express your thoughts and emotions clearly, and you also begin to listen actively to understand others' viewpoints. This can lead to improved relationships based on mutual respect, trust, and understanding. Effective communication can also help you avoid misunderstandings, and resolve conflicts peacefully.

In the workplace, strong communication skills can be the key to success. Employers value employees who can communicate effectively with their colleagues, clients, and customers. When you can convey your ideas and collaborate effectively, you can achieve better outcomes, and improve your chances of being promoted to higher positions.

Effective communication can also help you establish yourself as an expert in your field. When you communicate your ideas and opinions with clarity and confidence, you can build a reputation as a thought leader in your industry. This can enhance your credibility and increase your chances of being noticed by potential employers or clients.

Author's Personal Story: 'How Tailoring Your Communication Style Can Lead to Success'

Effective communication isn't just about passing on knowledge; it's also about building trust, understanding, and rapport. As a mind trainer and a motivational speaker, I have seen personally how communication can be a powerful tool for both personal and professional success.

When I spoke at a business event a while back, it was a great example of how important it is to communicate well. It was a high-stakes situation with a big group of people from different backgrounds and countries, so I had to plan ahead to make sure my message went over well.

I spent a lot of time researching and learning about the audience's cultural norms, beliefs, and ways of communicating to get ready for the event. I knew that people from different cultures might have different ideas about how to talk to each other and that it was important for me to change my way to fit their needs.

I did a lot of practice with my speech, paying close attention to my tone, body language, and pace. I also made sure to use personal stories and examples that would help the audience understand the message and connect with it.

During the event, I tried to speak in a way that was clear, polite, and interesting. I took the time to thank the crowd for coming and let them know I appreciated them being there, which helped make the room feel friendly and open.

Several people came up to me after the event to say how much they liked my talk. They said that the material was interesting and helpful, and that my way of talking to them helped them understand the material better.

This experience showed me again how important it is to communicate well if you want to build good relationships and be successful. By taking the time to understand the people I was talking to and changing the way I talked to them, I was able to build a sense of connection and trust that led to a successful outcome.

Exercises for you

- Practice active listening by having a conversation with a friend or family member and focusing solely on listening to them.
- Role-play assertive communication scenarios and practice expressing your needs and boundaries.
- Practice conflict resolution by identifying a recent conflict and brainstorming ways to resolve it peacefully.

Share your Thoughts

Congratulations on making it to the end of this chapter on the art of effective communication! Speaking of effective communication, have you heard the one about the scarecrow who won an award for communication skills? It goes like this: "Why did the scarecrow win an award for communication skills? Because he was outstanding in his field!" While it may be a silly pun, it also highlights the importance of being confident and comfortable in your own space, just like the scarecrow was in his field. So keep practicing your communication skills, and you'll be outstanding in your field too!

I want to ask, "do you feel more confident in your communication skills after reading this chapter?" Remember, effective communication is not just about speaking but also listening and understanding. It is about being able to convey your message clearly and also being able to receive and interpret messages accurately.

In the spirit of keeping things light, allow me to share a communication tip that has helped me. When in doubt, smile! A simple smile can go a long way in making the other person feel more comfortable and open to what you have to say.

Now, I want to hear from you. What communication successes or challenges have you faced recently? I encourage you to leave a review and share your thoughts and experiences with others. Your feedback can help other readers and also motivate them to work on their own communication skills.

Writing a review is easy and only takes a few minutes. Simply visit this book's page on Amazon and leave a rating and some comments about your experience with this book. Have you implemented any of the tips from this chapter in your personal or professional life? What worked well for you? Leave a review and share your thoughts - I can't wait to read them!

As a token of appreciation, I am offering an incentive to those who write a review. After writing the review, if you inform my office at sworld.mind@gmail.com, we will send you the 'Author's Draft' of this chapter. The Author's Draft contains extended details and research that may not have made it into this final published version.

Conclusion

In this chapter, we explored the art of effective communication, which is essential for personal and professional success. We discussed verbal, nonverbal, and written communication, and how to use them to convey your message effectively.

We also talked about communication in relationships and how to build strong, healthy connections with others through open and honest communication. Similarly, we explored communication in the workplace and how to communicate effectively with colleagues and bosses to achieve common goals. We also looked at cross-cultural communication and how to navigate communication differences in a diverse world. Finally, we shared personal stories and case studies that illustrate how effective communication can transform your personal and professional life.

The key takeaway from this chapter is that effective communication is a skill that can be developed and mastered with practice. By being mindful of your words, body language, and written communication, you can convey your message with clarity and impact. Effective communication is the foundation of strong relationships, successful careers, and personal growth

XIII. Wrap up

Congratulations for completing this chapter on effective communication. Remember, communication is not just about talking, it's also about listening and understanding. By being mindful of your communication style and practicing effective communication strategies, you can build stronger relationships, enhance your career prospects, and achieve your personal goals.

Developing effective communication skills requires practice, patience, and a willingness to learn. It may take time to overcome communication challenges and establish trust with others, but the effort is worth it.

To truly develop your communication skills, you must put what you've learned into practice. Start by paying attention to how you communicate with others, both verbally and nonverbally. Practice active listening, speak clearly and confidently, and be aware of your body language.

Remember, effective communication is not just about getting your message across but also about building meaningful relationships with others. Whether it is in your personal life or your career, strong communication skills can take you a long way. So, keep practicing and refining your communication skills, and you'll soon see the positive impact it has on your life.

Keep reading, keep learning, and never stop striving for personal development. With dedication and perseverance, you can continue to grow and become the best version of yourself.

"Effective communication is 20% what you know and 80% how you feel about what you know."

– Jim Rohn

❑

CHAPTER 8

Tapping into Your Emotional Intelligence

"Emotional intelligence is not the opposite of intelligence, it is the integration of intelligence and emotions."

– John Mayer

Introduction

Have you ever wondered why some people seem to have a natural ability to connect with others, handle stressful situations with ease, and lead successful lives both personally and professionally? The answer lies in their emotional intelligence.

In the previous chapter, we learned about the importance of effective communication in all aspects of our lives. Now, we will explore another crucial aspect of personal development: emotional intelligence, also known as EQ, which is the ability to recognize, understand, and manage our own emotions, as well as understand and influence the emotions of others. Emotional Intelligence plays a crucial role in personal and professional success, and is a skill that can be developed over time.

Through this chapter, you will learn about the different components of Emotional Intelligence, including self-awareness, self-regulation, motivation, empathy, and social skills. You will also explore the importance of Emotional

Intelligence in the workplace, and how it can impact your career growth and success.

Are you ready to develop your Emotional Intelligence and take your personal and professional life to the next level? Let's dive in and get started!

What is Emotional Intelligence

Emotional intelligence is a term that has become increasingly popular in recent years. Simply put, emotional intelligence refers to our ability to recognize, understand, and manage our own emotions, as well as the emotions of others. It involves several key components such as, self-awareness, self-regulation, motivation, empathy, and social skills.

In our personal lives, emotional intelligence can help us to better navigate our relationships with friends, family members, and romantic partners. It enables us to communicate effectively, resolve conflicts, and build stronger, more meaningful connections with those around us. On the other hand, in our professional lives, emotional intelligence can help us to be more successful in our careers. It can make us better leaders, more effective communicators, and more empathetic team members.

One of the most significant benefits of emotional intelligence is its ability to help us manage our own emotions. When we are emotionally intelligent, we are better equipped to identify and regulate our emotions. This means that we can respond to situations in a more measured and appropriate way. For example, if we are feeling angry, emotional intelligence can help us to express our anger in a constructive manner, rather than lashing out and causing harm to ourselves or others.

In addition to managing our own emotions, emotional intelligence also enables us to understand and empathize with the emotions of others. This is particularly important in our personal relationships, as it helps us to be more supportive, caring, and understanding partners and friends. It also enables us to build trust and rapport with others, which is essential in professional settings.

Self-Awareness

In many ways, self-awareness is the foundation upon which emotional intelligence is built. When we are self-aware, we are better able to identify our emotions, understand their triggers, and manage them in a healthy and productive manner. For example, if we are aware that we tend to feel anxious in certain situations, we can take steps to manage our anxiety, such as practicing mindfulness or deep breathing exercises.

Self-awareness helps us to understand how our emotions and behavior affect those around us. This is particularly important in our personal relationships, as it enables us to be more empathetic, understanding, and supportive partners and friends. It also helps us to communicate more effectively, as we are better able to express ourselves in a way that is both honest and respectful.

One way to develop self-awareness is through reflection and introspection. Taking time to reflect on our thoughts, feelings, and actions can help us to become more aware of our emotions and how they impact us. Journaling, meditation, and therapy are all effective tools for cultivating self-awareness.

Another way to develop self-awareness is to seek feedback from others. Asking trusted friends, family members, or colleagues for feedback can provide valuable insight into our strengths and weaknesses, as well as how we are perceived by others.

Recognizing and understanding personal emotions and triggers

To recognize personal emotions, it's essential to pay attention to our thoughts, feelings, and behaviors. It's natural to experience a range of emotions throughout the day, and identifying them can be a challenge. However, we can practice mindfulness, which means being fully present in the moment and being aware of our thoughts and emotions. When we practice mindfulness, we can observe our thoughts without judgment and identify the emotions we're experiencing.

Keeping a journal can be an excellent tool for recognizing and understanding personal emotions and triggers. Writing down our thoughts and feelings can help us process and understand them better. We can also identify patterns in our emotions and recognize what triggers them. For example, we might notice that we feel anxious when we have a deadline approaching, or we feel angry when someone criticizes us. By identifying these triggers, we can take steps to manage our emotions and respond to situations more effectively.

Another helpful strategy is to pay attention to our bodies. Our bodies often give us physical cues that we're experiencing an emotion. For instance, we might feel our heart rate increase when we're angry, or we might notice tension in our shoulders when we're stressed. By paying attention to these physical cues, we can become more aware of our emotions and recognize what triggers them.

Exercise: A self-reflection exercise to help you identify your emotional strengths and weaknesses

Self-reflection is an essential tool for personal development, and it can be particularly helpful for developing emotional intelligence. Here is an exercise that readers can use to identify their emotional strengths and weaknesses:

Step 1: Set aside some time to reflect on your emotions. Find a quiet, comfortable place where you can focus without distractions.

Step 2: Take a few deep breaths and relax your body. Close your eyes if it helps you to concentrate.

Step 3: Think about a recent situation that triggered an emotional response in you. It could be a positive or negative emotion. Try to recall the details of the situation, including how you felt and how you responded.

Step 4: Ask yourself the following questions:

- What was the emotion I felt in this situation?
- How did I express that emotion?
- Was my response appropriate for the situation?
- Could I have handled the situation differently?
- What did I learn about myself and my emotions from this situation?

Step 5: Repeat this exercise with different situations and emotions. As you reflect on your emotions, look for patterns and themes that emerge. Identify your emotional strengths and weaknesses based on your reflections.

Step 6: Create an action plan. Once you have identified your emotional strengths and weaknesses, create an action plan to help you improve. For example, if you struggle with expressing your emotions, you might work on communicating more effectively. If you tend to react impulsively, you might work on developing strategies for managing your emotions in the moment.

By regularly reflecting on your emotions and identifying your strengths and weaknesses, you can develop greater emotional intelligence. This, in turn, can help you to manage your emotions more effectively, communicate better with others, and build stronger relationships.

Self-Regulation

Self-regulation is an essential component of emotional intelligence. It's the ability to manage our emotions, thoughts, and behaviors effectively, even in challenging situations. When we can regulate our emotions, we're better equipped to handle stress, make rational decisions, and respond to situations in a constructive way.

One of the keys to self-regulation is being aware of our emotions. We need to be able to recognize when we're feeling strong emotions, such as anger, fear, or frustration. When we can identify our emotions, we can take steps to manage them effectively. For example, we might take a few deep breaths to calm ourselves down or take a break from a stressful situation to clear our heads.

Another essential aspect of self-regulation is learning how to control our impulses. We all have impulses that can lead us to make rash decisions or act impulsively. However, when we can regulate these impulses, we're better able to make deliberate and thoughtful decisions. For example, if we're feeling frustrated with a coworker, we might be tempted to lash out or say something hurtful. However, if we can regulate that impulse, we can take a step back and consider the consequences of our actions.

Self-regulation also involves setting boundaries for ourselves. It is important to know our limits and to say no when we need to. For example, if we're feeling overwhelmed with work, we might need to set boundaries with our colleagues or managers to ensure that we're not taking on too much.

Developing self-regulation takes time and practice. It's not something that happens overnight, but with dedication and effort, we can improve our ability to manage our emotions and impulses. By doing so, we can improve our relationships with others, make better decisions, and achieve greater success in our personal and professional lives.

Managing personal emotions and reactions

Managing personal emotions and reactions is a crucial part of emotional intelligence. It's important to be able to control our emotions, especially in situations that are stressful, challenging, or triggering. Here are some tips on how to manage your emotions and reactions in different situations:

1. In stressful situations

Stressful situations can trigger strong emotions, such as anxiety or frustration. To manage these emotions, it's important to take a step back and evaluate the situation objectively. Try to identify the source of your stress and focus on finding a solution. It can also be helpful to practice relaxation techniques, such as deep breathing, to calm your mind and body.

2. In conflict situations

Conflict situations can be emotionally charged, and it can be easy to react impulsively or defensively. To manage your emotions in conflict situations, it's important to stay calm and listen actively. Try to understand the other person's perspective and avoid making assumptions or judgments. Focus on finding a resolution that is fair and respectful to all parties involved.

3. In difficult conversations

Difficult conversations can be uncomfortable or confrontational, which can trigger emotions such as fear or anger. To manage your emotions in these situations, it's important to communicate effectively and assertively. Be clear and concise in your communication, and try to avoid blaming or accusing the other person. Use 'I' statements to express your feelings and needs, and be open to feedback and compromise.

4. In personal relationships

Personal relationships can also trigger strong emotions, such as jealousy or insecurity. To manage these emotions, it's important to practice self-awareness and self-regulation. Be honest with yourself about your emotions and triggers, and take steps to manage them effectively. Communicate openly and respectfully with your partner or loved ones, and focus on building trust and understanding.

Managing personal emotions and reactions takes practice and self-awareness. By learning to manage your emotions effectively, you can improve your relationships, communicate more effectively, and achieve greater success in your personal and professional life.

Case study: An example of a successful self-regulation strategy used in a challenging situation

Mina Parker is a high-level executive at a company that does business all over the world. She is a hard worker with a focus on her goals who is committed to her work. But she is known to have a short fuse and get upset easily, which has led to problems in the past.

One day, Mina was in a meeting with the company's board of directors when she was asked a tough question, to which she didn't know the answer. She felt her heart beat faster and her palms start to sweat right away. In the past, she might have gotten angry or defensive when someone asked her a question, but she had been working on her self-control and knew that this wasn't the best way to act.

Instead, Mina took a deep breath and said in a calm voice that she didn't know the answer but would be happy to give the board the information they needed after the meeting. The conversation then shifted to a related subject that she was more knowledgeable about. Mina was able to stay calm and handle the situation in a professional and effective manner by controlling her emotions.

Mina used her self-regulation skills well in this situation because she was able to recognize her emotional reaction, take a moment to calm down, and then respond in a calm and thoughtful way. She was able to stop herself from acting rashly or defensively and instead chose a better course of action. This kept her credibility with the board and kept her professional reputation intact. Mina showed how important it is to be able to control yourself at work by showing how well she handled her feelings in a tough situation.

Motivation

Motivation is an essential component of emotional intelligence. Without motivation, it can be difficult to stay focused, engaged, and resilient in the face of challenges. Motivation is the driving force that helps us pursue our goals, overcome obstacles, and achieve success in our personal and professional lives.

Motivation can be divided into two types: intrinsic and extrinsic. Intrinsic motivation comes from within and is driven by our internal desires, values, and interests. Extrinsic motivation, on the other hand, is driven by external rewards or incentives, such as money, recognition, or praise.

Research has shown that intrinsic motivation is a key factor in emotional intelligence. When we are intrinsically motivated, we are more likely to experience positive emotions such as joy, interest, and enthusiasm. We are also more likely to be persistent, resilient, and adaptable in the face of challenges.

One way to cultivate intrinsic motivation is to align our goals with our values and interests. When we pursue goals that are meaningful and relevant to us, we are more likely to be motivated and engaged. It's also important to set realistic and achievable goals, and to track our progress along the way.

In addition to intrinsic motivation, social support can also be a powerful motivator. When we have a strong support network of friends, family, and colleagues, we are more likely to feel motivated and engaged in our personal and professional lives. Social support can also help us cope with stress and adversity, and provide a sense of belonging and purpose.

Values and Goals Drive Motivation

Our personal values and goals are powerful drivers of motivation. When we align our goals with our values, we are more likely to feel motivated, engaged, and fulfilled in our pursuits. Personal values are the beliefs and principles that guide our behavior and decision-making, while goals are the specific outcomes we want to achieve.

To use personal values and goals to drive motivation, it is important to first identify our values and set meaningful goals. Reflect on what matters most to you in life, what you stand for, and what you want to achieve. This can help you clarify your personal values and set goals that are aligned with them.

Once you have identified your values and goals, it is important to break down your goals into smaller, achievable steps. This can help you stay motivated and make progress towards your goals. Set deadlines and track your progress, celebrating your successes along the way.

Another way to use personal values and goals to drive motivation is to visualize success. Visualize yourself achieving your goals and experiencing the benefits that come with them. This can help you stay focused and motivated, even in the face of challenges and setbacks.

Do stay flexible and adaptable in your approach to achieving your goals. If you encounter obstacles or setbacks, don't give up. Instead, reassess your goals and adjust your approach as needed.

Exercise: A goal-setting exercise to help you identify personal motivations and how to achieve them.

1. Choose a specific goal. To start, choose a specific goal that you want to achieve. It could be a personal or professional goal, but it must be something important to you.
2. Link the goal to your personal values Write down the things you care about and how achieving this goal will help you live your life in line with those things.
3. Break the goal down into smaller steps. Once you have determined the goal and how it relates to your personal values, you can break it down into smaller, more manageable steps. Write down each step you need to take to achieve your goal.
4. Establish a deadline: Decide when each of the smaller steps will be completed. This will keep you on track and help you move closer to your goal.

5. Set up a system of accountability. Tell someone you trust, like a friend, family member, or mentor, about your goal and your plan. This can help you keep track of what you are doing and keep you going throughout the process.
6. Celebrate milestones: As you advance towards your goal, take time to celebrate milestones along the way. This will help you keep going and keep your mind on getting to the end goal.

Remember that achieving a goal is a process that takes time, work, and motivation. By figuring out what your personal values are and breaking your goal down into smaller steps, you can make a plan that fits your values and motivations and take steps that will help you achieve your goals.

Empathy

Empathy is a critical component of emotional intelligence, as it enables us to understand and connect with others on a deeper level. It involves the ability to recognize and understand the emotions and perspectives of others, and respond in a way that is appropriate and supportive.

When we practice empathy, we are better able to communicate and collaborate with others, build strong relationships, and resolve conflicts in a positive way. By showing empathy towards others, we also tend to inspire trust and respect, which can be especially important in leadership roles.

Developing empathy requires us to be open-minded and non-judgmental, and to be willing to listen to the perspectives of others. It requires us to be patient and understanding, and to be willing to put ourselves in someone else's shoes. By practicing empathy, we can become more compassionate, caring, and effective communicators, and build stronger relationships with those around us.

How to recognize and understand the emotions of others

The first step in recognizing the emotions of others is to pay attention to their body language, facial expressions, and tone of voice. These nonverbal cues can often provide important clues about how someone is feeling. For example, a person who is hunched over and avoiding eye contact might be feeling sad or depressed, while someone who is standing up straight and speaking confidently might be feeling happy or excited.

It is also important to listen carefully to what someone is saying, as well as how they are saying it. Sometimes people will say one thing, but their tone of voice or the way they say it will indicate a different emotion. For example, someone might say "I'm fine," but their tone of voice might suggest that they are actually upset or angry.

In addition to paying attention to nonverbal cues and listening carefully, it is also important to ask questions and show genuine interest in the other person. By asking questions and showing that we care about their feelings, we can help them to feel heard and validated. It is also important to avoid making assumptions about how someone is feeling, and instead to ask them directly if we are unsure.

Case Study: Using Empathy to Improve a Personal Relationship

Sourav and Koyal had been close friends since childhood. However, as they grew older, their busy schedules and different priorities led to a strain in their relationship. Sourav felt that Koyal was always too busy for him, while Koyal felt that Sourav was too demanding and didn't understand her commitments.

One day, Sourav decided to try and mend their relationship by using empathy. He put himself in Koyal's shoes and realized that she had a lot going on in her life, including a demanding job and taking care of her elderly parents. He decided to express his understanding of her situation and offered his help in any way possible.

He called her up and said, "Koyal, I understand that you have a lot on your plate right now. I just wanted to let you know that I am here for you and if there's anything I can do to help, just let me know. I don't want to add to your stress, but I also miss our friendship and I hope we can find a way to make it work."

Koyal was touched by Sourav's understanding and willingness to help. She realized that she had been too caught up in her own problems and had neglected their friendship. She apologized for not being there for him and promised to make more time for their friendship.

From that day on, Sourav and Koyal made a conscious effort to stay in touch, even if it was just a quick text or call. They also started making plans to hang out and catch up on each other's lives. By using empathy, Sourav was able to repair their friendship and bring them closer than ever before.

Social Skills

Social skills are an essential component of emotional intelligence. They involve the ability to communicate effectively, build relationships, work collaboratively, and lead others. People who possess strong social skills can create and maintain positive connections with others, handle conflicts constructively, and influence and inspire others towards a common goal.

In the workplace, for example, employees with strong social skills can communicate effectively with colleagues, build relationships with clients and customers, and collaborate with team members towards a shared objective. Additionally, social skills are important in leadership positions, where individuals must be able to inspire and motivate their team, handle conflicts effectively, and build a positive work environment.

Social skills also play a crucial role in personal relationships. Individuals with strong social skills can communicate effectively with their friends and family, build and maintain positive relationships, and handle conflicts constructively. They are able to listen attentively, express themselves clearly, and respond to the needs and emotions of others.

Developing social skills requires practice and self-awareness. It involves being mindful of one's communication style, understanding nonverbal cues, and actively seeking to understand and empathize with others. It also involves being aware of one's emotions and how they affect others, and learning how to regulate one's emotions in different social situations.

How to communicate effectively, build relationships, and collaborate with others

To communicate effectively, it is important to choose your words, tone, and body language carefully. This helps you to convey your message in a clear and respectful manner. You should also consider the person or people you are communicating with, and adjust your style accordingly.

Building relationships with others takes time and effort. Relationships are based on mutual trust, respect, and shared experiences. It is important to invest time and energy in building relationships, whether they are personal or professional. You can do this by being present, actively listening, showing interest and support, and being reliable.

Collaboration involves working together towards a common goal. This often involves a group of people with diverse skills and backgrounds. To collaborate effectively, you need good communication, mutual respect, trust, and a shared understanding of the goals and expectations. Each person's contribution should be recognized and appreciated. You should also be willing to compromise and adapt as necessary.

Exercise: A role-playing exercise to help readers practice effective social skills

1. Choose a partner to practice with.
2. Decide who will play the role of the speaker and who will play the role of the listener.
3. The speaker will talk about a personal experience or a topic of their choice for two minutes.
4. The listener will listen actively, showing interest and support, and ask relevant questions to demonstrate their understanding.
5. After two minutes, switch roles and repeat the exercise.
6. After both partners have had a chance to speak and listen, discuss how it felt to be the speaker and the listener. Share what worked well and what could be improved.
7. Practice the exercise again, incorporating the feedback and focusing on improving your communication skills.

This role-playing exercise helps in developing active listening skills, showing empathy, and asking relevant questions to gain a better understanding of others' perspectives. By practicing and incorporating the feedback, readers can improve their social skills and build stronger relationships with others.

Emotional Intelligence in the Workplace

Managing your emotions at work is a crucial part of emotional intelligence. This means being able to recognize and control your own emotions, even in challenging situations. It also means understanding how your emotions may affect those around you and adjusting your behavior accordingly.

Emotional intelligence is not just about managing your own emotions. It is also about building positive relationships with everyone in your workplace, including your coworkers, clients, and bosses. Strong relationships based on trust, respect, and empathy can help you succeed and advance in your career.

Effective communication is the key to building positive relationships in the workplace. You need to listen actively to others, speak clearly and respectfully, and use appropriate body language and tone of voice. You also need to adjust your communication style to suit different people and situations.

Emotional intelligence also means being able to handle conflicts and difficult situations in a constructive way. This involves understanding other people's perspectives, staying calm and focused, and working together to find a solution that works for everyone.

How to use emotional intelligence to become a better leader

Leadership requires a range of skills, and emotional intelligence is one of the most critical. Effective leaders need to be able to understand and manage their own emotions, as well as the emotions of those around them. This involves being aware of the impact of your emotions on others, and using this awareness to make sound decisions and manage conflict constructively.

To become a better leader, it is important to develop self-awareness and self-regulation. This means taking the time to reflect on your emotions and behavior, and developing strategies to manage them effectively. It also means recognizing and managing stress, both in yourself and in others.

Leaders who make an effort to understand the viewpoints and requirements of others can establish better relationships with them, resulting in increased loyalty and commitment. Achieving this requires listening carefully, being attentive and involved, and displaying authentic concern and curiosity for others.

Effective communication is another key skill for leaders, and emotional intelligence can help in this regard as well. By being able to adapt your communication style to different situations and individuals, you can build stronger connections and influence others more effectively. This involves being clear and concise in your communication, using appropriate body language and tone of voice, and being open to feedback and input from others.

By being able to understand and manage emotions, and by demonstrating empathy and good communication skills, leaders can help to resolve conflicts constructively and find mutually beneficial solutions. This involves being able to remain calm and focused in challenging situations, and working collaboratively with others to find common ground.

Personal story: An individual shares how they improved their emotional intelligence in a professional setting.

Marketing expert Xavier Gomes, who is 32 years old, is known for his strategic and analytical skills. But he didn't have good emotional intelligence, which led to problems with his colleagues and made it hard for him to manage his team. Xavier had become interested in developing his skills to improve his leadership abilities after realizing the effects of his low emotional intelligence. As a result, he is excited to talk about his journey to improve his emotional intelligence.

I have always been a driven and goal-oriented person, but in my early years as a manager, I had trouble with emotional intelligence. When things didn't go as planned, I would often get angry and lose my temper, and it was hard for me to get along with the other people on my team. I didn't realize I needed to improve my emotional intelligence until I was working on a particularly hard project. After some self-reflection, I realized that my lack of emotional intelligence was causing stress and conflict within my team that didn't need to be there. I made the decision to act, and I began by becoming more self-aware. I thought about my strengths and weaknesses as a leader and where I needed to improve.

Emotional regulation was one of the most important things I needed to work on. I found that taking deep breaths and practicing mindfulness helped me manage my emotions in a healthier way. This helped me deal with situations in a more productive and logical way, even when I was stressed. I also worked to improve my verbal and nonverbal communication skills. I tried to listen carefully and understand what my team members were saying. I also worked on being clear and concise when I spoke.

Over time, I discovered that my efforts have started paying off. My team started to trust me more, and we were able to communicate more freely and effectively. We were able to work together more effectively and efficiently, and the project turned out to be a huge success.

It wasn't easy to improve my emotional intelligence, but it was definitely worth the effort. It not only made me a better leader, but it also helped me get along better with my colleagues and even in my personal life.

Personal Stories and Case Studies

Examples of Individuals Who Improved Their Emotional Intelligence and Achieved Success

1. Adam Grant is a psychologist and author who has written a lot about leadership, teamwork, and creativity. His work emphasizes the importance of emotional intelligence in these areas, and he has been named one of the world's top management thinkers.

2. Tony Hsieh was the CEO of Zappos, and he was known for his emphasis on employee happiness and well-being. He set up programs to help employees improve their emotional intelligence because he thought it was important for fostering a positive work environment.

3. Greta Thunberg is a climate activist who has become a global icon for her leadership and advocacy. People have praised her emotional intelligence,

which includes her ability to understand how climate change affects people and her willingness to take decisive action to solve the problem.

Emotional intelligence can lead to improved relationships and career success

Emotional intelligence is becoming a more important skill for both personal and professional success. One of the ways it can make a big difference is by making people's relationships better. By improving their emotional intelligence, people are better able to recognize and respond to the feelings of others, as well as understand and control their own emotions. This improves relationships' communication, cooperation, and trust, which can lead to better results and more success.

Emotional intelligence can be very helpful in the workplace when it comes to building and keeping relationships with colleagues, bosses, and clients. Leaders with high emotional intelligence are often able to connect with their team members on a more personal level, understand their needs and concerns, and offer support and guidance that is tailored to each person's needs. This can improve teamwork, make people happier at work, and lead to better performance and career success.

Emotional intelligence can help you become more self-aware and grow as a person, in addition to improving your relationships with other people. By being aware of and in control of their own emotions, people can become more resilient and flexible, making it easier for them to deal with challenges and setbacks in their careers. Emotional intelligence can also help people make better decisions, allowing them to make choices that are more strategic and in line with their values and objectives.

Author's Personal Story: 'My Journey of Developing Emotional Intelligence'

My path to developing emotional intelligence has been difficult but rewarding. When I was younger, I found it difficult to control my emotions and often acted impulsively. As a result, I often found myself in conflicts and experienced tension in my relationships with both family and friends. This has been a persistent issue for me.

I didn't realize how important emotional intelligence was to building strong relationships and achieving success until I started my career in motivational speaking. As I started learning a lot about the subject, I began researching it deeply. As I learned more, I started putting the ideas into practice in both my personal and professional lives.

I worked on becoming more self-aware and began to notice how my own feelings affected how I interacted with other people. I also tried to develop empathy by putting myself in other people's shoes and trying to understand their points of view. This helped me build stronger relationships as well as a deeper connection with my audience.

As I kept working on my emotional intelligence, I saw a big difference in my personal happiness and professional success. I was able to build a strong network of helpful relationships, talk to people better, and settle disagreements in a friendly way.

I firmly believe that emotional intelligence is a fundamental component in establishing fulfilling relationships and achieving success in all aspects of life, whether it be personal or professional. My own journey is a testament to the transformative power of emotional intelligence, as it has allowed me to overcome obstacles, connect more deeply with others, and achieve my goals. I encourage you to develop their emotional intelligence skills, as it can truly change your life for the better. Remember, with emotional intelligence, anything is possible!

Exercises for you

- Practice emotional self-awareness by identifying and labeling your emotions.
- Practice emotion regulation by using a technique, such as deep breathing or journaling, to calm yourself when feeling overwhelmed.
- Practice empathy by putting yourself in someone else's shoes and considering their perspective.

Share your Thoughts

We have reached the end of the chapter and I hope that you have found it to be informative and enlightening.

As you reflect on the chapter, I would like to ask if you have learned something new about emotional intelligence that you didn't know before. Emotional intelligence is an important aspect of personal development, and I believe that we can all benefit from improving our emotional intelligence skills. I sincerely encourage you to continue exploring this fascinating topic.

Speaking of exploration, I'd like to share a personal experience where emotional intelligence played a key role. One time, I accidentally spilled coffee on my boss's shirt during a meeting. Instead of getting upset, my boss simply laughed it off and made a joke, diffusing the tension in the room. This showed me how emotional intelligence can help us handle unexpected situations with grace and humor.

As we come to the end of this chapter, I would like to encourage you to leave a review and share your own emotional intelligence insights. Your feedback is invaluable to me.

If you are unsure how to write a review, don't worry, I can guide you through the process. Simply visit Amazon and on this book's page, leave your review there. It doesn't have to be lengthy or formal, just an honest reflection of your thoughts on this book.

And to sweeten the deal, I would like to offer you an incentive to write a review. After writing the review, if you inform our office at sworld.mind@gmail.com about the review, we will send over the 'Author's Draft' of this chapter. The Author's Draft contains extended content, details and research on this chapter that did not make it into this published version.

Thank you for taking the time to read this chapter, and I hope that you have found it helpful in your personal development journey.

Conclusion

In this chapter, we discussed the important role emotional intelligence plays in our personal and professional lives. We explored the five key components of emotional intelligence: self-awareness, self-regulation, motivation, empathy, and social skills. We also highlighted how emotional intelligence can help us build positive relationships with those around us, handle conflicts constructively, and become better leaders.

We delved deeper into emotional intelligence in the workplace, discussing the importance of managing emotions and relationships with coworkers and clients.

By developing our emotional intelligence, we can become more self-aware, manage our emotions effectively, build positive relationships, and achieve our personal and professional goals.

Wrap up

Congratulations on making it to the end of this chapter! By taking the time to learn about emotional intelligence, you have already taken the first step towards improving your personal and professional relationships. Remember that developing emotional intelligence takes time, effort, and patience, but it's a journey worth taking.

As you continue on this journey, I encourage you to practice self-awareness, self-regulation, motivation, empathy, and social skills regularly. Take time to reflect on your thoughts, feelings, and behaviors and how they impact those around you. Seek feedback from trusted friends, family, or colleagues and use it to improve yourself.

Remember that emotional intelligence is not a one-time accomplishment, but a continuous process of growth and development. Don't be afraid to make mistakes or face challenges, as they are opportunities to learn and improve. With dedication and practice, you can tap into your emotional intelligence and reach your full potential in all aspects of your life.

"When dealing with people, remember you are not dealing with creatures of logic, but creatures of emotion."

– Dale Carnegie

❑

CHAPTER 9

Cultivating Meaningful Relationships

"The quality of your relationships, whether they are spiritual, personal, or professional, determines the quality of your life."

– Avadhut das

Introduction

Have you ever struggled with building or maintaining relationships in your personal or professional life? Do you find yourself constantly at odds with people or unable to establish trust and respect? If so, you're not alone. Building strong, healthy relationships is a vital part of personal development and can greatly impact your overall happiness and success.

In the last chapter, we discussed the importance of emotional intelligence in personal and professional growth. In this chapter, we'll explore the different types of relationships and the importance of trust, and respect in building and maintaining them. We'll also delve into conflict resolution and setting healthy boundaries for yourself to maintain positive relationships.

We will also examine how building relationships in the workplace, where we spend a significant amount of time, can have a positive impact on our career growth and success. Additionally, we will explore strategies for cultivating positive relationships with colleagues, managers, and clients.

As always, we'll be incorporating personal stories and case studies to illustrate these concepts and provide practical tips for applying them in your own life. By the end of this chapter, you will have a better understanding of the key elements that contribute to building strong and healthy relationships, and how you can apply them in your personal and professional life. So, let's dive in and explore the power of building positive relationships!

Importance of building positive relationships

We thrive on relationships, whether personal or professional. Relationships bring us joy, meaning, and purpose in life. They make us feel connected, valued, and appreciated. Positive relationships can impact our mental and emotional wellbeing, our career, and our overall quality of life.

The importance of building positive relationships cannot be overstated. They help us grow, learn, and become better individuals. Positive relationships foster mutual respect, trust, and understanding. They create a safe and supportive environment where we can express ourselves freely and share our thoughts and feelings without fear of judgement or criticism.

Building positive relationships is not always easy. It requires effort, patience, and empathy. It is essential to be mindful of our behavior, communicate effectively, and practice active listening. We must also be willing to invest time and energy into developing and maintaining relationships. We cannot expect to have strong, healthy relationships without putting in the necessary work.

To build positive relationships, it is crucial to be authentic and genuine. Honesty and transparency create trust, and trust is the foundation of any successful relationship. We must also be willing to compromise, show empathy, and accept others for who they are. When we take the time to understand and appreciate others, we create a positive, supportive, and nurturing environment.

Types of Relationships

There are various types of relationships that are significant in our lives, and each type of relationship has its own set of advantages. Here are some examples of different types of relationships and their importance:

Because they give us a sense of belonging and support, family relationships are some of the most important relationships in our lives. Strong family ties can help people develop a sense of identity, values, and traditions. They can also help us deal with problems in life and offer emotional support when things are hard.

Because they give us company, help, and fun, friendships are crucial to our health. Positive friendships can help us feel better about ourselves, get along better with other people, and feel less stressed. They can also give us different points of view and insights, which can help us grow and change as people.

Romantic relationships are important for emotional and physical closeness, as well as for companionship and support. Positive romantic relationships can help us build trust, communication skills, and emotional fortitude. They can also give us a sense of safety, acceptance, and love.

Having professional relationships is important for moving up in your career and being successful. Positive professional relationships can help us build our network, get better at communicating and negotiating, and give us chances to work with others and get better. They can also give us advice and mentorship that will help us achieve our professional objectives.

How to prioritize and maintain different types of relationships

Putting different types of relationships first and keeping them going requires a balanced approach that takes into account the different needs and demands of each relationship. Here are some tips for putting different kinds of relationships first and keeping them going:

Family relationships should be a top priority for most people. To ensure that the relationship is positive and fulfilling, it is important to maintain healthy boundaries and clear communication with family members. Regularly spending time together, sharing important moments, and showing appreciation and support is essential for maintaining strong family relationships.

Maintaining friendships takes work and care. It is important to put the most important relationships first and devote time and effort to maintaining them. This can include regular communication, checking in on each other, and making time for shared activities or experiences.

Romantic relationships take work and dedication to maintain. To make a relationship stronger, it is important to put communication, intimacy, and quality time together first. Maintaining a healthy romantic relationship also requires regular expressions of appreciation, support, and affection.

Maintaining professional relationships requires a different strategy than maintaining personal relationships. In all interactions, it is important to be responsive, reliable, and professional. Regularly staying in touch, offering help or support, and recognizing achievements or milestones are also important for building and maintaining positive professional relationships.

A self-reflection exercise

An exercise to think about the important relationships in your life:

1. Take a few minutes to think about the various relationships in your life. Consider your family, friends, romantic partner, and professional contacts.
2. Write down the names of the most important people to you in each of these categories. Some names may cross over into multiple categories, which is fine.
3. Write why you care about each person next to their name. What do you value about them? How have they affected your life?

Example

Family

1. Mom: She has always been there for me and is my biggest supporter.
2. Dad: He's taught me valuable life lessons and has been a positive role model.
3. Sister: We have a close bond and always have fun together.

Friends

1. Rupa: We've been friends since childhood and always support each other.
2. Nilesh: He's a great listener and always offers me sound advice.
3. Nitin: He's my workout partner and we have a shared interest in fitness.

Go on like this.

Once you've listed all of your relationships and what you know about them, step back and look at the list as a whole. Do you feel like you've been ignoring any relationships? Are there any that you want to give more priority to in your life?

Think about ways you can strengthen the important relationships in your life. This could mean making plans to spend more quality time with people you care about, setting limits to protect your time and energy, or working on your communication skills.

Trust and Respect

Building strong, healthy relationships, both personally and professionally, requires trust and respect. All relationships are built on trust, and healthy relationships are built on respect. Relationships can easily get strained or even break apart without these two essential elements.

Trust is important for building strong relationships because it makes people feel safe, secure, and reliable. When we trust someone, we think they will do what's best for us and tell the truth. Trust also allows us to be open and vulnerable with others, which is important for making deeper emotional connections.

Because it allows us to value and appreciate others for who they are, respect is equally important in building strong relationships. When we respect someone, we recognize their value and the special contributions they make to the relationship. Respect allows us to communicate honestly and with kindness and empathy, which builds trust and connection.

People are more likely to feel valued and supported when there is trust and respect in a relationship. They are also more likely to be honest and open with each other, which makes for better communication, collaboration, and teamwork. Strong relationships built on trust and respect also increase happiness, fulfillment, and success.

When trust and respect are absent from a relationship, on the other hand, people may feel abandoned, disrespected, or even betrayed. This can lead to miscommunication, fights, and, in the end, the end of the relationship.

How to build and maintain trust and respect in different relationships

Here are some tips on how to build and maintain trust and respect in different types of relationships:

Family relationships

To build trust and respect in family relationships, it is important to listen actively, show empathy and understanding, and communicate honestly and openly. Regularly expressing gratitude and showing appreciation can also help to strengthen these relationships. To keep these relationships strong, it is important to talk often, spend quality time together, and be there for each other when things get hard.

Friendships

It is important to be a good listener, keep secrets, and be honest and reliable if you want to build trust and respect in your friendships. Regularly expressing gratitude and showing appreciation can also help to strengthen these relationships.

To keep these relationships going, it is important to talk to each other often, be there and offer support during hard times, and find time to do things or have common experiences together.

Romantic Relationships

To build trust and respect in romantic relationships, it is important to talk openly and honestly, be honest, and show affection and appreciation often. Respecting each other's boundaries and feelings is also important in building trust and respect. To keep these relationships strong, it is important to spend quality time together, be supportive and understanding during hard times, and keep talking openly and honestly.

Professional contacts

To build trust and respect in professional relationships, it is important to be reliable, competent, and respectful in all interactions. Building trust and respect also requires active listening, responsiveness, and adherence to commitments. To keep these relationships going, it is important to talk to them often, help or support them when they need it, and treat them with respect and courtesy at all times.

Exercise: A trust-building exercise to help you develop stronger relationships.

Step 1: Identify Areas of Mistrust

Consider a personal or professional relationship where trust may have been broken. Think about what happened to cause you to lose trust and how that affected your relationship.

Example: Jaya and Santosh have been friends for a long time, but a recent incident in which Santosh shared Jaya's personal information without her permission has caused mistrust in their relationship.

Step 2: Share Your Observations with the Other Person

Set up a time to meet with the other person and discuss the areas of mistrust. Use clear, non-judgmental language. Listen to what they have to say and try to see things from their point of view.

Example: Jaya meets with Santosh and tells him that she feels hurt and betrayed because he shared personal information about her without her permission. She explains how this has resulted in a loss of trust in their friendship.

Step 3: Discuss the Impact of Mistrust on the Relationship

Investigate the effects that a lack of trust has had on the relationship. Discuss how mistrust may have impacted the ability to communicate, collaborate, and build a strong relationship.

Example: Jaya and Santosh talk about how their lack of trust has caused them to communicate less and grow apart. They both agree that building trust is important for a strong and healthy friendship.

Step 4: Identify Actions to Rebuild Trust

Think of ways to re-establish trust in the relationship. Be specific and honest when identifying steps that both sides can take to build trust.

Example: Jaya and Santosh agree that Santosh can take steps to rebuild trust by apologizing for his actions, promising to keep personal information private in the future, and being more careful about how he shares information in their friendship. Jaya can start to rebuild trust by giving Santosh a chance to win back her trust and by working to get back together with him.

Step 5: Follow Through on Actions

Rebuild trust by carrying out the steps outlined in step 4. Regularly check on progress and talk about any problems or setbacks that come up.

Santosh apologizes to Jaya for his actions, promises to keep personal information private, and makes a conscious effort to be more careful about how he shares information in their friendship. Jaya appreciates Santosh's efforts and tries to be more open to building their friendship again.

By following this exercise, individuals can take actionable steps to rebuild trust in personal or professional relationships. It is important to remember that rebuilding trust takes time and effort from both parties. By being patient, committed, and consistent, individuals can build stronger relationships based on trust and respect.

Conflict Resolution

Conflict is a normal and unavoidable part of any relationship, but how people deal with and solve it can have a big effect on how strong the relationship is. Building and maintaining strong relationships, both personally and professionally, requires effective conflict resolution.

Conflict can happen when people have different ideas, values, expectations, or behaviors. If it isn't handled right, it can cause misunderstandings, resentment, and broken relationships. But if handled well, conflict can actually help strengthen relationships by increasing understanding and problem-solving.

Effective conflict resolution involves actively listening to each other, figuring out what the real problems are, expressing feelings and concerns in a constructive way, and working together to find a solution that works for both sides. Empathy, respect and a willingness to make compromises are necessary for this strategy.

By being willing to acknowledge and talk about concerns and differences, conflict resolution can also help to build trust and respect in relationships. It can also improve communication skills and problem-solving abilities and promote a more positive and productive environment.

On the other hand, trying to avoid or ignore conflict can lead to resentment, misunderstandings, and a break in the relationship. Aggressive or confrontational actions can also hurt relationships because they make it harder for people to trust, respect, and understand each other.

How to use conflict resolution strategies

To find a solution that works for both sides of a conflict, you need to understand and use different strategies. Compromise and collaboration are two common strategies.

Finding a solution that works for both sides is part of the compromise, even if it means giving up something. For this strategy to work, both sides must be clear about what they want and what they value most. They should also say where they are flexible and where they aren't. By understanding each other's points of view, they can look for solutions that work for both of them.

For example, imagine a couple trying to decide where to go on vacation. One partner wants to go to the beach, and the other wants to go camping. They could compromise by spending half their vacation at the beach and the other half camping in the mountains.

Collaboration means working together to find a solution that meets the needs and interests of both parties. This strategy requires active listening, empathy, and creativity. Both sides should be willing to express their needs and worries without being judged. They should also be willing to listen to new ideas and try out different options.

For example, a manager and an employee might need to figure out how to meet a hard deadline at work. They could work together to find a solution that works for both of them by coming up with new ideas, using the employee's knowledge, and brainstorming new ideas.

When using either of these strategies, it is important to respect, be flexible, and be willing to compromise. The relationship should be strengthened, and both parties should work towards a win-win solution.

Case study: An example of a successful conflict resolution strategy used to improve a personal or professional relationship.

Nazma and Farah, two cousins, were at odds over where Nazma should have her wedding. Farah wanted a modern wedding in a hotel ballroom, while Nazma wanted a traditional wedding at their family home. They had been fighting for weeks, and the situation was getting worse.

They made the decision to work together to find a solution to the conflict. They sat down together and discussed what was on their minds and how they felt. Nazma discussed how important it was for her to have a traditional wedding that honored their family's customs and heritage. Farah expressed her worries about the logistics and space requirements of holding the wedding at their family's ancestral home.

Together, they came up with ideas that would work for both of them. They came up with a plan to have the wedding ceremony at their ancestral home and the reception in a nearby hotel ballroom that could hold all of the guests. They also agreed to work together to decorate the family home for the wedding.

Nazma and Farah were able to find a solution that met both their needs and preserved their relationship as cousins. They continued to respect each other's points of view, listened carefully, and kept their minds open. Their relationship strengthened as a result, and they learned to respect each other's differences.

A similar conflict resolution strategy could be applied in a professional setting. For instance, a group of colleagues could work together to solve a problem at work. They could find a solution that meets everyone's needs, strengthens their relationships, and helps the team succeed by being open about their ideas, listening to each other, and treating each other with respect.

Boundaries and Self-Care

Setting boundaries involves defining and communicating the l of what is acceptable behavior from others. By setting boundaries, people can communicate their needs, expectations, and values to others, which helps build respect and trust in relationships. When people have clear boundaries, they are less likely to feel taken advantage of or overburdened, which can prevent resentment and conflict.

Self-care is also important for building strong relationships because it allows people to take care of their physical, emotional, and mental health. When people put themselves first, they are better able to deal with the stresses and demands of relationships. Exercise, healthy eating, getting enough sleep, taking breaks, and doing things that make you happy and fulfilled are all examples of self-care practices.

Setting boundaries and taking care of yourself in relationships can also keep people from becoming too dependent on others for their happiness or health.

How to identify personal boundaries and communicate them effectively

Identify your values and needs first. This involves thinking about your personal values and needs, as well as what makes you feel comfortable or uneasy in different situations. Ask yourself questions like, "What are my values?" "What are my needs?" and "What do I want from different relationships?" This will help you define your boundaries.

Second, be aware of when your boundaries are being pushed. Pay attention to situations where you feel uncomfortable or disrespected. These are frequent signs that your boundaries are being crossed. For example, if a friend consistently cancels plans at the last minute or a colleague makes inappropriate comments, these are signs that your boundaries may have been crossed.

Third, state your boundaries in a clear and firm manner. Once you've determined your boundaries, it is important to tell other people about them in a clear and assertive way. Use 'I' statements to express your feelings and needs, and avoid blaming or accusing others. For instance, "When you make remarks about how I look, it makes me feel bad. Please stop saying those things." Be clear about the behaviors you want to change.

Fourth, consistently enforce your boundaries. It is important to stick to your boundaries and be consistent with how you enforce them. This could mean saying no to requests that go against your boundaries or separating yourself from people who repeatedly ignore them.

Be willing to compromise and negotiate. While it is important to set and maintain your boundaries, it is also important to be open to negotiation and compromise in certain situations. This may involve finding a middle ground that respects both your needs and the needs of others. For example, if you don't want to talk about a certain subject, you could suggest a different subject that you'd rather talk about.

Personal story: How setting personal boundaries improved relationships

I am David, and I have been a professional DJ for the past 8 years. I really enjoy my job, but it can be hard work at times. I used to think that I had to be available 24/7 for my clients and fans, but that started to hurt my mental health and my relationships.

I can recall a time when I had to cancel plans with my family because I got a last-minute gig. I felt bad, but I didn't want to let my fans down or miss out on the chance. After that, I started to dislike my job, and it started to show in how well I did it. I then realized I needed to establish personal boundaries. I began by figuring out what was most important to me. For me, it was my family and my mental health. I told my clients that, unless it was an emergency, I wouldn't be available for last-minute gigs.

At first, it was hard to say 'no' to potential gigs, but I soon realized that my fans and clients respected my boundaries. They even started giving me more notice when they needed me to perform, which helped me make better plans and keep from getting too tired. I also started prioritizing self-care by taking time off to spend time with my family, meditating, and working out regularly. This not only helped me improve my mental and physical health, but it also gave me more energy and creativity to put into my performances.

My relationships have significantly improved since then. My family and friends are happier because they know I won't ignore them for work, and my clients and fans respect my boundaries and value my performances even more. Setting personal boundaries has been a game-changer for me overall. It has helped me improve my mental health, prioritize my relationships, and become a better DJ.

Building Relationships in the Workplace

One of the primary benefits of building relationships in the workplace is networking. Networking involves establishing connections with people who can offer us career advice, job opportunities, or other forms of professional support. By building relationships with coworkers, we can expand our professional network and gain access to new opportunities that can help us achieve our career goals. Networking can also help us stay updated on industry trends and changes, which is crucial for staying relevant and competitive in today's job market.

Another important aspect of building relationships in the workplace is collaboration. Collaboration involves working together with coworkers to achieve a common goal. When we build strong relationships with our colleagues, we are more likely to communicate effectively, share ideas, and work well together. This can lead to better outcomes, increased productivity, and innovation. Collaborating with coworkers can also help us build our skills and knowledge, as we learn from others who may have different expertise or perspectives.

Mentorship is another important benefit of building relationships in the workplace. Mentors are individuals who provide us with guidance, advice, and support as we navigate our careers. By building relationships with senior colleagues, we can gain access to valuable mentorship opportunities. Mentors can provide us with insight into the industry, help us develop our skills, and provide us with the necessary support to overcome challenges and achieve our goals.

Creating a positive work environment is also crucial for building strong relationships in the workplace. When we have positive relationships with our coworkers, we are more likely to enjoy our work and feel valued by our colleagues. This can increase job satisfaction, reduce stress, and improve overall well-being. In turn, this can lead to increased productivity and better outcomes in our work.

Effective Communication, Conflict Resolution, and Constructive Feedback in the Workplace

Effective communication is essential for building strong relationships in the workplace. It involves expressing ourselves clearly and listening actively to others. When we communicate effectively, we can prevent misunderstandings, build trust, and collaborate more effectively with our colleagues.

To use effective communication in a professional setting, it is important to be clear and concise in our messages. This means using simple and direct language, avoiding jargon, and being mindful of our tone and body language. It is also important to actively listen to our colleagues, seeking to understand their perspective and asking clarifying questions when necessary.

Example of Effective Communication: An employee is presenting a project proposal to their supervisor. To communicate effectively, the employee should:

- Use clear and concise language to explain the project proposal
- Avoid jargon or technical terms that the supervisor may not understand
- Use visual aids, such as graphs or charts, to help illustrate key points
- Ask clarifying questions to ensure the supervisor understands the proposal
- Listen actively to the supervisor's feedback and adjust the proposal as necessary

When people have different opinions, values, or expectations at work, it can lead to conflict and stress. It is important to handle conflicts by being open-minded and willing to listen to the other person's point of view. First, you should identify the problem and describe it without blaming anyone. Then, you should work together to find a solution that works for everyone by coming up with ideas and compromising.

Example of Conflict Resolution: Two colleagues have different opinions about how to approach a project. To resolve the conflict, they should:

- Identify the specific issue causing the conflict, such as the approach to the project
- Express their viewpoints objectively and avoid personal attacks or blame
- Listen actively to each other's perspectives and seek to understand their point of view
- Brainstorm ideas for a solution that satisfies both parties
- Evaluate each idea and choose a mutually agreeable solution

It is also important to be open to feedback and to provide constructive feedback in a professional and respectful manner. Feedback can help us improve our communication skills and build stronger relationships with our colleagues. When providing feedback, it is important to focus on specific behaviors or actions, rather than personal traits or characteristics.

Example of Constructive Feedback: An employee is giving feedback to a colleague on their presentation skills. To provide constructive feedback, the employee should:

- Focus on specific behaviors or actions, such as eye contact or vocal inflection
- Provide examples of both positive and negative aspects of the presentation
- Offer suggestions for improvement, such as practicing in front of a mirror or taking a public speaking course
- Be respectful and professional in their delivery of the feedback
- Listen actively to the colleague's response and address any questions or concerns they may have

Case Study: Building Trust and Respect through Collaborative Problem-Solving

Vikram is a project manager at a manufacturing company. He is responsible for ensuring that production goals are met within a tight timeline. However, he is facing some challenges with one of his team members, Rohit, who is a skilled technician. Rohit is often late to meetings and misses deadlines, which is causing delays in production. Vikram is frustrated with Rohit's performance and is unsure how to address the issue without damaging their professional relationship.

To improve his relationship with Rohit, Vikram decides to take a collaborative approach to problem-solving. He sets up a meeting with Rohit to discuss the challenges they are facing in meeting production goals. During the meeting, Vikram starts by acknowledging Rohit's expertise and the value he brings to the team. He then shares his concerns about the delays and asks Rohit for his input on how they can work together to address the issue.

Rohit opens up about some personal challenges he is facing, which have been affecting his performance. Vikram listens patiently and offers support, suggesting some resources that could help Rohit address his personal issues. Together, they come up with a plan to improve communication and set clear expectations for deadlines and responsibilities.

As a result of their collaborative problem-solving approach, Vikram and Rohit develop a stronger professional relationship based on trust and respect. They are able to work together more effectively, and production goals are met within the desired timeline.

This case study highlights the importance of taking a collaborative approach to problem-solving to build trust and respect in professional relationships. By acknowledging the expertise and value of team members and working together to find solutions, it is possible to improve professional relationships and achieve shared goals.

Personal Stories and Case Studies

There are many individuals who have built strong relationships and achieved personal and professional success. Here are a few examples:

1. Indra Nooyi: She is the former CEO of PepsiCo and is known for her strong relationships with her employees. She focused on creating a supportive and inclusive work environment, and this helped her build a strong team that was dedicated to the company's success.
2. Dr. Vivek Murthy: He is a physician and public health advocate who served as the 19th Surgeon General of the United States. He has emphasized the importance of building relationships and addressing loneliness as a public health issue. He also encourages people to cultivate strong relationships with others as a way to improve their overall well-being.

3. Dr. Geetha Manjunath: She is the CEO and founder of Niramai, a startup that uses AI-powered technology for early breast cancer detection. She has built strong relationships with her team and investors, and her company has won numerous awards and recognition for its innovative approach to healthcare.

These individuals demonstrate the importance of building strong relationships in achieving personal and professional success, whether it be through creating a supportive work environment, collaborating with partners and grantees, building relationships with local communities, or fostering strong relationships with team members and investors.

Improved well-being and career success

When we have good relationships in our lives, it can improve our mental and emotional well-being. The same is true in the workplace. Building strong relationships with coworkers can help us be more successful in our careers. Having supportive people in our lives can reduce stress, anxiety, and depression, and help us cope with difficult situations. It also gives us a sense of belonging and connectedness, which can reduce feelings of loneliness and increase our self-esteem and confidence.

When we have good relationships with our colleagues, it can increase our job satisfaction and lead to higher productivity, better performance, and job retention. Strong relationships with our managers and supervisors can help us advance in our careers by opening up opportunities for professional development, promotions, and pay raises. Building strong relationships with coworkers can also provide us with networking opportunities and help us expand our professional connections.

The Author's Journey to Success Through Relationship Building

My journey began when I started working as a trainer. I was very passionate about assisting people in realizing their potential and achieving their goals at the time. But I quickly realized that this wasn't enough. To be successful in this field, I needed to develop relationships with my clients and colleagues.

I started going to networking events and conferences to meet people who shared my interests. I also made it a point to keep in touch with my clients and follow up with them on a regular basis. My clients soon started referring their friends and family to me as a result of this, which helped me gain trust and credibility.

I also made it a point to keep a good attitude and treat everyone with respect, regardless of their position or status. This helped me get along well with everyone, which led to opportunities for my career to grow.

As I continued to build and maintain relationships, I realized that it wasn't just about doing well in my job. It was also about enhancing my general health. I found that having a supportive network of friends and colleagues helped me stay motivated and inspired, even during challenging times.

Building and keeping relationships has been very important for me to achieve my goals and do well in my career. It has also helped me improve my overall health and live a fuller life. I encourage you to make an effort to build and maintain relationships, as it can have a positive impact on all aspects of your life.

Exercises for you

- ❖ Attend a networking event and practice introducing yourself and building connections.
- ❖ Schedule time to nurture important relationships with friends and family members.
- ❖ Identify a difficult relationship and practice setting boundaries and communicating effectively.

Share your Thoughts

As we come to the end of this chapter, I want to ask you something. Based on the knowledge you have gained, do you now feel more equipped to build and maintain meaningful relationships in your life?

Speaking of meaningful relationships, let me share a funny story that happened with my own friends. One day, a childhood friend of mine, Rumi decided to surprise our common childhood friend Juhi by showing up unannounced at her doorstep. But as soon as Juhi opened the door, Rumi tripped and fell into her, sending them both sprawling onto the floor. They both lay there laughing, and Juhi exclaimed, "Well, I guess this is the closest we have been in years!" This hilarious moment brought them even closer and made them appreciate their friendship even more.

If you have also had some funny or heartwarming moments with your friends or loved ones that helped improve relationships, we would love to hear about them. Additionally, I encourage you to leave a review of this chapter and share your own experiences with cultivating relationships.

Writing a review is easy. Simply visit this book's page on Amazon, and share your thoughts.

And finally, as an incentive for you to leave a review, if you inform our office at sworld.mind@gmail.com about your review, we will send over the 'Author's

Draft' of this chapter. This version contains additional insights, stories, and research that didn't make it into this final published version. We hope this will further enrich your understanding of how to cultivate meaningful relationships in your life.

Conclusion

In this chapter, we explored the importance of cultivating meaningful relationships in our personal and professional lives. We discussed the different types of relationships, the significance of trust, respect, conflict resolution, boundaries, and self-care. We also looked at building positive relationships in the workplace and shared personal stories and case studies.

The key takeaways from this chapter are that building positive relationships requires effort, patience, and empathy. We must be authentic, genuine, and willing to compromise, show empathy, and accept others for who they are. Trust, and respect are essential building blocks for any successful relationship. Conflict resolution, boundaries, and self-care are also critical elements in maintaining healthy relationships.

Having meaningful relationships in our lives can have a significant impact on our mental and emotional health, career success, and overall happiness. When we have healthy relationships, we feel valued, loved, and appreciated. These positive feelings can improve our mood, reduce stress, and increase our overall life satisfaction.

Wrap up

Congratulations on completing this chapter on cultivating meaningful relationships! As you have learned, building positive relationships is crucial for personal and professional growth. I encourage you to take the lessons you have learned in this chapter and apply them to your life.

Building positive relationships is an essential part of the journey. It requires effort, patience, and empathy, but the rewards are immeasurable. By investing in your relationships, you create a support system that can help you through any challenge.

Don't be afraid to show your true self, be genuine, and willing to compromise. Remember that trust and respect are the foundation of any successful relationship. Practice conflict resolution, set boundaries, and take care of yourself. When you do, you'll notice a positive impact on both your personal and professional life.

By building strong relationships, you will gain a sense of belonging and connectedness that can boost your mental and emotional well-being. And when you establish yourself as a valuable team member through positive relationships at work, you increase your chances of career success. You will have opportunities for professional development, promotions, and networking that can take your career to new heights.

So, don't wait any longer. Start investing in your relationships today and watch as they enhance your life in ways you never imagined. Remember, building positive relationships is not just a nice-to-have, it is an essential part of personal development. Let's do this together!

"Trust is the glue of life. It is the most essential ingredient in effective communication. It is the foundational principle that holds all relationships."

– Stephen Covey

❑

CHAPTER 10

Breaking Free from Fear

"You can conquer almost any fear if you will only make up your mind to do so. For remember, fear doesn't exist anywhere except in the mind."

– Dale Carnegie

Introduction

In the last chapter, we discussed the importance of building strong relationships and the various factors that contribute to healthy relationships. Now, we move on to a topic that can hinder our ability to build relationships and achieve our goals - fear.

Have you ever felt held back by fear? Has fear ever stopped you from pursuing your dreams or taking action towards your goals? Fear is a natural emotion, but it can also be debilitating if we allow it to control us.

We will begin by exploring the nature of fear and its impact on our lives. We will also discuss different strategies for overcoming fear, including techniques for managing anxiety, reframing negative thoughts, and facing our fears head-on. Additionally, we will explore the importance of taking action, even when we are afraid, and how it can help us build confidence and achieve our goals.

We will then discuss how to apply these strategies in the workplace and share personal stories and case studies to help illustrate their effectiveness. By the end of this chapter, you will have the tools and knowledge to overcome your fears and take action towards achieving your personal and professional goals. So let's dive in and start overcoming our fears together!

How fear can hold individuals back from achieving their potential

Fear is a powerful emotion that can have a significant impact on our lives. It is an instinctive response to a perceived threat, whether real or imagined. While fear can be helpful in certain situations, such as alerting us to danger, it can also hold us back from achieving our full potential.

One of the most common fears that people experience is the fear of failure. This fear can be paralyzing, preventing individuals from taking risks and pursuing their goals. They may be afraid of making mistakes or not living up to their own expectations, which can lead to feelings of inadequacy and low self-esteem. As a result, they may avoid new challenges and opportunities, limiting their growth and potential.

Another common fear is the fear of rejection or criticism. People may be hesitant to put themselves out there or share their ideas for fear of being judged or rejected. They may worry about what others will think of them, which can hold them back from expressing themselves authentically and pursuing their passions.

And then there is the fear of the unknown. This fear can arise when we are faced with new situations or challenges that we have never encountered before. We may be afraid of the risks involved or uncertain about the outcome, which can lead to anxiety and avoidance.

Whatever the source of our fears, it is important to recognize that they can have a significant impact on our lives. When we allow fear to control us, we miss out on opportunities for growth and development. We may remain stuck in our comfort zones, unable to take the necessary steps to achieve our goals and aspirations.

Understanding Fear

Fear is an emotion that we all experience in our lives, and it can hold us back from reaching our full potential. One of the most common fears is the fear of failure, which can make us hesitant to take risks and pursue our goals. When we let this fear control us, we may miss out on opportunities for growth and development, and it can also lead to feelings of inadequacy and low self-esteem.

Another common fear that can hold us back is the fear of rejection. This fear can arise in different situations, whether it is in social or professional settings. It can be difficult to overcome because it's often tied to our need for social acceptance and belonging. We may fear being judged or criticized by others or excluded from a group. However, it is important to remember that rejection is a natural part of life and it is not a reflection of our worth.

The fear of the unknown is another type of fear that can hold us back. It can arise when we encounter new situations or challenges that we have never experienced before. We may be uncertain about the outcome or afraid of the risks involved. This fear can lead to anxiety and avoidance, preventing us from taking necessary steps towards our goals and aspirations.

Fear can manifest in different ways for different people. Some may experience fear as a feeling of panic or dread, while others may feel uneasy or uncomfortable. Fear can also vary in intensity, ranging from mild to severe. The source of our fears can be influenced by past experiences, upbringing, and cultural conditioning.

It is important to recognize that fear is a normal part of the human experience. However, when we allow fear to control us, we miss out on opportunities for growth and development. We may remain stuck in our comfort zones, unable to take the necessary steps to achieve our goals and aspirations. By acknowledging our fears and taking steps to overcome them, we can break free from their hold and reach our full potential.

How fear can manifest in different ways and hold individuals back

Procrastination is a common way that fear shows itself. People who are afraid of something might put off doing important tasks or projects because they are afraid of failing or not knowing what to do. For example, a student who is worried about getting a bad grade on an assignment may put it off and wait until the last minute to start it. This can hurt their performance in the long run.

Self-doubt is another way that fear can manifest itself. Fear can give people a sense of self-doubt, which can make them question their skills, worth, or even who they are. When it comes to personal development, this can cause negative self-talk and a lack of confidence. For example, someone who thinks they aren't creative enough might not try to be creative and might not come up with new ideas, which can limit their growth and success.

Fear can make people avoid things or situations they think are dangerous or uncomfortable. Preventing them from trying new things or taking risks, can limit their personal growth and development. For example, someone who is afraid of public speaking might avoid speaking in front of others and miss out on chances to improve their communication skills and confidence.

Exercise: A self-reflection exercise to help you identify your fears and how they may be impacting your life

Step 1

Set aside some time in a quiet, distraction-free place where you can concentrate on your thoughts. Example: Set aside an hour on your calendar to think about your goals and fears in a quiet place, like a library or a peaceful park, without any distractions.

Step 2

Make a list of your goals and aspirations, both big and small. Example: Create a list of your goals and aspirations, such as finishing a project at work, learning a new skill, traveling to a new country, or improving your health and fitness.

Step 3

For each goal or dream, ask yourself, "What worries or fears do I have about achieving this goal?" Write down any fears you have, no matter how big or small. Example: If you want to finish a project at work, you might worry that you don't have the skills or knowledge to finish it on time or that you might make a mistake that will hurt your performance.

Step 4

Next, look at each fear on your list and ask yourself, "How does this fear affect my life?" Does it stop me from working toward my goals? Does it lead to procrastination, avoidance, negative self-talk, or self-sabotage? Example: You might realize that your fear of making a mistake is causing you to put off working on the project because you keep second-guessing your work and never feel satisfied with it. This fear is keeping you from taking steps toward your goal and is leading to negative self-talk.

Step 5

Finally, ask yourself, "What can I do to overcome these fears and take action toward my goals?" Write down any strategies or solutions that come to mind, such as asking for help from others, practicing self-compassion, or breaking the goal into smaller, more manageable steps. Example: To overcome the fear of making a mistake, you could seek feedback from a trusted colleague or mentor, break the project into smaller tasks, and celebrate each completed task as a win. Practicing self-compassion and acknowledging that mistakes are a natural part of the learning process can also help overcome this fear.

The Impact of Fear

Fear can get in the way of personal growth and development in many ways, but one of the main ways is by making people less willing to take risks. When people are afraid of failing or being rejected, they may not take advantage of challenging opportunities or try new things. This can keep them from learning new skills and achieving their goals.

Fear can also hold people back by making them doubt themselves and talk negatively about themselves. When individuals are afraid of failure, they may question their abilities and worthiness, leading to a lack of confidence and motivation. This can cause people to give up on their goals or settle for less than they are capable of.

Fear can also make people focus only on short-term goals instead of long-term ones. People may be so focused on avoiding potential threats or challenges that they fail to consider the bigger picture and the potential benefits of taking risks and pursuing long-term goals. This can result in missed opportunities for professional and personal development and lower one's chances of success.

Fear can impact mental health and well-being

Fear can have a big effect on both short-term and long-term mental health and well-being. In the short term, fear can set off the body's stress response, which can cause symptoms like a faster heartbeat, more sweating, and tense muscles. This can help in some situations, like when we need to react quickly to a perceived threat. But fear and stress that last for a long time can hurt your mental and physical health.

For example, fear of social situations or rejection can lead to social anxiety disorder, which can cause people to avoid social situations and become isolated. Feelings of loneliness, depression, and low self-esteem may result from this. Fear of failing can cause perfectionism and excessive self-criticism, which can lead to anxiety and depression.

Aside from the physical effects of fear, long-term fear, and stress can also weaken the immune system, making people more susceptible to disease and illness. Fear can also make it hard to sleep, which can make mood disorders like depression worse.

Fear can also affect mental health and well-being by making it harder to feel positive emotions and do things that make you happy. For example, someone who is afraid of heights might not be able to enjoy outdoor activities like hiking or rock climbing, which can make them feel disappointed and frustrated. People may not pursue hobbies or interests they enjoy out of fear of failing, which can make them feel less fulfilled and happy in life.

Personal story: Urmi, shares how She overcame her fear

I am Urmi, a 26-year-old chartered accountant, and mother of two. Fear had a tight hold on me, and it prevented me from achieving both personal and professional success. But because I was determined and brave, I was able to get over my fear and do more than I ever thought I could.

My fear was sparked when I was offered the chance to lead a project at work. It was a big responsibility, and I didn't feel ready for it. I was afraid of failing and letting my clients and colleagues down. I was hesitant to take on the project because I didn't want to disappoint anyone.

But deep down, I knew I had to get over my fear if I wanted to advance in my career. So, I mustered the courage to face the challenge. I spent more time studying and getting ready for the project, and I also asked my colleagues for help and advice.

As I started working on the project, I discovered that I was actually enjoying it. I was learning new things and discovering skills I didn't know I had. I was also becoming more confident in my abilities.

The project was a resounding success, and both my colleagues and clients praised me highly. It was a turning point for me, and I realized that I had let my fear hold me back for far too long.

I was motivated to face my own fears after overcoming my fears at work. Public speaking was one of my biggest fears, so I had always tried to avoid it. But I decided to push myself and signed up for a public speaking class.

At first, it was terrifying to stand up in front of a group of strangers and speak. But with practice and determination, I started to feel more comfortable and confident. I was able to give speeches without stumbling over my words, and I even started to enjoy it.

These experiences taught me that fear is not something to be avoided or feared. Fear can be a sign of development and progress. By facing my fears head-on and taking calculated risks, I was able to achieve personal and professional growth I never thought possible.

I am proud of what I have done and excited about what the future holds. I know that there will be more challenges and opportunities for growth in the future, but I am no longer afraid to take them on.

Strategies for Overcoming Fear

Getting over your fears is a hard but necessary step on the path to personal growth and development. There are many ways for people to get over their fears and build resilience. One good way to deal with fear is to face it head-on. This entails facing the thing or situation that makes you scared and becoming less afraid of it over time. This method can help people build confidence and feel more in control of their fears.

Another method for getting over fear is to change the way you think about things. Fear is often based on negative assumptions and beliefs that may not be true. People can feel less anxious and more confident if they question these beliefs and replace them with ones that are more positive and realistic. This may require asking if one's fears are true and looking for proof to back up more positive beliefs. For example, someone who is afraid of public speaking may change their thoughts from "I am terrible at speaking in public" to "I am nervous, but I am well prepared and have practiced a lot."

Getting assistance from other people can also help you get over your fears. Talking to a trusted friend or family member, joining a support group, or working with a mental health professional may be necessary. Assistance from others can provide encouragement, constructive feedback, and practical advice for conquering fear and anxiety. This can be very helpful for people who are dealing with very strong or crippling fears.

How to create an action plan to overcome fear

Making an action plan to get over fear can help break down a big, scary task into smaller, more manageable steps. Finding the specific fear or phobia that is causing anxiety is the first step in making an action plan. This could mean taking some time to think about what led to the fear in the first place, such as a bad experience or negative thoughts about oneself.

Once the fear has been identified, the next step is to break it down into smaller steps. This can be done by making a list of things or situations that people are afraid of, with the least scary thing at the bottom and the scariest thing at the top. For example, someone who is afraid of flying might start by looking at pictures of planes, then watch videos of take-off and landing, and finally go on a short flight.

After breaking the fear into smaller parts, the next step is to make sure that each part of the plan has goals that can be achieved. This means setting specific goals for each step of the plan and keeping track of how close you are to achieving those goals. For example, a goal for someone who is afraid of heights could be to climb a flight of stairs without feeling scared in the next week.

Case study: Overcoming Fear - Rani's Journey to Building Confidence as a Nurse

Fear can be a strong emotion that can affect our ability to perform well at work. In this case study, we follow Rani's journey to overcome her fear of caring for accident victims as a nurse. Rani found herself feeling overwhelmed and uncertain in emergency situations, despite her extensive training and experience. Rani's story is a testament to the strength of facing fear head-on and the positive effects it can have both personally and professionally.

Rani was constantly worried about helping accident victims because she was afraid of hurting them. Even though she had been trained and worked as a nurse for years, she felt overwhelmed and unsure of what to do in emergency situations. She felt terrible about not being able to give her patients the best care possible.

Rani knew that if she wanted to be the best nurse she could be, she would have to get over her fear. She started by identifying her fear and acknowledging how it affected her work. She was constantly questioning her abilities and wondering if she had what it took to handle emergency situations.

But Rani was determined to get over her fear. She started to fight her negative thoughts by reminding herself of her training and the skills she had picked up over the years. She also worked on changing her perspective and concentrating on the positive aspects of helping others in need.

Rani did not find it easy to gain confidence. She went to training programs and workshops to learn more about emergency care and improve her skills. With each step forward, she felt a renewed sense of purpose and commitment to her patients.

Rani's exposure therapy was probably the hardest part of her journey. She volunteered to work in the hospital's emergency room even though she knew she would have to deal with things that scared her. She watched her colleagues and learned from their experiences, gradually gaining the experience and confidence to handle emergency situations on her own.

Rani turned to her colleagues and seniors for help throughout it all. Their advice and encouragement gave her the strength and drive to keep going, even when things seemed too hard. She also joined a group of nurses who had gotten over their own work-related fears. Sharing her experiences with people who understood what she was going through was an important part of her healing process.

Rani's journey was not easy, but it was rewarding. She rewarded herself for her progress by taking some time to think about what she had done well and the positive effects she was having on her patients. She felt a lot of happiness and pride when she shared her accomplishments with her friends and family.

Rani is now a better nurse and an important part of her community. She knows she still has a lot to learn and that there will be new challenges ahead, but she is confident in her abilities to handle whatever comes her way. By taking steps to deal with her fear, Rani has given herself new personal and professional opportunities. She is a great example of how powerful it is to be determined and keep going even when you are scared.

Taking Action

Fear often causes people to avoid situations or tasks that make them anxious or uncomfortable. However, this avoidance can reinforce the fear and make it stronger, leading to a cycle of anxiety and avoidance. By taking action and facing one's fears, one can break this cycle and start to feel more in control.

Taking action to confront your fears can boost your self-confidence and self-esteem. By facing your fears, you may discover that you are capable of more than you thought, which can make you feel good about yourself and inspire you to take on more challenges.

Taking action can also help you feel a sense of power and achievement, which can give you a greater sense of control over your fears. As a result, you may find that you are able to do things that you previously avoided due to fear or anxiety, leading to an improved quality of life.

Identifying fears and action plan to overcome them

Step 1: Write Down Your Fears

Write down all the fears that come to your mind. Don't hold back and be honest with yourself. This list can include anything from fear of failure to fear of rejection or fear of the unknown.

Step 2: Analyze Each Fear

Next, take each fear and analyze it. Ask yourself: Why am I afraid of this? Is this fear based on past experiences or future concerns? Is this fear rational or irrational? Because of this fear, what am I losing out? What could I have gained if I didn't have this fear? Write down your answers next to each fear.

Step 3: Prioritize

Prioritize them in order of importance. Which fear is causing you the most distress or holding you back the most? Start with that fear and work your way down the list.

Step 4: Create an Action Plan

Based on your analysis of each fear, set a specific, measurable, and achievable goal. Break the goal down into smaller steps, and write down a timeline for the completion of each. Write down the actions you need to take to achieve each goal.

Step 5: Take Action

Start with the first item on your priority list and take the actions you have planned. Remember, taking action can be daunting, but it is the only way to move past your fears and achieve your goals.

Step 6: Seek Support

Seek support from friends, family, or a professional therapist. Sometimes it is helpful to have someone to talk to who can offer guidance and support as you work through your fears.

Repeat this exercise as many times as needed to overcome all of your fears and unlock your full potential.

Some examples of action plans to overcome fears

Overcoming the fear of flying:

1. Educate yourself: Learn about the safety measures and statistics of air travel to help ease your fears.
2. Use relaxation techniques: Practice deep breathing, visualization, or meditation to calm your nerves before and during the flight.
3. Distract yourself: Bring a book, music, or other distractions to help take your mind off of your fears.
4. Seek professional help: Consider working with a therapist or counselor who specializes in anxiety or phobias.

Overcoming the fear of darkness:

1. Identify the fear: Acknowledge that you have a fear of darkness and try to understand why it makes you anxious.
2. Challenge negative thoughts: Recognize that the darkness itself is not harmful and that your fear may be based on irrational or exaggerated thoughts. Challenge negative thoughts by reminding yourself that you are safe and there is nothing to fear.

3. Gradual exposure: Start by exposing yourself to small amounts of darkness, such as dimming the lights in a room or closing your eyes in a dark room. Gradually increase your exposure to darkness by spending time in a dark room for a few minutes at a time, then gradually increasing the time spent in darkness.
4. Use relaxation techniques: Practice deep breathing, visualization, or meditation to calm your nerves before and during exposure to darkness.
5. Create a positive association: Associate darkness with positive experiences, such as a refreshing warm bath or a cozy night in with a good book.
6. Seek professional help: If your fear of darkness is severe or interfering with your daily life, consider seeking help from a therapist or counselor who specializes in anxiety or phobias.

Overcoming Fear in the Workplace

People's fears can sometimes keep them from achieving their full potential at work. It can stop people from taking risks, grabbing growth opportunities, and making important decisions. Fear can have a big effect on a person's career success and growth at work, as it can limit their chances of moving up and getting better at their job.

Fear of failure is one of the most common ways that fear hurts career success. This fear can keep people from taking on new opportunities and challenges that could help them advance in their careers. For example, a person may not take on new responsibilities or projects out of fear of failing, which can hurt their chances of getting ahead in their career and being successful.

Fear can also make it hard for people to talk to each other while at work. If someone is afraid to speak up or share their ideas, they might miss out on chances to help with important conversations or projects. This can make it hard for them to get along well with their colleagues and leaders, which can hurt their chances of getting ahead and growing in the company.

Fear can also make people doubt their own skills, which can stop them from pursuing their career goals and taking risks. For example, if someone is afraid of being turned down, they might not apply for a job or promotion they want. This can cause people to miss out on opportunities to move up in their careers and limit their ability to grow in their field.

How to overcome fear and take action in a professional setting

People can get over their fear of failing or doubt in their abilities by changing the way they think about things. Instead of thinking about what could go wrong, they can reframe their thoughts to think about what could go right and what they could learn. For example, if someone is hesitant to start a new project, they can change the way they think about it by thinking about the new skills and experiences they will gain from it.

One may also overcome their phobias by taking small-small actions. Instead of trying to do everything at once, they can break their goals down into smaller tasks that are easier to handle. For example, if someone is afraid to speak up in meetings, they can start by speaking up in smaller group discussions or sending an email to their team with their ideas.

You can also get over your fears and act by asking for help from fellow employees or a mentor. Having someone to talk to and get feedback from can be encouraging and help you move forward. For example, if someone is afraid to apply for a job or promotion because they think they won't get it, they can get help from a mentor who can give them advice and help them get ready for the application process.

Case study: A successful strategy used to overcome fear and achieve success.

The story of Amy Cuddy, a social psychologist, and professor at Harvard Business School.

In her early academic career, Cuddy suffered a traumatic brain injury that left her struggling with cognitive and speech impairments. She feared that she would never be able to complete her graduate studies and become a successful academic.

To overcome her fear, Cuddy adopted a strategy of 'fake it till you become it'. She researched the psychological effects of body language and began experimenting with power poses, such as standing with her feet shoulder-width apart and her hands on her hips. Through this practice, she discovered that adopting a confident posture could actually increase her feelings of confidence and competence.

Cuddy then went on to conduct a study on power posing, which demonstrated that adopting high-power poses for just two minutes could increase levels of testosterone (the hormone associated with dominance) and decrease levels of cortisol (the hormone associated with stress).

Cuddy's strategy of 'fake it till you become it' has not only helped her overcome her fear and achieve professional success but has also led to important scientific discoveries and helped countless individuals improve their own confidence and performance.

Personal Stories and Case Studies

Examples of individuals who have overcome fear and achieved personal and professional success.

1. Simone Biles: Simone Biles is a world-famous gymnast who has won a lot of medals at the Olympics and World Championships. She got over her fear of falling and getting hurt so she could become one of the best gymnasts ever. Even though she has been criticized and watched closely, she continues to encourage young people to follow their dreams and get over their fears.
2. Jay-Z: Born Shawn Corey Carter, Jay-Z is a rapper, songwriter, record producer, and business owner. He has won several Grammy Awards and sold more than 100 million records around the world. He has also built a successful business empire that includes the music streaming service Tidal, the clothing line Rocawear, and the sports agency Roc Nation Sports. Even though he grew up in poverty, he got over his fear of failing and followed his dreams, which led to him becoming one of the richest and most influential people in the entertainment industry.
3. Halle Berry: Halle Berry has been in a lot of movies and TV shows and has won awards for her work. She got over her fear of being turned down and followed her dream of being an actress. For her role in 'Monster's Ball', she won the Academy Award for Best Actress. She has also been a vocal advocate for women's rights and mental health awareness.

How taking action can lead to improved well-being and career success

Taking action despite our fears is a powerful way to build confidence in ourselves. By facing our fears and pushing ourselves outside of our comfort zones, we discover that we are capable of overcoming obstacles and achieving our goals. This builds a sense of self-efficacy and resilience, which can improve our overall well-being and happiness. When we take action despite our fears, we realize that our fears are not insurmountable barriers, but rather temporary obstacles that we can overcome with effort and perseverance.

Moreover, taking action can also lead to career success. When we take initiative and pursue our goals, we demonstrate to our employers and colleagues that we are driven, motivated, and capable of achieving great things. This can lead to greater recognition, promotions, higher salaries, and more job satisfaction. People who take action and overcome their fears are often seen as leaders and role models in the workplace. By pushing themselves outside of their comfort zones and taking risks, they inspire others to do the same and contribute to a positive, high-performing work culture.

However, it's important to note that taking action does not always guarantee success or positive outcomes. Sometimes our efforts may not lead to the results we hoped for, and we may face setbacks and failures along the way. It's important to approach these challenges with a growth mindset, viewing them as opportunities for learning and growth rather than as signs of failure. By reflecting on our experiences and learning from our mistakes, we can become more resilient, adaptable, and better equipped to face future challenges.

From the Author's Desk: My Journey to Becoming a Motivational Speaker by Conquering My Fears

Are you letting fear stop you from getting what you want? Because I was a shy and quiet child, I know how fear can make you miss out on opportunities. I was afraid that people would judge or reject my ideas, so I kept quiet and avoided getting anyone's attention.

As I was growing up, I realized I couldn't live my life this way any longer. I had to face my fears and hesitations head-on if I wanted to make a difference in the world. So, I took small steps to get over my hesitancy of speaking in front of people. I started by giving speeches to my closest friends and worked my way up to larger groups over time.

Yes, I had setbacks and failed attempts along the way, but I never gave up. Through years of practice, dedication, and self-reflection, I finally overcame my hesitancy of public speaking. Not only that, but I also found that I was naturally good at using my words to motivate and inspire other people.

Now that I have been a successful motivational speaker for over 3 and a half decades, I have helped a lot of people get over their fears and achieve their goals. And when I think back on my journey, I am proud of how far I have come and how I have helped other people.

Remember that you can also overcome your fears and achieve your goals. Stop letting fear hold you back. Take steps towards your goals, keep going even when things don't go as planned, and your life will change.

Exercises for you

- Identify a fear that is holding you back from achieving a goal and create a plan to overcome it.
- Practice taking small, incremental actions towards a goal to build confidence and momentum.
- Practice self-compassion and forgiveness when faced with setbacks or failures.

Share your Thoughts

Congratulations on finishing this chapter on breaking free from fear. I hope it has given you the tools to empower yourself to face your fears head-on. Do you feel more empowered to conquer your fears after reading this chapter? I truly hope so.

Let me share this story of Jim conquering his fear of the unknown. Jim walks into a library, approaches the librarian, and asks for books about paranoia. The librarian whispers, "They are right behind you!"

Jim felt a chill run down his spine as he heard the librarian's words. He slowly turned around, expecting to see someone or something lurking behind him. To his surprise, there was no one there. Jim's heart raced as he realized the librarian was just joking. He laughed nervously, feeling foolish for letting his paranoia get the best of him. In that moment, Jim made a decision to confront his fear and not let it control him. He checked out a book on managing anxiety and left the library, determined to overcome his fear of the unknown.

Do you have a story to tell? I encourage you to leave a review or share your stories or own experiences with facing your fears. It might inspire someone else to take that first step towards overcoming their fears.

To share your story, give a feedback, or write a review, simply go to this book's page on Amazon and find the section for leaving a review. Your insights and feedback are invaluable to me, and they can also help other readers who are struggling with their own fears.

In order to thank you for taking the time to leave a review, I want to offer you an incentive. If you inform my office at sworld.mind@gmail.com about your review, we will send over the 'Author's Draft' of this chapter to you. The Author's Draft of the chapter contains extended details and research on this chapter that did not make it into this published version.

Thank you for reading this chapter, and I wish you all the best in your journey to conquer your fears. As you move forward on this journey, I wish you all the very best in your pursuit of a life free from the limitations of fear.

Conclusion

In this chapter, we explored the concept of fear and its impact on personal and professional growth. We learned that fear is a natural emotion that can manifest in various ways, and it can hold us back from reaching our full potential.

We discussed several strategies for overcoming fear, including identifying the source of fear, reframing our thoughts, practicing mindfulness, and taking action.

By taking action despite our fears, we build confidence in our abilities and learn that we are capable of facing challenges and overcoming obstacles. We also discovered that breaking free from fear is essential for personal growth and success.

We also explored how fear can affect us in the workplace, leading to missed opportunities, decreased productivity, and lower job satisfaction. We discussed strategies for overcoming fear in the workplace, such as seeking support from colleagues and mentors, taking calculated risks, and focusing on learning and growth.

We also heard personal stories and case studies of individuals who faced their fears and overcame them, achieving great success and personal growth. These stories showed us that it is possible to break free from fear and achieve our goals and dreams.

Yes, breaking free from fear is not easy, but it is necessary for personal and professional growth. By taking action, seeking support, and reframing our thoughts, we can overcome our fears and achieve our full potential.

Wrap up

Congratulations on making it this far in your personal development journey! Breaking free from fear can be a challenging and a daunting task, but remember that it is possible. It takes courage, determination, and a willingness to face your fears head-on and work on personal development, and you should be proud of yourself for taking this step.

Remember that personal development is a lifelong journey, and overcoming fear is just one aspect of it. Don't be discouraged by setbacks or failures. Instead, use them as opportunities to learn and grow. Keep pushing yourself out of your comfort zone, taking risks, and pursuing your passions.

It can be helpful to have a support system in place, whether it's friends, family, or a coach or mentor. Don't be afraid to reach out and ask for help when you need it. And most importantly, be kind to yourself throughout the process. Celebrate your successes, no matter how small, and don't beat yourself up for mistakes or setbacks.

Remember, you have the power to overcome fear and achieve your dreams. Keep working on your personal development, and you'll be amazed at what you can accomplish!

"Start viewing fear as an opportunity for personal growth, and you will develop the strength to overcome any obstacles that may come your way."

– Avadhut das

❑

CHAPTER 11

How Mindfulness can Change Your Life

"Your light cannot shine without fuel. Practicing self-care is like filling the lantern with fuel to keep your light shining brightly."

– Avadhut das

Introduction

Have you ever felt overwhelmed by the demands of daily life? Do you find yourself constantly on the go, juggling various tasks and responsibilities, and feeling like there's never enough time in the day? In our fast-paced world, it's easy to get caught up in the hustle and bustle of life and neglect our own well-being. That's why in this chapter, we'll explore the concepts of mindfulness and self-care and how they can help us manage stress, improve our overall health and well-being, and live more fulfilling lives.

In the last chapter, we discussed the importance of overcoming fear and taking action to achieve our goals. In this chapter, we'll be delving deeper into what mindfulness and self-care are, why they're crucial to our personal development journey, and strategies for incorporating them into our daily lives. We'll also be exploring how mindfulness and self-care can be applied in the workplace to improve productivity, creativity, and overall well-being.

As always, we'll be sharing personal stories and case studies to illustrate the benefits of mindfulness and self-care. By the end of this chapter, you'll have a better understanding of how to cultivate these practices in your life, leading to greater self-awareness, happiness, and success. So, let's dive in!

The importance of mindfulness and self-care for personal development

Mindfulness is a practice that can transform your life and bring about positive changes in your overall well-being. It involves being present in the moment, without any judgments or distractions. By practicing mindfulness, you can learn to become more aware of your thoughts and emotions, and respond to them in a constructive manner. This can help you reduce stress, improve focus, and enhance your overall well-being.

Self-care is another essential component of personal development. It involves taking care of yourself physically, mentally, and emotionally. This includes practicing healthy habits such as exercise, meditation, getting enough sleep, eating well, and taking breaks from work or other responsibilities. When you take care of yourself, you become more resilient and better equipped to deal with life's challenges.

By incorporating mindfulness and self-care into your daily life, you can improve your mental and emotional health. Mindfulness helps you to observe your thoughts and emotions without judgment, which can help you develop greater self-awareness and self-compassion. Self-care practices, such as meditation, exercise, and good nutrition, can also improve your physical health, which is essential for overall well-being.

When you practice mindfulness and self-care, you learn to prioritize your well-being and take responsibility for your own happiness. You learn to become more aware of your thoughts and emotions, and how they affect your well-being. This can help you develop greater self-awareness and emotional intelligence, which can improve your relationships with others.

Understanding Mindfulness

Mindfulness is a powerful practice that can improve many aspects of our lives. One of the most significant benefits is its ability to reduce stress and improve mental health. When we are mindful, we are fully present and engaged in the moment, which can help us to better understand our thoughts and emotions. This, in turn, can help us to manage stress and anxiety in a more constructive way, leading to a greater sense of calm and clarity.

But mindfulness isn't just about reducing stress. It can also help us to improve our relationships with others. By being more present and attentive in our interactions with others, we can develop greater empathy and understanding. This can lead to more meaningful and fulfilling relationships, as well as avoiding misunderstandings and conflicts that can harm our relationships.

Another key benefit of mindfulness is its ability to improve focus and concentration. When we are mindful, we train our brains to be more focused and less distracted, which can be particularly helpful for individuals who struggle with attention-related issues such as ADHD. By improving our ability to concentrate and avoid distractions, we can become more productive and achieve our goals more effectively.

Mindfulness also helps us to develop greater resilience. When we are mindful, we learn to approach challenges with a more adaptive and flexible mindset. This can help us to overcome setbacks and achieve our goals more effectively, even in the face of adversity. By developing greater resilience, we can become more confident in our abilities and better equipped to navigate life's ups and downs.

Exercise: An actual mindfulness meditation to help you experience its benefits

1. Find a quiet, comfortable place to sit or lie down without distractions. It is important to find a place where you won't be disturbed, so you can concentrate. You might want to find a quiet place at home, at work, or even in nature. Make sure you feel safe and at ease in the space you choose.
2. Make sure you are sitting in a way that's comfortable and lets you stay calm and alert. Choose a position that is comfortable for you, such as sitting on the floor with your legs crossed, sitting in a chair with your feet on the floor, or lying on your back. Whatever position you choose, make sure your spine is straight and your shoulders are relaxed.
3. Take a few deep breaths to help you relax and center yourself. Take a deep breath in through your nose, then slowly let it out through your mouth. You might want to close your eyes to help you focus on your breath and let go of any tension or stress in your body.
4. Focus on the feeling of your breath, such as the rise and fall of your chest or the expansion and contraction of your stomach. Once you feel calm and in control, pay attention to your breathing. Take note of how the air feels as it enters and exits your body. You might want to concentrate on your chest rising and falling or how your stomach grows and shrinks. As you focus on

your breath, allow yourself to become fully present in the moment, letting go of any thoughts or distractions.

5. Pay attention to your breath without trying to change it. At this stage, the goal is to simply pay attention to your breath as it naturally moves in and out of your body without trying to control or change it in any way. This means you shouldn't try to slow down or deepen your breath; instead, you should just watch it as it is. As you do this, you may feel your breath, such as how cool the air feels when you breathe in and how warm it feels when you breathe out. Simply observe these feelings without judging or analyzing them.

6. When you notice that your attention has wandered away from your breath during meditation, simply bring it back with kindness and compassion. During a single meditation session, this may happen more than once. That's fine; bringing your attention back to your breath is an important part of the practice. Try not to get angry at or judge yourself for getting side-tracked, as this can add stress and tension that you don't need.

7. If your mind is especially busy or distracted, it can help to use a mental cue to bring your focus back to your breath. You could, for instance, silently say 'inhale' to yourself as you breathe in and 'exhale' as you breathe out. This can help you keep your mind from wandering as much by giving you something to focus on.

8. Allow your awareness to grow to include the entire present moment as you keep your attention on your breath. Take note of any sounds you can hear, any physical feelings you have, and any thoughts that come and go in your mind. Instead of getting caught up in these things, just watch them with curiosity and an open mind, without judging or analyzing them. This can help you develop a sense of mindfulness and presence, which can help you be more present in the here and now.

9. During meditation, it is common to experience a wide range of thoughts and emotions, such as stress, anxiety, happiness, and excitement. Instead of getting caught up in these thoughts and feelings or judging them as good or bad, just watch them come and go. This can help you develop a sense of detachment from your thoughts and feelings, which can help you deal with stress and anxiety in your daily life.

10. If your mind is especially restless or you can't keep your attention on your breath, you can use a mental anchor to bring your attention back to the present moment. Counting your breaths or silently repeating a soothing word or phrase like 'relax' can help you focus and ground your attention during meditation.

11. Mindfulness Meditation is a technique for increasing awareness and clarity in your life. Try not to go into the practice with a specific goal in mind, but rather

with an open mind and a sense of curiosity. This can help you be more present and open to whatever comes up during your meditation practice.

12. Be kind and gentle with yourself as you learn to cultivate greater awareness and clarity in your life. Mindfulness is not something you can learn overnight; it is important to keep that in mind. It is a practice that needs consistency, patience, and self-compassion. If your mind wanders or you find it hard to stay focused while you are meditating, try not to judge yourself or get discouraged. Simply acknowledge the feeling and come back to your breath. Over time, you may find that your ability to stay present and focused during meditation gets better, giving you more clarity and awareness in your daily life.
13. As your meditation comes to an end, it is important to gently exit the practice. Take a few deep breaths to ground yourself, and then slowly open your eyes and take in your surroundings. This can help you focus on the here and now and keep you from feeling lost or scattered as you go about your day.

Take a moment to check in with yourself and see how you feel after you meditate. You might feel calmer, more in control, or more clear-headed. If you do feel calm or relaxed, enjoy this feeling for a few minutes and let it stay with you as you go about your day. In your daily life, this can help you maintain mindfulness and presence.

Understanding Self-Care

Self-care refers to the practice of taking intentional actions to care for your physical, mental, and emotional well-being. It involves prioritizing your own needs and taking time for yourself, in order to maintain a healthy and balanced lifestyle. Self-care is important for personal development because it helps to prevent burnout, reduce stress, and improve overall well-being.

Many people mistakenly believe that self-care is selfish or indulgent, but in reality, it is essential for maintaining good health and preventing negative outcomes such as stress-related illnesses, depression, and anxiety. When we neglect our own needs, we become less productive, less creative, and less able to cope with the challenges of daily life.

In addition to improving our own health and well-being, self-care also helps us to be more effective in our relationships with others. When we take care of ourselves, we are better able to be present and engaged in our interactions with others, and we are more able to offer support and care to those around us.

Self-care can take many forms, from simple acts such as taking a relaxing bath or getting enough sleep, to more complex practices such as regular exercise or mindfulness meditation. The key is to find activities that are enjoyable and fulfilling for you, and to make them a regular part of your routine.

In order to practice self-care effectively, it is important to prioritize your own needs and to make time for self-care activities, even if it means saying no to other demands or commitments. It is also important to be gentle and compassionate with yourself, and to avoid self-judgment or self-criticism when things don't go as planned.

Self-care for mental health and well-being

While self-care may seem like a luxury or something that can be put off until later, it is actually a crucial component of personal development and overall well-being.

When we neglect self-care, we can experience negative consequences on our mental health and well-being. For example, neglecting self-care can lead to burnout, which is a state of emotional, mental, and physical exhaustion caused by excessive and prolonged stress. This can lead to feelings of apathy, detachment, and decreased productivity, among other symptoms. Additionally, neglecting self-care can lead to increased levels of stress and anxiety, as well as a decreased ability to manage these feelings effectively.

On the other hand, engaging in regular self-care practices can have a significant positive impact on mental health and well-being. For example, regular exercise, healthy eating habits, and getting enough sleep can help to reduce stress levels and improve mood. Other self-care practices, such as journaling, practicing mindfulness, or engaging in hobbies, can also help to improve mental health by reducing stress, improving self-awareness, and increasing feelings of happiness and fulfillment.

Personal story: 'How Self-Care Transformed My Life as a Banker'

Meet Priyanka Choube, a successful banker with over a decade of experience. With a demanding job that frequently required long hours and high-pressure situations, Priyanka found herself struggling to balance her work and personal life. Over time, she started to feel burned out, stressed, and exhausted. She didn't start to notice a change in her life until a friend suggested that she start practicing self-care. Priyanka was able to improve her health and happiness through mindfulness meditation and other self-care practices. This helped her handle her work and personal life with more ease and efficiency.

As a banker, my job is hard. I often have to work long hours and deal with situations that are very stressful. For a long time, I had trouble juggling my job and taking care of myself. To keep up with the demands of my job, I would often work late into the night, skip meals, and not exercise. Over time, I started to feel burned out, stressed, and exhausted.

A friend once suggested that I try mindfulness meditation as a way to deal with stress and improve my overall health. I was initially hesitant. I didn't think that spending a few minutes each day sitting still and focusing on my breath could make a big difference in my life. But I decided to give it a shot, and the results were pleasantly surprising.

I started meditating for ten minutes every morning before I went to work, and after a few weeks, I started to notice changes in my mood and energy levels. I felt more calm, more focused, and more clear-headed. As a result, I was able to approach my work with greater clarity and efficiency, and I felt more motivated and inspired to deal with the challenges of my job.

Along with meditation, I started putting other self-care practices first in my life. I made sure to get enough sleep every night, even if it meant leaving work a little earlier than usual. I also started taking breaks throughout the day to stretch, go for a walk, or just sit and breathe for a few minutes. I made sure to eat healthy meals and do things that made me happy, like reading, cooking, and spending time with loved ones.

As I kept putting self-care first in my life, I could tell that my overall health was getting better. I was more energized, focused, and motivated, and I could do my work more easily and quickly. I felt closer to my friends and family, and I was able to handle the challenges and stress of my job better.

I can now thrive both personally and professionally thanks to self-care, which has truly changed my life. By making time for my own needs and well-being, I have become a more effective, resilient, and happy person, and I am thankful for the many benefits that self-care has brought into my life.

Strategies for Practicing Mindfulness and Self-Care

Incorporating mindfulness and self-care into our daily routine is crucial for personal development and well-being. There are many strategies that we can use to practice mindfulness and self-care. Here are some effective ways to do it:

Meditation: One of the most popular ways to practice mindfulness is through meditation. Meditation involves sitting quietly and focusing on your breath, thoughts, and sensations. This practice can help you calm your mind, reduce stress, and increase self-awareness.

Exercise: Exercise is not only good for your physical health but also for your mental health. Regular exercise can help you manage stress, boost your mood, and improve your sleep quality. You can choose any form of exercise that you enjoy, such as running, cycling, swimming, or yoga.

Spending time in nature: Spending time in nature can help you connect with yourself and the world around you. It can also help you reduce stress and improve your mood. You can go for a walk in a park, hike in the mountains, or simply sit outside and enjoy the fresh air.

Journaling: Journaling is a great way to practice self-care and self-reflection. Writing down your thoughts and feelings can help you gain clarity, reduce stress, and improve your emotional well-being.

Creative activities: Engaging in creative activities such as painting, playing music, or writing can also be a form of self-care. These activities can help you reduce stress, improve your mood, and boost your self-esteem.

Mindful eating: Eating mindfully means paying attention to the taste, texture, and smell of your food. It can help you slow down and enjoy your meals, which can lead to better digestion and improved overall health.

Incorporating these strategies into your daily routine can help you cultivate a sense of mindfulness and self-care, which can lead to improved mental health and well-being. Start with small steps and gradually build up to a routine that works for you. Remember, taking care of yourself is not a luxury, it's a necessity.

How to create a self-care plan and incorporate mindfulness into daily life.

Step 1: Identify Areas of Self-care

The first step in creating a self-care plan is to identify areas of self-care that are important to you. Self-care includes physical, emotional, social, intellectual, spiritual, and occupational areas. Some examples of self-care activities in each area include:

1. **Physical:** Regular exercise, eating nutritious meals, getting enough sleep, taking breaks to stretch or move around during the day, and staying hydrated.
2. **Emotional:** Journaling, therapy, practicing self-compassion, setting boundaries, and expressing emotions through creative outlets like art or music.
3. **Social:** Spending time with loved ones, joining a club or group, volunteering, attending social events, and practicing communication skills.

4. **Intellectual:** Learning new skills or hobbies, reading, attending workshops or seminars, participating in online courses or communities.
5. **Spiritual:** Reading spiritual books, discussions with spiritualists, attending spiritual classes, performing spiritual services, and visiting spiritual places.
6. **Occupational:** Taking breaks during the workday, setting realistic goals, delegating tasks, practicing time management, and pursuing career development opportunities.

Step 2: Evaluate Your Current Self-care Practices

The next step is to evaluate your current self-care practices. Take some time to reflect on the following questions:

1. What self-care practices do you currently engage in?
2. How frequently do you engage in these practices?
3. Which areas of self-care are you neglecting?
4. What are the barriers preventing you from engaging in self-care?
5. What self-care practices do you enjoy and find helpful?
6. Are there any self-care practices that you want to try?

Step 3: Set Realistic Self-care Goals

After evaluating your current self-care practices, set realistic self-care goals. Choose one or two areas of self-care that you want to focus on and set specific, achievable goals. For example, if you want to improve your physical self-care, a specific goal could be to exercise for 30 minutes three times per week. If you want to improve your emotional self-care, a specific goal could be to practice journaling for 10 minutes every night.

Step 4: Create a Self-care Plan

Now that you have identified areas of self-care, evaluated your current practices, and set realistic goals, it is time to create a self-care plan. Your plan should include specific self-care activities, the frequency of these activities, and the duration of each activity. Write down your plan and include it in your daily or weekly schedule.

Step 5: Incorporate Mindfulness into Daily Life

1. Start your day with mindfulness. Begin your day with a few minutes of mindfulness practice. This could be meditation, deep breathing, or simply sitting quietly and focusing on your breath.

2. Practice mindfulness during everyday activities. You can practice mindfulness during everyday activities such as brushing your teeth, washing the dishes, or taking a shower. Focus on the sensations you are experiencing in the present moment.
3. Take mindfulness breaks during the day. Take a few minutes throughout the day to practice mindfulness. You can do this by taking a few deep breaths, closing your eyes and focusing on your breath, or simply taking a short walk outside and observing your surroundings.
4. Practice mindfulness during meals. Mindful eating is a great way to practice mindfulness and improve your relationship with food. Focus on the taste, texture, and smell of your food, and take your time eating, without distractions.
5. Practice gratitude. Practicing gratitude is a form of mindfulness that can help you cultivate a positive outlook on life. Take a few minutes each day to reflect on things you are grateful for, and focus on the positive aspects of your life.
6. Use mindfulness apps. There are many mindfulness apps available that can help you incorporate mindfulness into your daily life. Some popular apps include Headspace, Calm, and Insight Timer.

Examples of Self-Care Plans

Example 1: Physical Self-Care Plan

Goal: To improve physical health and well-being by incorporating regular exercise and healthy eating habits into daily life.

Self-Care Activities:

- Exercise for 30 minutes, three times per week
- Take a walk outside during lunch break
- Drink at least 8 glasses of water per day
- Eat at least 3 servings of vegetables per day
- Get at least 6 hours of sleep per night

Example 2: Emotional Self-Care Plan

Goal: To improve emotional well-being by practicing self-compassion, setting boundaries, and expressing emotions through creative outlets.

Self-Care Activities

- Journal for 10 minutes every night
- Practice saying no to commitments that don't align with values and priorities
- Schedule time for creative activities such as painting, drawing, or writing
- Set aside time for self-care activities, such as taking a bath or getting a massage
- Practice mindfulness and deep breathing exercises when feeling stressed or overwhelmed.

Example 3: Spiritual Self-Care Plan

Goal: To improve spiritual well-being by incorporating spiritual practices into daily life.

Self-Care Activities:

- Meditate for 10 minutes every morning
- Read spiritual books every morning for 10 minutes
- Attend a spiritual class once per week
- Prepare and eat spiritual food a minimum of 2 times a day
- Go for a short pilgrimage once every 5 months
- Host a short spiritual function once every quarter

Case study: An example of a successful strategy used to practice mindfulness and self-care

An example of a successful strategy used to practice mindfulness and self-care is that of Arianna Huffington, co-founder and former editor-in-chief of The Huffington Post. Huffington's strategy involves prioritizing sleep, unplugging from technology, and taking breaks throughout the day to recharge.

Huffington emphasizes the importance of getting enough sleep, stating that "sleep is a fundamental human need and the foundation of physical, emotional, and mental well-being." To prioritize her sleep, Huffington sets a regular bedtime and wakes up at the same time each day. She also creates a relaxing bedtime routine, such as taking a warm bath or reading a book, to help her unwind and prepare for sleep.

In addition, Huffington believes in the importance of unplugging from technology to reduce stress and increase mindfulness. She recommends turning off electronic devices at least 30 minutes before bed.

Finally, Huffington emphasizes the importance of taking breaks throughout the day to recharge and reduce stress. She suggests taking a few deep breaths or going for a short walk to clear the mind and increase energy.

These strategies have been successful for Huffington and have helped her to prioritize self-care and maintain a healthy work-life balance. As she stated in an interview with Oprah Winfrey, "We need to move from a culture of burnout to a culture of self-care."

Source:

❖ Huffington, A. (2016). The Sleep Revolution: Transforming Your Life, One Night at a Time. Harmony.

Mindfulness and Self-Care in the Workplace

In today's fast-paced and competitive world, it's common for individuals to feel stressed, overwhelmed, and burnt out in their jobs. Many people believe that working harder and longer hours is the key to success in their careers. However, this approach can often lead to burnout and poor mental health, ultimately hindering career success.

Mindfulness and self-care practices can play a crucial role in achieving career success and well-being in the workplace. Mindfulness practices can help individuals improve their focus, attention, and productivity, allowing them to work more efficiently and effectively. When we are mindful, we are more aware of our thoughts, emotions, and physical sensations, which can help us manage stress and work more efficiently.

Self-care practices such as regular exercise, healthy eating habits, and getting enough sleep can also significantly impact our performance and well-being at work. When we prioritize our physical and mental health, we are better equipped to handle work-related stressors and challenges.

In addition to improving individual performance, mindfulness and self-care practices can also foster positive workplace cultures. When individuals prioritize their well-being, they are more likely to exhibit positive behaviors such as collaboration, empathy, and creativity. These positive behaviors can ultimately lead to a more productive and harmonious work environment.

Employers are increasingly recognizing the importance of mindfulness and self-care in the workplace and are implementing wellness programs to support their employees' well-being. By encouraging employees to prioritize their physical and mental health, companies can improve employee satisfaction, retention rates, and ultimately, the bottom line.

Mindfulness and self-care in a professional setting

Start by taking breaks throughout the day. Even a short five-minute break can be incredibly beneficial to reset your mind, stretch your body, and come back to your work with renewed focus. Use this time to practice deep breathing or a quick meditation to calm your mind.

Try to create a comfortable workspace that promotes relaxation. Add some plants, artwork, or personal items to your desk to make it a calming and inviting space. You can also consider using essential oils or a diffuser to create a relaxing atmosphere.

Incorporate physical activity into your workday. Take a quick walk around the office or do some light stretching at your desk. You can also consider doing some office exercises with your colleagues.

Practice mindful eating. Instead of rushing through your lunch break, take the time to savor and appreciate your food. Pay attention to the flavors and textures and take a moment to be grateful for the nourishment it provides your body.

Set boundaries around work hours and stick to them. This means avoiding checking emails or taking work calls outside of designated work hours. Create a schedule that allows for adequate time for work, self-care, and personal time.

Practice gratitude. Take a few moments at the end of each day to reflect on what you are grateful for in your professional life. This could be a supportive colleague, a successful project, or a kind email from a client.

You could organize a group meditation session or a team outing to a nature park. This will not only benefit you individually but also help to build a more mindful and supportive team environment.

Incorporating mindfulness and self-care practices into your professional life can be challenging, but by taking small steps every day, you can create a more peaceful, productive, and fulfilling work environment.

Personal story: Practicing mindfulness and self-care

Officer Kabir is a devoted police officer who has been with the force for more than ten years. Throughout his career, he has been through a lot of terrible things that have hurt his mental and emotional health. Officer Kabir has decided not to let the stress of his job get the best of him. Instead, he is putting his health first by practicing mindfulness and self-care.

In this personal story about Officer Kabir, we can see how incorporating self-care and mindfulness into his daily life has helped his career and overall health. Officer Kabir became a more effective and caring police officer by taking the time to work on his mental and emotional health. This also improved the quality of his life outside of work.

Officer Kabir has seen a lot of traumatic things during his career, which has hurt his mental and emotional health. Over time, he began to notice that the demands of his job were making him feel more and more stressed, anxious, and overwhelmed.

This is when Kabir decided to look into how mindfulness and self-care could help him in his work and personal life. He started by incorporating small practices into his daily routine, such as taking a few deep breaths before responding to a stressful situation or taking a short walk during his lunch break. He also started doing a few minutes of mindfulness meditation every morning, which helped him clear his mind and focus on the present.

As Kabir continued to put mindfulness and self-care at the top of his list of priorities, he saw big changes in how he felt and how well he did at work. He became more understanding and patient with the people he helped, and he was better able to talk to and connect with his colleagues. He also discovered that he could deal with stressful situations better because he had learned how to control his feelings and stay in the present.

Mindfulness and self-care have helped Kabir's career, as shown by a stressful situation where he had to help an armed suspect in a potentially dangerous situation. Before acting on impulse, Kabir was able to stop, take a deep breath, and think about what was going on. This gave him the ability to approach the situation with a clear head, talk to the suspect in an empathic way, and ultimately de-escalate the situation without hurting anyone.

Kabir's dedication to self-care has also helped him keep a good balance between work and life, which has improved his overall health. He now takes time away from work to do things like work out and spend time with his family. This helps him relax and feel less stressed. He also prioritizes getting enough sleep and eats well, which have improved his physical health and energy levels.

Kabir's journey to put mindfulness and self-care first has made his personal and professional life better. By taking the time to focus on his health, he has become a more effective and caring police officer, and he has also improved the quality of his life as a whole.

Kabir knows that practicing mindfulness and taking care of himself is an ongoing process, and he keeps looking for new ways to include these practices in his life. To learn more and improve his skills, he attends mindfulness workshops and reads books about the topic. He also tells his colleagues that their health should be a top priority and tells them about the benefits he has seen from practicing mindfulness and self-care.

Kabir thinks that putting mindfulness and self-care first has not only made his own life better but also helped the people he works with. He believes that by being more patient, understanding, and grounded, he can connect with and help the community better.

Ultimately, Kabir's story shows how mindfulness and self-care can help improve one's professional success and overall health. By putting these things first, he has become a better and more caring police officer and has also made his life better.

Personal Stories and Case Studies

Examples of individuals who have practiced mindfulness and self-care and experienced personal and professional benefits.

1. Ellen DeGeneres: Ellen DeGeneres is a television host and comedian who has spoken publicly about her daily meditation practice and the benefits it has had on her life. She has stated that mindfulness has helped her to deal with anxiety and stress, and has also made her more present and focused in her work.
2. Misty Copeland: Misty Copeland is a professional ballerina who has spoken publicly about the benefits of mindfulness and self-care in her rigorous training schedule. She has stated that practicing mindfulness helps her to stay present and focused during performances, as well as manage the physical and mental demands of her profession.
3. Miranda Kerr: Miranda Kerr is a supermodel and entrepreneur who has spoken publicly about the benefits of mindfulness and self-care in her personal and professional life. She has stated that practicing mindfulness has helped her to stay grounded and focused, and has also helped her to manage stress and anxiety.
4. Jocko Willink: Jocko Willink is a retired Navy SEAL and author who has spoken publicly about the benefits of mindfulness and self-care in his life. He has stated that mindfulness practices have helped him to manage stress and stay focused during high-pressure situations, both in his military career and in his professional life as an author and speaker.

When we take care of ourselves, we are better able to handle challenges and perform at our best. When we are mentally and physically healthy, we are better able to focus on our work, make good decisions, and communicate with others. We are also more likely to have the energy and motivation to work towards our goals and take on new challenges.

Putting mindfulness and self-care at the top of our lists help us learn important skills like emotional intelligence, empathy, and resilience. These skills can be very helpful in both personal and professional relationships because they help us connect with people more deeply, deal with difficult situations with grace and compassion, and get back on our feet after any setbacks.

The Author's Personal Journey on How Mindfulness and Self-Care Transformed His Life

Due to the demands of the type of work I do, I noticed several years ago that I was constantly on the move, meeting new people and giving speeches, but I wasn't taking care of myself. I found it increasingly difficult to focus, communicate effectively, and connect with my audience.

That's when I decided to make self-care and mindfulness part of my daily routine. I started by giving myself a few minutes every morning to practice mindfulness meditation, which helped me clear my mind and focus on the present. I also made a conscious effort to prioritize self-care by doing things that were good for my mind and body, like working out regularly and spending time in nature.

As I kept putting mindfulness and self-care at the top of my list of priorities, I saw a big change in my mental health and overall well-being. I was better able to manage my stress levels, stay focused and present during my work engagements, and connect more authentically with my audience. I also discovered that I was able to find a better balance between work and the rest of my life, which gave me more time for the things that deeply mattered to me.

Also, the good things that happened in my personal life had an effect on how well I did at work. I started getting more requests to speak, and my speeches got better and more well-liked. My productivity, creativity, and overall job satisfaction had all increased.

My experiences with mindfulness and self-care taught me that it is important to take care of my mental and physical health if I want to be successful in all areas of my life. By prioritizing my well-being, I have been able to improve my personal and professional life, and I am more fulfilled and energized than ever before.

Exercises for you

- Practice mindfulness meditation for 10 minutes a day.
- Create a self-care routine and prioritize it in your daily schedule.
- Practice self-compassion and forgiveness when faced with setbacks or failures.

Share your Thoughts

I hope that this chapter on mindfulness has provided you with valuable insights on how this practice can transform your life. As you reflect on what you have learned, I would like to ask you, do you feel more present and aware of your thoughts and emotions after reading this chapter? If so, congratulations! You are one step closer to living a more fulfilling and meaningful life.

Here is a funny incident with mindfulness that illustrates the importance of accepting and laughing at the unexpected. After hearing so much about mindfulness from me, my friend Anup attempted to meditate. However, he couldn't stop thinking about the delicious pizza he had the night before. He tried to refocus his mind, but the scent of the leftover pizza in his apartment was too strong. Feeling frustrated, Anup decided to open his eyes and found his dog sitting next to him, munching on a pizza slice. The sight was hilarious, and Anup realized that mindfulness can involve accepting and finding humor in the present moment.

In my own experience, I have found that the 'body scan' technique can be a powerful tool for cultivating mindfulness. By bringing attention to each part of the body and releasing any tensions or sensations, this practice helps me connect with my physical body and attain a sense of relaxation and inner peace. While different mindfulness practices may work better for different people, I have found the body scan to be a helpful way to ground myself in the present moment.

I would love to hear about your experiences with mindfulness and how it has impacted your life. I encourage you to leave a review and share your insights with other readers. Your review could help someone else discover the power of mindfulness and improve their well-being.

To write a review, simply share your thoughts on what you found most helpful or insightful in this chapter. Share it on Amazon on this book's page. You can describe how you plan to apply these ideas in your own life or share any challenges you might be facing. Your feedback is important to me, as it helps me improve and tailor my content to your needs.

As a token of my appreciation, I would like to offer you an incentive to write a review. If you email my office at sworld.mind@gmail.com to let us know that you have written a review, we will send you the 'Author's Draft' of this chapter. This version contains additional research and insights that didn't make it into this final published version, so you can delve deeper into the topic of mindfulness and continue your journey of personal development. Thank you for your support, and I look forward to hearing your thoughts!

Conclusion

In this chapter, we have learned about the importance of mindfulness and self-care for personal development. Mindfulness is the practice of being present and fully engaged in the current moment, which can help reduce stress and anxiety, improve mental and physical health, and maintain balance in our lives. Self-care is essential for personal development because it helps us prioritize our well-being and prevent burnout.

We discussed various strategies for practicing mindfulness and self-care, including simple techniques like deep breathing and body scans, as well as guided meditations and mindfulness apps. We also explored how mindfulness and self-care can be integrated into the workplace to improve productivity and job satisfaction.

Lastly, we shared personal stories and case studies that demonstrate the transformative power of mindfulness and self-care. By practicing mindfulness and prioritizing self-care, we can unlock our full potential and achieve our goals with greater ease and joy.

Wrap up

Don't be intimidated by the idea of mindfulness or self-care, you don't need to be an expert overnight. Just start small and gradually incorporate these practices into your daily routine.

Prioritizing your physical and mental health is crucial for personal development, whether you are at work or home. Don't neglect your needs, take regular breaks, get enough sleep, and engage in activities that bring you joy. Remember, self-care is not selfish, it is a necessary component for your growth and well-being.

Believe in your power to transform your life through mindfulness and self-care. It is important to be kind to yourself along the way and not beat yourself up if you slip up. With consistency and dedication, you can achieve your personal development goals and live the life you desire. Keep pushing forward and never give up. The path to personal development may not always be easy, but it is worth it. So stay motivated, stay focused, and keep moving forward towards a better and more fulfilling life.

"Self-care is giving the world the best of you,
instead of what's left of you."

- Katie Reed

❑

CHAPTER 12

Personal Development for Life

"The future belongs to those who learn more skills and combine them in creative ways."

– Robert Greene

Introduction

In the previous chapter, we discussed the importance of mindfulness and self-care in personal development. Congratulations on completing your personal development journey so far! You have learned so much about yourself and how to grow as a person. But remember, personal development is a continuous journey, not a destination. In this final chapter, we will discuss how you can continue your journey of personal development and growth.

Welcome to the final chapter! Now, as you come to the end of this book, you may be wondering, "What's next?"

The answer is simple - your personal development journey never truly ends. The skills and knowledge you have gained through this book are only the beginning. This last chapter is all about continuing your personal development journey and setting yourself up for long-term success.

This chapter will help you set new goals, reflect and evaluate on your progress, seek new learning opportunities, incorporate feedback, overcome setbacks, and celebrate your successes. Whether you're looking to further develop your personal or professional life, these tips and strategies will help you get there.

Through personal stories and case studies, you will be inspired by the journeys of others and gain valuable insights into what it takes to continue growing and developing over time. So, let's get started on this final chapter, and continue your personal development journey!

Why is it so important to continue your personal development beyond this book?

The answer is simple - because personal development is not a one-time event but a continuous process. Just like you need to exercise regularly to maintain your physical health, you need to continue working on yourself to maintain your personal growth and development.

By continuing your personal development journey, you will keep yourself motivated and engaged in life. You will also discover new opportunities and experiences that you may not have otherwise encountered. It is important to challenge yourself and push yourself out of your comfort zone to grow and evolve.

The world is constantly changing, and you need to keep up with the changes to stay relevant and competitive. The skills and knowledge that were once valuable may no longer be relevant today. By continually learning and developing new skills, you will keep yourself up-to-date and increase your marketability.

By continually working on yourself, you will improve your self-confidence, self-esteem, and self-awareness. You will also develop better relationships, improve your communication skills, and be better equipped to handle the challenges and stressors that life throws your way.

Setting New Goals

Setting new goals after achieving initial personal development goals is crucial because it allows you to maintain your progress and momentum. Personal growth is a journey, not a destination, and it requires continuous effort and commitment. Without new goals to work towards, it can be easy to lose motivation and become stagnant in your personal development journey.

Moreover, setting new goals allows you to challenge yourself and push beyond your current limitations. It enables you to acquire new skills, knowledge, and experiences that can help you grow both personally and professionally. This helps to keep your development journey dynamic, interesting, and fulfilling.

Another important reason for setting new goals is that it helps you adapt to changes in your circumstances. Life is unpredictable, and new challenges and opportunities may arise that require you to adjust your goals. By setting new goals, you can navigate these changes and continue making progress towards your desired outcomes.

Setting new goals after achieving initial personal development goals also helps you to maintain a sense of purpose and direction in life. Without a clear sense of direction, it can be easy to feel lost or aimless. Setting new goals helps you to identify what you want to achieve and work towards it, which provides a sense of meaning and fulfillment.

How to set new, challenging goals to continue personal growth

It is important to think about one's strengths, weaknesses, interests, and values in order to set new, challenging goals. This kind of thinking can help one figure out where they want to improve and grow, and it can also help them set goals that are both hard and important. Also, it is important to set goals that fit with your overall personal and professional goals.

If you want to set new, hard goals, you could try taking on new challenges or going after new opportunities. For example, if a person's goal was to get better at public speaking and they achieved that, they might want to set a new goal of becoming a mentor or coach for other people who want to get better at public speaking. This goal not only pushes them to keep improving their skills, but it also gives them a chance to help others grow.

Focusing on personal growth and development outside of work is another way to set new, challenging goals. For instance, someone who has completed a marathon may want to set the goal of completing a triathlon. This goal not only pushes them physically, but it also gives them a chance to try out new hobbies and interests.

Setting new, challenging goals can involve getting more education or training. For example, someone who has learned a new language may want to set a new goal of getting a higher degree in a related field. This goal not only makes them think harder, but it also gives them new information and skills that can help them achieve their personal and professional goals.

Exercise: A goal-setting exercise to help you set new personal development goals

Step 1: Reflection

Take some time to think about how far you've come in your personal development so far. Think about the goals you've accomplished and the skills you've gained. Ask yourself: What have been the most important and rewarding parts of my personal development journey so far? What have been the hardest things I have had to deal with, and how did I get through them? What are my strengths and weaknesses?

Step 2: Identify New Areas for Growth

Based on what you've learned, think about where you want to keep growing and improving. Think about both your personal and your professional lives. Ask yourself, "What skills or knowledge do I want to develop more of?" What experiences do I want to have? What are my personal and professional goals?

Step 3: Set SMART Goals

Set SMART goals that are specific, measurable, achievable, relevant, and time-bound based on the areas where you need to improve. For each goal, ask yourself, "What exactly do I want to accomplish?" How will I track my development? Is this goal attainable? Is it relevant to my personal or professional goals? When do I want to accomplish this goal?

Step 4: Create an Action Plan

Create an action plan for each goal. Determine the steps you must take to achieve your objectives and any resources or assistance you may require. Think about potential problems and how you will solve them. Set deadlines for each step to hold yourself accountable.

Step 5: Track Progress and Adjust Goals If Necessary

Monitor your development toward your objectives on a regular basis and make necessary adjustments. Celebrate your successes along the way, and be kind to yourself if you face problems or setbacks. Remember, personal development is a journey, and it is important to enjoy the process.

For example, if you accomplished your goal of developing a healthier lifestyle, you may choose to focus on improving your mental health and set a goal of meditating for 20 minutes every day for the next three months. Your action plan might involve researching different meditation techniques, finding a suitable time and place to meditate, and tracking your daily progress. You can monitor your progress by keeping a journal of your meditation practice and noting any changes in your mental well-being.

Reflection and Evaluation

It is important to keep track of how far you've come towards your goals so you can decide what needs to be changed, improved, or kept the same. Without thinking about how far you've come, it is easy to get comfortable or lose sight of the bigger picture, which can hurt your personal development. By looking back on progress and evaluating goals, people can learn more about their strengths and weaknesses, make changes to their action plans, and take the steps they need to take to achieve their goals.

Evaluating personal development goals is also important because it helps people know if they are on the right track or not. In some cases, goals may need to be changed because they are no longer important or doable because circumstances or priorities have changed. When a person evaluates their personal development goals, they can see if they are in line with their overall vision and values and if they are still applicable to their current situation. This process helps people stay focused on what really matters to them and decide what needs to be changed or adjusted based on good information.

Maintaining motivation and enthusiasm requires reflecting on progress and evaluating personal development goals. Celebrate small wins along the way to feel good about yourself, boost your confidence, and keep a positive attitude. It is also important to recognize and learn from any failures or setbacks that have occurred, as these can provide valuable lessons and insights into what needs to be done differently. Individuals can stay motivated and inspired to continue their personal development journey, even when the going gets tough, by reflecting on progress and evaluating personal development goals.

Evaluation methods to determine what worked and what did not work in the personal development journey.

1. Self-reflection

In this method, you think about your own experiences and figure out what went well and what didn't. Individuals can ask themselves questions like, "What did I learn from this experience?" "What problems did I have to deal with?" and "What could I have done differently?" By thinking about these questions, people can learn more about their personal development journey and use this knowledge to decide what needs to be changed.

2. Feedback from others:

Getting feedback from friends, family, mentors, or coaches can help you evaluate your personal development goals. In areas that need improvement, these people can offer constructive criticism and feedback. It is important to ask for feedback from people who care about your growth and development and are willing to give you honest, objective feedback.

3. Goal progress tracking:

Another efficient method of evaluation is keeping track of progress towards specific personal development goals. This can be done with a journal, a progress report, or a mobile app. For example, if the goal is to read a certain number of books in a year, keeping track of the number of books read each month can help identify areas that need improvement.

4. Data analysis:

In this technique, progress is measured and areas for improvement are found by analyzing data. For example, if the goal of personal development is to increase productivity, keeping track of the number of tasks completed each day and analyzing this data can give insights into areas where improvements can be made.

Personal story: A Journey of Personal Growth - Reflections and Evaluations at age 89

Meet Devika Sen, an 89-year-old woman who has lived a long and fulfilling life. She has worked hard to improve herself and make a positive difference in the lives of those around her throughout her journey. The story of Devika is a great example of how reflection and evaluation can help a person grow. She has learned from her experiences that self-reflection and evaluation are crucial for personal growth and overcoming challenges. In this story, we will follow Devika as she reflects on her journey of personal growth. She realizes that there's always room for growth and improvement.

As I sit in my cozy armchair, surrounded by family photos and mementos of a life well-lived, I can't help but reflect on my personal development journey. At this age, I have been through a lot, and when I think back on my journey, I feel both nostalgic and proud.

As a young girl growing up in a small village, I never thought I'd be sitting in this cosy home in Mumbai with my family. But I was able to make a life for myself and my family through hard work and determination.

When I look back on my life, I can see that setting and achieving goals has been a big part of my personal growth. From learning English to starting my own business, each goal I set for myself was a step towards a more fulfilling life.

But as I look back on my journey, I also see that there were times when I didn't achieve my goals. I remember a time when I wanted to be a doctor, but I couldn't afford it, so I had to give up on that dream. At the time, it felt like a failure, but now that I look back, I can see that it was just a change in direction that led me to where I am now.

Journaling has been one of the most helpful ways for me to evaluate things. I have kept a journal throughout my life where I write down my thoughts, feelings, and experiences. Reading through my old journals now, I can see how much I have grown and changed. I can also see patterns in my actions and thoughts that have either helped or hurt my personal growth.

I have also found it helpful to get feedback from trusted friends and family. They have helped me understand my strengths and weaknesses in ways that I might not have seen on my own. As I continue to think about and evaluate my journey of personal development, I feel grateful for everything I have accomplished and experienced. I am also reminded that personal development is a lifelong journey, and there is always room for growth and improvement.

Seeking New Learning Opportunities

Seeking new learning opportunities allows one to stay up-to-date with the latest developments in their field or area of interest. It also helps them to keep their skills and knowledge relevant and applicable to changing circumstances and environments.

Moreover, seeking new learning opportunities provides individuals with the chance to develop new skills and knowledge that they may not have previously had, which can help them to expand their horizons and become more versatile in their personal and professional lives. It can also give them the opportunity to learn from other experts, which can broaden their perspectives and give them new ideas to apply in their personal and professional lives.

Seeking new learning opportunities makes individuals avoid becoming complacent or stagnant in their personal growth and instead helps remain motivated and engaged in their personal development journey.

Different learning opportunities

People who want to keep learning new things and growing as individuals have many options available to them. Workshops, courses, and mentorship programs are a few examples of learning opportunities.

Workshops are short learning sessions that focus on one topic or skill at a time. They can be done in person or online and are usually led by an expert. Workshops are a good way to learn new things quickly and to meet people who share your interests. They can also be affordable for people who don't have a lot of time or money.

Courses are more organized and thorough than workshops. They cover a wider range of topics and usually take place over a longer period of time. Courses can be done in person or online, and they can lead to a certification or degree. Taking a course is a good way to learn about a subject in depth and can be helpful for your resume or portfolio.

Mentorship programs are another way to learn and grow. These programs match people with a mentor who has more experience and can offer advice, support, and feedback on personal and professional goals. Mentors can help people deal with new challenges, find ways to improve, and provide guidance based on their own experiences.

Case study: Continuing Personal Development Through Seeking New Learning Opportunities

One example of an individual who continued his personal development through seeking new learning opportunities is Warren Buffett, the billionaire investor and philanthropist. Despite his immense success, Buffett continues to prioritize learning and seeking out new knowledge.

Buffett has famously stated that he spends 80% of his day reading and thinking. He believes that continuous learning is essential to success, stating in his annual letter to shareholders, "The more you learn, the more you'll earn."

In addition to reading books and newspapers, Buffett also seeks out opportunities to learn from others. He has said that one of the most important things he learned was from his mentor, Benjamin Graham, who taught him the principles of value investing.

Furthermore, Buffett has also made a point of attending various educational programs throughout his life, including courses on economics and business at Columbia University and the University of Nebraska-Lincoln.

Buffett's commitment to learning has undoubtedly played a role in his success as an investor and businessman. He stated, "I just sit in my office and read all day."

Source:

❖ Schroeder, A. (2008). The Snowball: Warren Buffett and the Business of Life. Bantam.

Incorporating Feedback

Seeking and using feedback shows that you have a growth mindset and want to learn and get better. It shows that you are open to constructive criticism and value other people's opinions and perspectives. You can build a reputation as a proactive, self-aware, and dedicated professional by actively seeking out feedback and using it to make targeted improvements. This can help you build strong relationships with colleagues, supervisors, mentors, and clients, which can lead to greater success in your personal and professional life.

Friends and colleagues are a good source of feedback. Based on their own experiences working with you, they can offer insightful advice. Such peer feedback can be informal, like a casual chat over lunch, or more formal, like a peer review process. To get the most out of feedback from peers, you should go into these conversations with an open mind, be willing to listen to constructive criticism, and use the feedback to figure out where you can improve.

Supervisors and managers can also give important feedback on performance and growth. This can take the form of regular performance reviews, one-on-one meetings, or feedback on specific projects or tasks. To make the most of feedback from supervisors, you should be open to it, ask for clarification or more information when you need it, and work with the supervisor to come up with a plan for improvement.

In addition to these sources, feedback can also come from customers or clients. For instance, a business owner might use customer feedback to make their products or services better. To get the most out of customer feedback, it is important to actively look for it, respond to it quickly, and use it to make specific changes that will help both the customer and the business.

Exercise: A feedback exercise to help you solicit and incorporate feedback

Receiving feedback, can be difficult, especially when it is negative or constructive. So, it is important to come up with a feedback exercise that can help you ask for and use feedback for your own personal development. Here is a thorough feedback exercise that you may use to get feedback and use it to help grow as a person.

Step 1: Define Your Goals

Defining your goals is the first step in the feedback exercise. You need to figure out what parts of yourself you want to improve. This could be anything from enhancing leadership abilities to improving communication skills. The key is to be clear about the areas you want to improve and make sure they align with your goals for personal growth.

Step 2: Identify Feedback Sources

Identifying feedback sources is the second step. Feedback can come from many different sources, including friends, family, colleagues, mentors, and coaches. Choose someone you trust and respect and who has knowledge and experience in the areas you want to improve. It is important to choose someone who will tell you the truth and help you improve.

Step 3: Request Feedback

The third step is to solicit feedback. Once you've chosen your sources of feedback, it is time to ask for it. Be clear about the kind of feedback you want and why it matters to you. Make it clear that you welcome constructive criticism and value their input.

If you want to get better at talking to people, for example, you could ask a friend or family member, "Please give me some feedback on my communication skills? I want to improve as a listener, speaker, and writer, and I'd like your honest opinions." If you want to improve your leadership skills, you could ask your boss, "Please give me feedback on my leadership abilities? I value your feedback as I work to develop my decision-making, delegation, and relationship-building abilities."

Step 4: Listen Actively

Active listening is the fourth step. It is important to listen carefully and not get defensive or dismissive when you get feedback. Try to understand the feedback from the other person's point of view and ask clarifying questions to make sure you understand it completely. If you need to, take notes, but don't talk over the person giving feedback or argue with them.

For example, if someone gives you feedback on your communication skills, listen carefully and ask questions like, "Please give me an example of a situation where my communication skills could have been better?" or "What specific actions should I take to improve my communication skills?" By paying attention, you will learn more about the feedback and how to use it to get better.

Step 5: Reflect on the Feedback

The fifth step is to consider the feedback. Take some time to think about the feedback you got and how it fits with your goals for personal growth. Think about how you can use the feedback to advance towards your goals and look for any patterns or themes in the feedback. Don't forget that feedback isn't just about finding mistakes; it is about finding ways to get better and grow.

For example, if you get feedback on your communication skills, think about the specific actions or circumstances where you could have communicated better. Think about what you can do differently to improve your communication skills in the future and how you can apply the feedback to your personal development journey.

Step 6: Make a Plan of Action

Making an action plan is the sixth step. Create an action plan based on the feedback you received to address the areas you want to improve. Set clear goals and figure out what you need to do to achieve them. Remember to set small, attainable goals that you can achieve over time.

For example, if you get feedback on your communication skills, your action plan could include going to a workshop on communication skills, practicing active listening, and reading books on effective communication. You can move closer to your personal development goals by breaking down your goals into smaller, more manageable steps.

Step 7: Implement Your Action Plan

The last step is to put your plan into action. Put your plan into action and keep track of your progress towards your personal development goals. Always ask for feedback and make necessary changes to your plan. Remember that personal development is an ongoing process and that making lasting changes takes time and work.

For example, if you go to a workshop on communication skills as part of your action plan, use the skills you learn in your daily interactions with others. See if the people around you notice any changes by asking them for their feedback. Keep track of how far you've gotten towards your communication goals, and change your action plan as necessary to keep moving forward.

Overcoming Setbacks

Setbacks are a part of personal development that cannot be avoided. Setbacks are unavoidable, whether you are attempting to learn new skills, change bad habits, or deal with personal issues. Setbacks can also be a chance for learning and growth. Here, we will discuss why setbacks are a normal part of personal development and how to overcome them.

Why Setbacks Are Normal

First, personal development is a journey, not a destination. It requires acquiring new skills, altering habits, and overcoming difficulties. This takes time, work, and persistence. Setbacks are a normal part of this journey because along the way, we may run into problems, make mistakes, or face problems we didn't expect.

Second, setbacks provide valuable feedback. When we experience setbacks, we can learn from them and change our strategy. This feedback can help us find areas for improvement and make our personal development goals more specific. In fact, setbacks can teach us more than successes because they make us look at what we're doing and make the changes we need to make.

Third, setbacks help people become more resilient. Resilience is the capacity to get back on your feet after a setback and deal with difficulties. Setbacks can be hard and discouraging, but they can also be a chance to build resilience. By facing setbacks head-on and sticking with them, we can build the mental and emotional strength we will need to deal with other problems in the future.

How to Overcome Setbacks

In order to overcome setbacks in personal development, there are a number of strategies that can be helpful. One of the most important is resilience, which means being able to get back up after a setback and keep going when things get hard. This means keeping a positive attitude, staying motivated, and keeping your eye on the big picture. Mindfulness, optimism, and coping mechanisms can all be used to build resilience.

Seeking assistance is another important strategy. This can mean asking for help, support, and advice from friends, family, or professional support networks. Support can take many different forms, including a mentor, coach, therapist, or support group. The key is to find someone who can give you good advice and help you come up with a plan for how to move forward.

Reframing the situation is another method for overcoming setbacks. This means viewing setbacks as chances for development and education rather than as failures. Reframing can help you change your mind and have a more positive outlook, which can make you more resilient and determined.

Self-care is an important strategy for overcoming setbacks. You can develop resilience and deal with stress by taking care of yourself physically, emotionally, and mentally. This can include getting enough sleep, eating healthy, working out regularly, and doing things that make you happy and calm down.

Personal story: Overcoming Adversity: Anu's Journey of Resilience and Triumph

This is the story of Anu, a new mom whose life got harder than she could have ever imagined after her husband died suddenly. Anu's journey is a heartbreaking story of loss and grief, but it is also a story of strength, courage, and hope. Even though Anu had to deal with emotional, financial, and social setbacks, she refused to let them define her. She looked for help, took steps to manage her finances, and tried to make new friends. Anu's journey taught her to find strength in weakness and to rise from the ashes of her tragedy. Her story shows how strong the human spirit is and how important community is when things are hard.

My name is Anu, and I am a new mother. I wish I could say that my journey as a new mother was full of joy and happiness, but that was not the case. A few months ago, when my husband died suddenly, my world was turned upside down. I have never faced anything like the emotional, financial, and social setbacks that followed. But I didn't want these setbacks to define me, and I knew I had to do something to get over them.

Emotional Setbacks

The emotional pain and grief I felt after losing my husband were indescribable. He was the love of my life, and we had been married for five years. He was my best friend, my confidant, and my rock. It was like losing a piece of myself when I lost him. I was confused and didn't know how to proceed. I was constantly crying, and it felt like the sadness would never go away.

I knew I needed support, so I went to my family and friends. During this difficult time, they were my lifeline, and they helped me get through the darkest days. They would come to my house to spend time with me and my daughter. They would bring food and offer to help with anything I needed. When I needed to cry, they provided me with comfort, and when I needed to talk, they served as a listening ear. They helped me remember that I wasn't alone and that I had people who would always be there for me.

Therapy was another thing that helped me get over my emotional setbacks. I started seeing a therapist, and it was one of the best decisions I have ever made. My therapist helped me deal with my grief and gave me tools to deal with my feelings. She also showed me that I was strong and could get through this hard time. She taught me coping skills like mindfulness and deep breathing, which helped me control my anxiety and stress.

Financial Setbacks

After my husband died, I was left to handle our finances on my own. I had never been in charge of our finances, so I had no idea where to start. I was worried about how I would pay the bills and take care of my daughter on my own.

I knew I had to take action to get over these financial setbacks. I made a budget and started tracking my spending. I talked to a financial advisor, who helped me make a plan for my and my daughter's futures. I started looking for ways to save money, such as cutting back on unnecessary expenses and finding ways to make more money. I started doing freelance work and started selling some of our old stuff.

It wasn't easy, but I was able to get a handle on our finances over time. I learned to be more responsible with my money and to organize my spending. I also learned the importance of having an emergency fund and insurance. I knew I needed to be ready for anything, so I set up a safety net.

Social Setbacks

Losing my husband also meant losing a big part of my social life. We had a lot of friends in common, and after he died, many of them seemed to stop talking to me. It felt like they didn't know how to be around me anymore, and that hurt me a lot.

I had to take initiative to get past these social setbacks. I started talking to people, even when it was hard or scary. I joined a group for widows and widowers, and it changed my life. I met other people who were going through similar experiences, and it was comforting to know I wasn't alone. I also tried to get in touch with old friends and make new ones.

I realized that I needed to surround myself with people who supported and encouraged me. I didn't have the energy or time for people who made me feel bad about myself or my situation. I concentrated on forming connections with people who gave me confidence in myself and inspired me to keep going.

My Journey Towards Personal Development

Through all of these setbacks, I learned a lot about who I was and what I was capable of. I discovered that I was stronger and more resilient than I had ever imagined. I learned that it was okay to ask for help and that it was not embarrassing to admit that I needed help.

As I moved forward on my path to personal development, I made new goals for myself. I started taking classes online to learn new skills and advance my education. I joined a gym and started working out regularly, which helped me manage my stress and anxiety. I also began to meditate, which helped me find inner peace and calm.

Setting boundaries was one of the most important things I did to advance my personal development. I learned to say no to things that didn't serve me or my goals, and I focused on doing things that made me happy and fulfilled. I stopped putting so much pressure on myself to be perfect, and I allowed myself to make mistakes and learn from them.

Now that I have made it this far, I am proud of how far I have come. I still have days when I miss my husband and feel overwhelmed, but I know that I have the tools and support I need to get through those difficult times. I am thankful for the lessons I have learned and the person I have become.

Conclusion

Losing a spouse is one of the hardest things anyone can go through, and it can be overwhelming to deal with the emotional, financial, and social setbacks that come with it. But, as I have learned from my own experience, it is possible to overcome those setbacks and come out on the other side stronger and more resilient.

I was able to find my way towards personal development and growth by asking for help, being proactive, and taking action. I am thankful for the people who were there for me when things were bad and for the chances that helped me grow and develop.

I have learned that it is never too late to start working on your personal development. There is always a way forward, regardless of the challenges you are currently facing or the setbacks you have experienced. It may not be easy, but anything can be overcome with time, support, and perseverance.

Celebrating Successes

Taking the time to recognize and appreciate one's achievements can boost self-esteem and confidence, which can lead to even more success in the future.

Celebrating successes can also be a chance to reflect and be thankful. By taking the time to think about how hard they had to work to achieve a goal, people can gain a better understanding of their own skills and strengths. This can contribute to general happiness and life satisfaction.

Celebrating successes in personal development can also give other people ideas and motivation. Sharing one's successes with others can encourage and inspire them to pursue their own personal growth journeys.

Celebrating success doesn't have to be expensive or extravagant. It can be as simple as recognizing one's progress, giving oneself a small reward, or telling friends and family about one's accomplishments. The important thing is to take the time to notice and value one's own growth and progress.

How to acknowledge and celebrate personal development achievements.

Recognizing and celebrating your personal development achievements helps you see how hard you've worked and gives you a sense of satisfaction and motivation to keep working towards your goals. Here are some ways to recognize and celebrate personal development achievements:

1. **Journaling:** Take some time to think about your journey and write down what you've done, how far you've come, and how you overcame obstacles. This can help you put things in perspective and see how far you've come. You can keep a physical or digital journal, whichever is more comfortable for you. Writing down your thoughts and progress can help you remember your personal growth journey and solidify your accomplishments.

2. **Treating yourself:** Give yourself a small reward for achieving a goal or a milestone. It can be as simple as treating yourself to a favourite dessert or giving yourself a small gift. Small rewards can help reinforce good behavior and keep you motivated to keep working towards your goals.

3. **Sharing your successes:** You can tell your friends and family who have helped you along the way about your accomplishments. Their praise and thanks can make you feel good about yourself and validate what you did. Sharing your journey with others can also encourage and inspire them to pursue their own personal development goals.

Case study: An example of Susan who celebrated her personal development success

Hello, my name is Susan, and I used to struggle with anxiety and self-doubt. I often second-guessed myself and avoided difficult situations, which made me feel unfulfilled and stuck. But I decided to take action and work on my personal development, and I am proud to say that this journey has changed my life.

I started by setting small goals for myself, like speaking up in meetings and trying new hobbies. As I achieved these goals, my confidence grew, and I became more comfortable pushing myself outside of my comfort zone. It wasn't easy, and there were times when I just wanted to give up, but I kept going and didn't give up.

I got some exciting news one day. At work, I had been offered a promotion. I was excited and terrified at the same time. This new job would give me more responsibility and require me to leave my comfort zone even more. But I knew I couldn't pass up this chance. I accepted the promotion and started getting ready for my new job.

As I settled into my new job, I realized that my newfound confidence and willingness to take risks had paid off in a big way. My colleagues were impressed with my dedication and hard work as I was performing well at work. I had also started a side business in my personal life, which was starting to do well. It was a lot of work, but I felt like I was finally on the right track.

To celebrate my personal development success, I decided to throw a party for my closest friends and family. I wanted to thank them for their support and also use the occasion to reflect on my growth journey. I spent weeks planning the perfect party, and I didn't cut any corners. I hired a caterer, ordered a custom cake, and rented a photo booth.

I was nervous but excited on the day of the party. From my mentor to my therapist, I had invited everyone who had helped me on my path to personal development. As my guests arrived, I greeted them warmly and thanked them for being in my life.

I felt appreciative and joyful the entire night to be with people who cared about and supported me. I spoke with each of my guests, sharing some of my struggles and successes with them. I told them how hard I had worked to get over my self-doubt and how proud I was of what I had done. My friends and family congratulated me and expressed their admiration for my tenacity.

The party got livelier as the night went on. The dance floor was packed, and the music was blasting. I was overcome with emotion as I looked around. I realized that my personal development journey had not only helped me grow as a person but had also strengthened my relationships with those around me.

As the party ended, I said goodbye to my guests, feeling thankful and happy. I went to bed that night feeling content and accomplished, knowing that my personal development journey had led me to this point. I was excited to see what the future held, and I knew I was ready to face any challenge.

Personal Stories and Case Studies

Here are some examples of individuals who, after achieving success in one area of personal development, continued on their personal development journey and experienced even higher personal and professional benefits:

1. Rabia got over her fear of public speaking by taking a course and getting better at it. Her hard work paid off when she gave a good presentation and got good feedback from colleagues and superiors. Her confidence was boosted by this achievement, which led her to take a leadership course to keep growing as a person.

   In this course, Rabia learned important skills in communication, resolving conflicts, and making decisions, which helped her do a great job as a manager. She was able to put together a team that did well, and upper management noticed her leadership abilities, which earned her a promotion. Rabia's journey of personal development not only helped her get over her fear of public speaking, but it also made her a better leader and helped her do better in her career.

2. Dinesh went to a workshop on time management to learn how to better manage his time and stop putting things off. He used the strategies he learned, and his stress levels and procrastination reduced. As a result of this success, his interest in further personal development led him to sign up for a productivity course.

   Dinesh took this course to learn how to improve his ability to focus and stay organized. This helped him take on more responsibilities at work and be considered for a management position. Dinesh's journey of personal development not only helped him overcome his time management issues but also allowed him to advance in his career and take on new challenges.

3. Amrita wanted to learn Spanish but didn't have the time. She enrolled in a beginner's course when she started working with Spanish-speaking colleagues, and her perseverance paid off. She was able to have conversations with her colleagues and get to know them better.

   This success made her want to keep growing as a person, so she took a more advanced course. She learned Spanish very well and was able to use it to get a new job with a company that did a lot of business in Latin America. Amrita's journey of personal growth helped her learn a new language, move up in her career, and learn more about other cultures.

How continuing personal development can improve mental health, well-being, and career success

Continuing personal development is not only important for personal growth and progress but also has a significant impact on mental health, well-being, and career success. In this section, we will discuss in-depth how continuing personal development can improve these areas of our lives.

Mental Health

Continuing personal development can have a positive impact on mental health. By learning new skills, gaining new experiences, and challenging ourselves, we can improve our self-esteem and build a sense of accomplishment. This can lead to a more positive outlook on life and reduce the risk of depression and anxiety. Additionally, by developing new coping mechanisms and resilience, we can better handle stressful situations and overcome obstacles, leading to better mental health.

Well-being

Continuing personal development can improve overall well-being. By setting and achieving new goals, we can build a sense of purpose and direction, leading to increased life satisfaction. Additionally, by learning new skills and taking up new hobbies or activities, we can reduce stress and enhance relaxation. By taking care of our physical, emotional, and social needs, we can promote overall well-being and lead a fulfilling life.

Career Success

Continuing personal development can also have a positive impact on career success. By learning new skills and staying up-to-date with the latest developments in our field or industry, we can become more competent and confident in our work. This can lead to better job performance, increased job satisfaction, and career advancement opportunities. Additionally, by expanding our network and building new relationships, we can increase our chances of finding new job opportunities and career growth.

The Author's Personal Journey of Continuous Personal Development

I have always had a strong belief in the power of personal development. Throughout my life, I have always sought out ways to improve myself, whether it was by reading books, going to workshops, or working with coaches.

When I decided to launch my own business as a subconscious mind trainer, that was a moment that stands out to me. It was a big job, and I knew I would have to keep learning and getting better if I wanted to do well.

So, I promised myself that I would regularly invest in my personal development. I went to conferences and workshops, read books, and worked with mentors and coaches. I learned a lot about communication, marketing, and sales, and I worked hard to become an expert in the field of training the subconscious mind.

My business started to grow and do well as a result of my dedication to personal development. I was able to get more clients, make more money, and offer more services. And perhaps most importantly, I experienced a sense of satisfaction and purpose in my work that I had never felt before.

But my journey of personal development wasn't just beneficial for my career. It also had a profound impact on my mental health and well-being. I learned how to manage stress and anxiety, develop positive habits, and cultivate a growth mindset. I felt more confident and resilient, and I was able to approach challenges with a superior sense of optimism and determination.

To sum it up, my personal experience with continuous personal development has taught me that investing in oneself is one of the most valuable things we can do. By continually seeking out opportunities to learn, grow, and improve, we can achieve our goals, maintain our success, and enhance our overall well-being.

Exercises for you

- Identify a new skill or subject you want to learn and create a plan to start learning.
- Find a support group or accountability partner to help you stay on track with your personal development goals.
- Celebrate your successes, no matter how small, and use them as motivation to continue your journey.

Share your Thoughts

As we come to the end of Personal Development Made Easy, I hope that you have found this book to be a valuable tool in your journey towards personal growth. In this final chapter, we discussed how personal development is a lifelong journey, and I want to know if you feel more confident in your ability to continue on this journey after reading it.

For me, personal development is a never-ending process. It's about constantly learning and growing, and I make it a point to prioritize my personal development every day. One habit that has been helpful for me is setting aside time for self-reflection and goal-setting. By taking time to reflect on my actions and behaviors, I'm able to identify areas where I can improve and set actionable goals to work towards.

I encourage you to leave a review of this book and share your own tips for sustaining personal development over the long term. Your feedback is valuable and can help others who are on a similar journey. To leave a review, simply go to Amazon and search for Personal Development Made Easy. You can write your review there and let others know how this book has helped you. To make it easier for you, here is a guide on how to write a review.

1. Start with a brief summary of this book and what you found most valuable about it.
2. Share how the book has impacted your personal development journey and any specific takeaways you have gained.
3. Offer your own tips and advice for others who may be looking to improve themselves.
4. Conclude with a suggestion on who you think would find this book helpful in their personal development journey.

To sweeten the deal, we are offering an exciting incentive to readers who write a review. Simply inform my office at sworld.mind@gmail.com about the review, and we will send you the first 5 chapters of our upcoming book, The Ultimate Sales Guide! This valuable resource will provide you with invaluable tips and strategies for improving your sales techniques and increasing your revenue. I am sure, you will like to seize this fantastic opportunity to continue your personal development journey while also taking your sales skills to the next level!

Thank you for joining me on this journey of personal development, and I hope that this book has inspired you to continue growing in several aspects of your life.

Conclusion

Congratulations! You have made it to the end of 'Personal Development Made Easy.' We hope that this book has served as a helpful guide on your personal development journey so far. By now, you must have made significant strides in your personal growth. Be proud of yourself for all the progress you have made. In this chapter, we have discussed several key aspects of continuing your journey and taking it to the next level. Let us take a moment to summarize what we have covered.

Firstly, setting new goals is crucial in keeping your personal development journey on track. It gives you a sense of purpose and direction and keeps you motivated. Secondly, reflection and evaluation help you assess your progress and identify areas that need improvement. Seeking new learning opportunities is also essential to keep growing and developing.

Incorporating feedback helps you to learn from your mistakes and improve your performance. Setbacks are inevitable, but it's important to persevere and keep pushing forward. Celebrating your accomplishments, no matter how minor, is a crucial aspect of sustaining motivation and confidence, as it keeps you inspired and energized throughout your personal development journey.

We hope that these points have inspired you to continue your personal development journey and to keep growing and improving yourself. We also hope that the personal stories and case studies have served as an inspiration and have provided valuable insights into how others have achieved personal growth.

Now, as you come to the end of this book, it is up to you to take the lessons you have learned and apply them to your life. You may use the tools and techniques you have learned to continue your personal development journey and achieve your goals.

Wrap up

As we bring this book to a close, we want to leave you with one final message: your personal development journey is never over. There will always be new challenges to face, new skills to learn, and new opportunities to grow.

The key is to keep moving forward, even when things get tough. Remember that personal development is not a one-time event but a continuous process of self-improvement. So, take the lessons you've learned from this book and apply them to your life every day.

Here are a few tips to help you continue your personal development journey:

To continue your personal development journey, it is important to set new goals that align with your values and aspirations. Having something to work towards can keep you motivated and moving forward. Regularly reflect on your progress and evaluate your actions to see if you are on track towards your goals. This can help you stay focused and make any necessary adjustments to your plan.

Staying curious and open-minded is important for personal growth. Seek new learning opportunities to expand your knowledge and skills. This can include taking courses, attending workshops, or simply reading books on topics that interest you. Feedback is essential for growth and development.

Incorporate feedback from others, learn from it, and use it to improve yourself. Setbacks are inevitable, but they are not permanent. Use setbacks as opportunities to learn and grow stronger. Celebrate your successes, no matter how small they may be. Recognize your progress and use it to motivate yourself to keep going.

We believe in you, and we know that you have the power to achieve great things. With hard work, dedication, and a commitment to personal growth, you can overcome any obstacle and achieve your dreams. So, go out there and make the most of every opportunity. Your future self will thank you for it.

"The future belongs to those who learn more skills and combine them in creative ways."

- Robert Greene

❑

Conclusion

This book is meant to be a complete guide to personal development that gives readers the tools and strategies they need to achieve their goals and be the best they can be. The book begins by looking at different facets of personal development, such as self-awareness, goal-setting, mindset, time management, communication, emotional intelligence, getting over fears, and mindfulness. Throughout the book, readers are encouraged to reflect on their own experiences, values, and beliefs and to take action to make positive changes in their lives.

One of the most important things to learn from this book is the importance of self-awareness. We can identify areas for improvement and set goals that are in line with our true selves by understanding our strengths and weaknesses, values and beliefs, and personality type. Another important thing to learn is the importance of having a 'growth mindset.' This means that we should welcome challenges, learn from our mistakes, and believe in our ability to get better. Effective communication, emotional intelligence, and relationship-building abilities are also crucial for both personal and professional success. By enhancing these abilities, we can forge strong relationships with others and handle problems and conflicts with poise and confidence.

The importance of self-care and mindfulness is also emphasized in the book. Taking care of our physical, mental, and emotional health is important for our overall happiness and success. We can cultivate a sense of peace and presence in our daily lives and enhance our capacity to handle stress and challenges by practicing mindfulness.

Encouragement

Congratulations on completing 'Personal Development Made Easy: A step-by-step guide to self-improvement'! By investing in your personal development, you have taken an important step towards achieving your goals and achieving your full potential. Remember, personal development is a lifelong journey, and there is always room for growth and improvement.

As you continue on your journey, I encourage you to stay committed to your goals and to keep taking action towards them. Remember to practice self-awareness and regularly reflect on your strengths, weaknesses, values, and beliefs. Set SMART goals that are aligned with your true self and create action plans to achieve them. Stay motivated and focused by celebrating your progress and learning from your failures.

Developing a growth mindset is also essential for personal growth and success. Embrace challenges as opportunities to learn and grow, and believe in your ability to overcome obstacles and achieve your goals. Cultivate positive habits, improve your time management and productivity, and practice effective communication, emotional intelligence, and relationship-building skills.

Remember to take care of yourself and practice mindfulness regularly. Take time to rest, recharge, and engage in activities that bring you joy and fulfillment. Seek support and accountability from friends, family, or a coach or mentor. Celebrate your successes and learn from your challenges.

With the practical strategies outlined in this book, and a willingness to learn and grow, you can unlock your full potential and achieve success. I wish you all the best on your personal development journey, and I hope that this book has inspired and motivated you to achieve your goals and dreams. So go out there and make the most of your life – the world is waiting for you!

❑

Appendix: *Additional Resources for Personal Development*

"Congratulations, dear reader, on completing this book. You have embarked on an inspiring journey towards self-improvement and personal growth. Now, to further enrich this beautiful journey, let me share some additional resources. These books will serve as your trusted guides, helping you navigate the path to your full potential and paving the way to success."

Books

'The 7 Habits of Highly Effective People' by Stephen Covey: This classic book provides a framework for personal and professional success based on seven key habits, such as being proactive and prioritizing important tasks. Covey's insights and practical strategies have helped millions of people worldwide.

'Mindset: The New Psychology of Success' by Carol Dweck: In this book, Dweck explores the power of mindset, specifically the difference between a fixed mindset and a growth mindset. She provides tools and strategies for cultivating a growth mindset and achieving greater success in all areas of life.

'Atomic Habits: An Easy & Proven Way to Build Positive habits & Break Bad Ones' by James Clear: This book offers a practical and science-backed approach to creating positive habits and breaking negative ones. Clear's strategies help readers to make small, incremental changes that add up to big results over time.

'Emotional Intelligence 2.0' by Travis Bradberry and Jean Greaves: This book provides a framework for understanding and improving emotional intelligence, including skills such as self-awareness, self-regulation, empathy, and social skills. The authors offer practical strategies and tools for developing emotional intelligence and improving relationships.

'The Power of Now' by Eckhart Tolle: Tolle's book focuses on the importance of living in the present moment and letting go of negative thoughts and emotions. Through his teachings, he helps readers to cultivate inner peace, mindfulness, and a deeper sense of purpose.

'You Can Heal Your Life' by Louise Hay: This transformative book focuses on the connection between our thoughts, emotions, and physical health. Hay provides practical strategies for healing and transforming our lives, including affirmations and visualization exercises. This book is a must-read for anyone seeking to improve their mental, emotional, and physical well-being.

'The Power of Positive Thinking' by Norman Vincent Peale: This book is a classic in the field of personal development, providing practical strategies for overcoming negative thinking and cultivating a positive mindset. Peale's teachings have helped millions of people worldwide to overcome obstacles and achieve their goals.

These books, filled with valuable insights, work hand in hand with 'Personal Development Made Easy', making your journey towards success smoother. They have the potential to gently nudge you towards a more successful version of yourself. These could be friends in your journey, helping you unfold your own story of growth. So, dear reader, enjoy the exploration, celebrate your progress, and keep going. Happy reading!

Websites

TED Talks - This website features inspiring and informative talks by experts in various fields, including personal development, motivation, and success.

Psychology Today - This website provides articles and resources on various topics related to personal development, including emotional intelligence, communication, relationships, and mindfulness.

Coursera.org - This website provides online courses on various topics related to personal development, including time management, leadership, emotional intelligence, and communication.

Courses

Dale Carnegie Training - Dale Carnegie offers a range of courses on personal and professional development, including leadership, communication, and interpersonal skills.

Subconscious World - A range of online LIVE workshops provided by the author of this book including, weekend subconscious mind training, money energy training, pendulum dowsing training, sales success training, and academic excellence training.

Tony Robbins - Tony Robbins offers a range of courses and seminars on personal development, including goal setting, mindset, and success.

Remember that personal development is a continuous journey, and these resources are just a starting point. Keep learning, growing, and evolving, and tailor these resources to your unique needs and circumstances. Best of luck on your personal development journey!

Author's Training Academy

Subconscious World
Email: sworld.mind@gmail.com
WhatsApp: +91 9836 338 102
Youtube: bit.ly/mindtrainer
Facebook: subconsciousworld

❑

Your Journey, Your Words

This space belongs to you, dear reader. Consider it your personal canvas. As you journey through the pages of this book, you might encounter ideas that resonate deeply, spark curiosity, or inspire a change. This is your space to capture those moments. Write down the insights that strike a chord, sketch the dreams that start to take shape, or outline the plans that begin to unfold.

By doing so, you are not just a passive reader, but an active participant, becoming a part of this book itself. Your thoughts, your reflections, your unique perspective - they all add a new dimension to this book, making it even more meaningful and personal.

Use these pages to reflect on your personal growth journey. Explore, create, and transform on this canvas. So, take a moment after each chapter or whenever inspiration strikes, and let your thoughts fill these pages. Make this space truly your own, and let it serve as a testament to your journey of personal development.